AN
Alphabetical
LIFE

Living It Up in the
World of Books

WENDY WERRIS

Carroll & Graf Publishers
New York

An Alphabetical Life
Living It Up in the World of Books

Carroll & Graf Publishers
An Imprint of Avalon Publishing Group, Inc.
245 West 17th Street, 11th Floor
New York, NY 10011

AVALON

Library of Congress Cataloging-in-Publication Data is available.

ISBN-13: 978-0-78671-817-7
ISBN-10: 0-7867-1817-X

9 8 7 6 5 4 3 2 1

DESIGNED BY PAULINE NEUWIRTH, NEUWIRTH & ASSOCIATES, INC.

Printed in the United States of America
Distributed by Publishers Group West

"The best memoirs are those in which you connect with the world by connecting with one life. *An Alphabetical Life* is one of those. It is a powerful and poignant book."

—**Michael Connelly**, author of *The Closers*

"**Wendy Werris has written a corker of a book: a memoir that is a brave, honest, and thoroughly engaging** narrative of her coming of age in the book business in 1970s Los Angeles and beyond. We join Werris on her journey from the venerable Pickwick Bookshop of Hollywood, cutting her teeth in an urban melting pot of high glamour and downright squalor, to the 1973 ABA book convention in downtown LA where she scores her first publishing job at a company called Straight Arrow in San Francisco, a subsidiary of *Rolling Stone*. Werris quickly figures out that an office job in marketing is not for her, and she lands a sales gig with a newly formed distributor called Two Continents Publishing, run by the legendary Leonard Shatzkin. This brings her back home to LA where she hits the road and becomes for all intents and purposes a 'young lady salesman.' She joins a commission group, Nourse-McKay, and gets the Southern California, Arizona, and New Mexico territory. She has the experience of handling a bestseller—*The World According to Garp*—for EP Dutton, for which she will later become a house rep. Werris forms her own commission group, I–5 Associates, with George Carroll and Jack O'Leary. She deftly describes the many eccentric bookshop characters she encounters; my favorite is the proprietor of Anne Chiquoine Books in tiny Ventura, CA, an heiress who runs her shop out of the local Elks lodge and affectionately calls Werris 'Poopsie.' It is oddball characters like this one, both famous and infamous, that populate Werris' memoir that make it crackle with energy. There is also quite a bit of pathos in Werris' life story, the decline of her father's writing career in Hollywood, the diminishing bookstore landscape in her territory, the early death of a close friend, and her own experience with sexual assault. Werris weathers the worst of it with humor and authority, and we begin to see a life that has been sustained through the business of books. Through it all she still has her customers, the lines she is selling, and the new books and personalities she encounters along the way. It's a rich ride, and I always knew that Wendy was cool, sitting in many publisher sales meetings with her year after year. I just wasn't sure exactly why she was so cool, and now I know and I'm very glad of it. **Werris has blazed a trail with her new book and become the poet laureate of publishers' reps.**"

—**Eric Miller**, President, National Association of
Independent Publisher Representatives

For
Penny Susan Rose
who heard every word, and always will

and in blessed memory of my parents
Charlotte Werris
1914–1978
Snag Werris, V.S.R.
1911–1987

and
Miriam "Micky" Hope Bass
1948–2003

It's all soul.
—JUNIOR WELLS

CONTENTS

Books seem to me to be pestilent things, and infect all that trade in them . . . with something very perverse and brutal. Printers, binders, sellers and others that make a trade and gain out of them have universally so odd a turn and corruption of mind that they have a way of dealing peculiar to themselves, and not conformed to the good of society and that general fairness which cements mankind.

—JOHN LOCKE

AN *Alphabetical* LIFE

One

A SOLILOQUY FOR PICKWICK BOOKSHOP

Some people never go crazy. What truly horrible lives they must live.

—CHARLES BUKOWSKI

WHEN I WALKED into the house that afternoon, my mother was at the dinette table eating a Limburger cheese sandwich, scallion on the side. She had a Chesterfield going in the ashtray by her elbow, and a copy of *Daily Variety* open in front of her.

"Ma," I announced, "I got a job today. I'm going to work in a bookstore." It was September 2, 1970.

My mother, Charlotte, finished swallowing the bite of her disgusting sandwich. It was a variation on the other bizarre and nauseating foods that were her favorites—pigs' feet in their jellied slime, something called "head cheese," calves' brains, and boiled coffee—which my sisters and I grew up around but, thankfully, were never forced to eat. Charlotte picked up her cigarette and took a puff.

"Good for you," she said, smiling. Her robust Brooklyn accent, ever at the ready despite having lived in Los Angeles for almost twenty years, made this sound oddly like goodfa ewe. "Which bookstore?"

I sat down across from her and lit a cigarette of my own. "It's our favorite one!" I said happily. "Pickwick Bookshop, up on Hollywood Boulevard."

"Oh, for God's sake! I love that place. Your father's going to be so proud of you when I tell him tonight," she exclaimed.

"Well, don't go too nuts over this," I told her. "I doubt I'll stay there more than a couple of months. It's just a temporary job, Mom, until I start college."

She snapped off a piece of scallion in her mouth and patted her bottle-blonde hairdo. "Don't be so sure," she said. "You never know where this might lead."

It was a time of restless ennui for me. After graduating from high school in Los Angeles in 1968, I enrolled at L.A. City College to take the additional classes I needed so I could enter a four-year university. When I was ready, I applied to San Francisco State in the hopes not only of scramming out of L.A. but to pursue my goal of becoming an English teacher. While awaiting word from the admissions office, I primarily spent my time getting high, reading and writing poetry, and longing for my father to return from his job in Miami. He'd been a staff writer on *The Jackie Gleason Show* for ten years at that point and could only be home when the show was on its annual four-month hiatus. By the middle of that peculiar summer of 1970, I was out of my mind with late-teenage anguish; getting a job seemed the sensible thing to do.

I was born in Brooklyn, but my father's career in show business motivated our move to Los Angeles when I was four years old. Snag Werris was a trouper all his life, starting out in vaudeville and burlesque as a teenager. He brought a myriad of talents to the stages of burlesque houses all over the country, including tap-dancing, singing, and playing piano, and acting as the "banana" (or straight man) for Eddie Cantor as half of a comedic duo. The butt of Cantor's jokes, Dad wore ridiculous costumes, took pratfalls, and suffered various humiliations, all for the sake of keeping the laughs coming.

Although my father had a flair for many theatrical skills, he knew that his greatest gift was for writing. It came naturally to him in a way that knew no bounds. This, along with an innate sense of humor that belied his dour Russian lineage, laid the groundwork for a successful life in show business. He filled dozens of notebooks with jokes scrawled in number one pencils and began selling them for two dollars apiece to comedians who worked the burlesque circuit in and around the Catskills. His reputation began to gather steam, and the demand for his jokes grew substantially.

Dad eventually struck it rich in radio in the 1940s, hired by Frank Sinatra, Bing Crosby, and others to write their shows. These were broadcast in the evenings to a nationwide listening audience that wanted only to be entertained and distracted from the awful reality of World War II. Comedy was always on the tip of Dad's tongue, and he was finally writing for a living full-time.

He and my mother first moved to Los Angeles in 1944 when Dad was hired by Paramount to rewrite screenplays for the studio. In time, he was writing original screenplays and light romantic comedies, and having the time of his life. Five years later, however, New York beckoned once again with the advent of television. My parents returned with my two older sisters in tow.

Dad was hired to write for one of the first variety shows on TV, the *Cavalcade of Stars*. The young comedian hired to be the first host and star of the show was Jackie Gleason, for whom Dad would work on and off for the next twenty years. Thanks to Jackie's support and loyalty, my family enjoyed a comfortable existence as my sisters and I grew up.

The sound of my father's typewriter keys lulled me to sleep nearly every night when I was a kid. It reached around hallway corners and through closed doors in our house; a rhythmic, metal-on-metal tapping that became the subconscious glue bonding me to Dad. The typewriter! Fresh sheets of white paper would be curled into the platen with a snap of the release pin. When paper was torn out in frustration, it ripped through the typewriter like an angry zipper, quickly destroyed in a crumpled mass tossed on to the floor of the study. This was the discordant music that led my father on a nightly journey toward the completion of a script, often until dawn. It was the sound of my childhood.

I've always thought it was my weird genetic goulash that pushed me into the book business, but it happened with such a gale force that I've been unable to leave—even after several free-wheeling decades now. Who the hell knows which chromosome it was? It burst open like a sweet, ripe melon that day I strolled into Pickwick. I entered through the doors to buy a copy of *Fire Station* by Charles Bukowski, and two hours later I walked out with a job. I swear to God, this wasn't intentional! It was a hot day;

the Santa Ana winds had kicked up the night before and the temperature hovered around ninety degrees. Seeking relief in the air-conditioned store, I stalled for time by talking, in the lovely chilled air, to the clerk who rang up my sale.

Then I noticed the help wanted sign by the cash register and on a whim inquired about the position. It had never occurred to me that I wanted to work in a bookstore, that I might actually be hired on the spot, or that if I'd waited just a short while longer I could have gotten the employee discount on the book I'd just paid my last three dollars for. Being the unrefined girl that I was, the concept of serendipity was still unfamiliar to me.

It only took a couple of minutes to fill out the job application, leaning against the front counter as I did it. When you're nineteen years old, your history is achingly brief. Mine included two part-time jobs—the first selling popcorn at a movie theater; the next answering phones at a hardware store—and a minor degree in English from a community college. On paper, my life showed little of merit.

I was directed up two flights of stairs to the administrative offices and, before I knew it, I was sitting across from Pickwick's personnel manager.

"I see you have no bookstore experience. Why do you want to work here, Miss Werris?" Shirley Arnold crossed her long legs and thrust the spike heel on her left foot in my general direction. I swallowed. She examined her fingernails, each an inch long and painted bright red. I stared at Shirley as she pushed her black hair back behind one ear, took a deep breath, and finally rested her hands in her lap.

"You see," I stammered, "I really love literature and I read

quite a lot so I'm *prettyknowledgeableaboutbooks*." My words ran
together in a fit of nerves. "And I spend so much time shopping
in here anyway *thatitalmostfeelslikehometome*.

"And I know how to make change!" Now my brains were
falling out of my mouth. Oh, god!

But Shirley understood; good old Shirley, with her blue eye
shadow, high heels, and uncanny intuition about people that
would later make me go running to her whenever I was in any
kind of trouble at the store. Sparing me further humiliation, she
smiled and said: "The most I can pay you is minimum wage—a
dollar sixty an hour. We need someone to work on the sales floor
and eventually manage the children's department upstairs. I like
you. You can start on Monday if you're interested." There was a
subtle shifting of her hips in the swivel chair that she occupied so
gracefully.

"Oh boy, thank you so much. I really appreciate it! Yes, I do.
Thanks!" I got up from my chair to shake Shirley's hand, drop-
ping the bag with *Fire Station* on the floor at the same time. "Oh.
I guess I'll see you on Monday. And you'll see *me* on Monday.
Wow! Thanks!"

Shirley bent to pick up my bag and handed it to me. She was
trying to keep a straight face, but it was difficult. "Be here at eight
thirty," she announced, "and you'll begin your training. You get
off at six and have an hour for lunch." She finally burst out laughing. "Listen, you've gotta relax! I can tell you're a natural for this
job." From your mouth to God's ears, I thought.

Pickwick Bookshop was known in all the literary, educated cir-
cles as the best bookstore west of the Mississippi. It had opened
in 1938 and was an enormous three-story structure on Hollywood

Boulevard that prided itself on the depth of its stock and almost supernaturally astute staff. Affectionately referred to as "The Big Bookshop," it was *the* place to browse, schmooze, and find books that no one else in town carried. Many of its customers were writers, artists, academics, and celebrities from all walks of life who knew that when they came to Pickwick, they would be treated with the utmost discretion and civility. Despite the crappy wage, I considered myself a lucky girl to be working at such an extraordinary place.

I loved it from the very first morning, when the staff gradually welcomed me from every corner of the store, emerging from behind bookcases and the rolling ladders attached to the walls for access to stock on the uppermost shelves. Some slid around from behind the long sales counter to greet me before counting the money in the cash drawers they'd just slipped into the registers. To a soul, everyone was friendly and, to varying degrees, seemed to hold the potential for madness.

That day, I met the kind of people I'd been subconsciously waiting for all my life. Mad poets. Gay men. Hilarious alcoholics. Old queens and struggling actors; street hustlers and college dropouts. I shook hands with frustrated novelists and capricious astrologers. They all worked at Pickwick and would soon become my extended family.

Until this time, my circle of friends had been made up of the high-school chums I'd known practically all my life. We all lived in the same neighborhood, a protective enclave of single-family dwellings in Los Angeles with no ethnic diversity and only a handful of people who could claim Semitic immunity. This was a world of white, heterosexual Jews and their ingenuous kids. My relationships with them were enjoyable but lacked the intrigue and challenge I was ready to experience.

It's not that I was entirely naïve about the world. From the time I was fourteen, I'd been sneaking out of the house to hitchhike with my girlfriends up to the Sunset Strip or the side streets off of Hollywood Boulevard to listen to music and dance in the clubs. We'd lie about our ages when necessary but more often than not were allowed inside to hear hippie bands like The Seeds and Arthur Lee's Love. I was smoking pot, smoking cigarettes, and reading the poetry of Kenneth Patchen and Baudelaire. My family, which orbited around my father's career in show business, was sophisticated enough to have instilled in me an awareness of liberal politics, the theater, and cultural diversity.

But despite my forbidden nights of trolling the underbelly of Los Angeles, including once hitching a ride in an old Volkswagen van from an unknown band called The Doors, and living in a relatively free-form household, nothing could have prepared me for the dense range of humanity that would tether me to Pickwick Bookshop in the years to come.

For the first six months there, I was a sales clerk behind the front counter; I also floated between book sections, managing the stock. Each day I took inventory of "my" books in the crafts, sports, and biography aisles and submitted yellow reorder slips to the buyers. We were never out of a title for very long. These slips of paper went into a tray on the desk of the backlist buyer, where they were then sorted and filed by publisher. Pickwick was a high-volume bookstore, so within a day or two there were usually enough books needed from one publisher to generate an order with an acceptable wholesale discount.

Computers weren't around back then, and we were blissfully unaware of the speed and efficiency they would later bring to inventory control and ordering. However, thanks to the system then in use at Pickwick, I became familiar with the hundreds of publishers whose books we stocked. It didn't take long before I made the important leap to connecting particular titles and authors with their respective publishers, an essential skill for booksellers.

I learned, for instance, that it was Dodd, Mead who published the Agatha Christie mysteries. Van Nostrand Reinhold specialized in art books, as did Dover and Abrams. Llewellyn published books on the occult, and we ordered *The Joy of Cooking* from Bobbs-Merrill (its original publisher). I had an excellent memory for such details and learned quickly. From the start, I made a good impression on the management at Pickwick.

Within a month or two I picked up on the rhythm of life at the bookstore. When we opened in the morning of a blank easel of a day, I was ready for anything. The breeze from Hollywood Boulevard carried a thousand scenes into Pickwick and dumped situations at our front door that I couldn't have made up if I'd tried. The street was always washed out in the early-morning light, not quite nine o'clock, too early for the Hare Krishna folks, bag ladies strolling their turf who would steal rolls of toilet paper from our bathrooms, the Jews For Jesus, and the drunks trolling for spare change. They'd all come calling later on. However, it was just the right time for a team of crazy booksellers to start their day.

Out there in the wilds of the aisles of biographies, Merck manuals, cookbooks, and Nancy Drew mysteries, we yawned and stretched. We often looked like we'd slept at Pickwick the night before, shuffling lazily while dusting the books and slurping coffee from Styrofoam cups. That blessed silence! It was the only time of day when the phones were quiet, cash registers still, and aisles empty of shoppers. On those mornings, it was easy to imagine Pickwick standing firmly on Hollywood Boulevard like the eighth wonder of the world; it seemed eternal to me. As the big security door was rolled up to let in the first customers of the day, we would all check to make sure our name tags were pinned on, the books on the front tables in perfect alignment.

We were all misfits in those days, not fitting in anywhere else except within the dusty confines of Pickwick. It was the start of the seventies, and Los Angeles was on a swing from antiwar hippiedom to the tentative rhythm of disco, from hallucinogens to cocaine, and from the "closet" attitude forced on homosexuals to a more openly gay lifestyle. I was part of an eccentric group of sales clerks, shipping and receiving pranksters, and brilliant book buyers. Between the employees and the clientele, we demonstrated the whole gamut of psychological diagnoses—from manic-depression to narcissistic tendencies.

John Fante wrote that "nostalgia is the whore of memory," and I bear that in mind while recalling, as ruefully as possible, what I was like at that time. I imagine a sassy, moody young woman with a passion for the Beatles, Laura Nyro, John Mayall, and Fred Neil. My taste in writers included Jack Kerouac, Knut Hamsun, Kenneth Patchen, and Pablo Neruda. How impatient I was to reach the legal drinking age! In the meantime I became addicted to amphetamines, furtively buying little "white cross" pills or rummaging through various medicine cabinets for prescription diet pills. Whether or not I was high, my mind smoldered with ideas and visions that I could barely keep up with. The poetry I was writing in those days was good enough to get me published in small literary journals. One was about working at Pickwick and reads in part:

> All day I glare at book spines
> and they read like pale applause;
> I sip and sway through coffee
> I sit, stunning,
> at the desk
> and my mouth is wet
> with an injured shine
> and the book spines
> at five o'clock
> stop translating.
> > Shelf after shelf
> > their profiles endure
> > to watch me curse and exit. . . .

As I approached the age of twenty, I was also wildly curious about, and participating in, sex with various young men from differing milieus. Most of them either wandered into the bookstore as customers or worked there as fair game for the likes of me. Each experience was fodder for my poetry, growing ever more evocative, and for my weirdly developing adult personality. Falling in love didn't interest me, but the knowledge of human complexities did. Self-involvement was the order of the day. I was a pleasant, funny person. I was a dreadful, selfish person. I loved people, then I hated them. And a grave self-awareness served as the umbrella over all that I was becoming.

My good mates at Pickwick ran the gamut from—as I've said—gay to straight, alcoholic to sober, comedic to despairing, intellectual to simple. Bob Glasscock was an astrologer with a wicked, smart playfulness to him that drew me in like a magnet. His best friend was Linda Goodman, the best-selling author of *Sun Signs*; she used to take us saplings out to coffee at the Bonanza, a down-on-its-heels coffee shop next door to Pickwick where we ate lunch nearly every day. Linda would tell our fortunes via crystal pyramids she'd hold over our palms.

Our shipping and receiving manager was a black drag queen named B. J. Johnson. He was in a never-ending bitchy mood, and he had a perfectly coiffed Afro, which I later learned was a wig that hid his bald head. B. J. strutted and preened like a peacock, reminding me of Pearl Bailey. The sweet drunk who managed the metaphysical section at the store was a southerner named Hugh Callens. He dabbled in the occult arts and expertly directed customers to the best books on auras, numerology, and Aleister Crowley's treatises on black magic. With his leonine blond hair and handlebar moustache, Hugh was our resident Buffalo Bill. He also introduced me to the deadly mai tais made at Don the Beachcomber's, across the street from the bookstore. On more than one occasion I was sent to retrieve Hugh from his bar stool at Don's, where he'd been drinking for a couple of hours.

I was mad for Charles Bukowski, whose poetry gained a popular momentum during my years at Pickwick. His work articulated the mental hoops I jumped through as a young woman; it was rife with brilliant street metaphors and lush, raw eroticism. I went to a group poetry reading in Hollywood one night with a friend. We met someone there who was friends with "Buk," and drove us over to his apartment on Lexington Avenue to introduce us to him. The screen door was open, and his friend walked right in.

Bukowski lived in a run-down building and had a one-bedroom flat that was littered with empty beer cans, half-empty bottles of rye, and dirty ashtrays that overflowed with both cigar and cigarette butts. I walked tentatively into this hovel, fearful of what I might find, not taking the risk of entering more than a few feet into the place. Bukowski had a brutal reputation for rants, and I was only twenty years old at the time. His friend called out to him, and he yelled something unintelligible from the bedroom.

When he staggered out, Bukowski was dressed in a dirty white T-shirt and a pair of crumpled chinos; his face was red, his hair a mess, the grin on his face lopsided and salacious. "How ya doin'?!" he bellowed, walking over to give his friend a bear hug. "And who are these fine ladies you've brought to me? My, *my!*"

I stayed right where I was, at a safe distance from the poet, and lit a cigarette with a pack of matches I found in the debris on his coffee table. Bukowski smiled at me, and I offered only a polite nod of the head in my suddenly mute state. I'll admit it: I was scared to death of the guy. His presence held such a corrupt sexuality that I suddenly forgot who he was. The writer whom I idolized, and all the memorized lines of his poetry stored in my head, vanished. In their place was a drunken old (to me, at least) man walking toward me with open arms. I backed away from him and stumbled out the door with my friend, running to the street in a panic.

We got ourselves to the nearest bus stop and exploded with laughter. I was such a silly girl that night! How well I now know that if I'd met Bukowski five or ten years later than that, he could have had me as a willing participant in his bed. Overall, however, that particular night was a lose-lose situation.

Penny Rose, the young woman at Pickwick in charge of special orders, soon became my best friend for life. The first time we met was in a tiny, eight-foot-square room in the back of the store that was more a cell than an office. She sat at a rickety desk with an old typewriter on it; a stack of order forms was on her right and an ashtray on her left. There she'd type up customer orders for books we didn't have in stock, and make sure they reached the buyer's desk for processing.

Everything about Penny seemed hidden and mysterious to me. She had thick, dark-blonde hair that reached the middle of her back and kept her face from view when she so desired. Her clothing was designed to keep her body cloaked and two-dimensional— ankle-length skirts, long-sleeved, billowy blouses, flat shoes, and black tights that covered her legs in the fashion of a nun. Penny would sit ramrod-straight in the hard wooden chair at her little desk, feet flat on the ground in a posture of perfect balance.

Her voice was deep and melodious, and she kept to a precise English that was measured and even; surely she seemed from another time. I was relieved when I first heard her burst with a laughter so raucous and dirty that it seemed to be coming from another person altogether. This showed the flip side of Penny's personality, the one that enabled me to first approach her.

Like me, she was a poet, and this common denominator first sparked our friendship. We were exactly the same age, Penny having been born just eight days before me in 1950, and both of us were voracious readers and lovers of books and words. While I was flirtatious and bold, Penny had a guarded reserve about her.

We each had something the other needed, the aim being some sort of inner balance, and we embarked on this adventure with the clumsiness of young adults who still much preferred sidesplitting giggles to serious discussions about our lives. There would be an abundance of the latter in the future as we grew older together.

Eventually Penny's broad understanding of Pickwick Bookshop led to a higher calling than sitting in what amounted to a large closet typing up order forms. She was promoted to a position upstairs where she worked for Alan Kahn, boy wonder of the industry and the head buyer for the Pickwick Bookshop chain. At the time, Alan was twenty-three years old. He had gone to work at the store while a student at Fairfax High School (my own alma mater) in the 1960s and gradually worked his way up the ladder at Pickwick, beginning as a part-time receiving clerk when he was fifteen years old. Catching the eye of Louis Epstein, the founder and owner of the store, Alan began a remarkable tutelage under the best mentor the book business has ever known.

Alan was tall and handsome, with a beautiful smile that redeemed his normally harried expression. I had never met anyone so thoroughly distracted. Alan always wore a suit and tie to work, but by noon his shirt had come untucked from his trousers, his tie would be askew, and he looked for all the world like a deranged Mr. Magoo. Penny would fill me in on what went on in that office between Alan's first cup of joe and lunchtime to cause such disarray.

If it wasn't Lou Epstein driving him crazy by *kvetching* about sales figures, there might be a publisher's rep in his office, a rep with an unfortunate personality irritating the crap out of Alan. Or Nick Clemente, Pickwick's advertising director (who originated the concept of co-op advertising, in which the publisher and bookstore share the cost of a book ad), would burst into Alan's office yelling about the books that hadn't arrived for Jacqueline Susann's appearance in the store the next day. Crises like these occurred every day, and it was no wonder that Alan was usually transformed into a maniac by lunchtime.

Penny had a small office directly next to Alan's, with a window in one of the walls looking into his domain. He was demanding and did not suffer fools easily. Hiring Penny Rose to be his secretary was a stroke of genius, because she was the only person at Pickwick with enough patience, good humor, and civility to not only stand up to Alan's scrutiny but also to calm and placate him. Penny was utterly without pride. They were a perfect match, calling one another "Boris" and "Natasha," names they chose from among the distinctive characters on the *Rocky and Bullwinkle* TV show. Alan grew to depend on her to bring order to his chaos, and with time she came to anticipate all his needs.

A perfect example of this involved Penny's transcriptions of the letters he dictated to her. These typically came in response to a publisher who'd given the wrong discount on a large order, or a customer with a house charge who was delinquent in paying a substantial bill for books he'd purchased.

Alan would call Penny into his office to take dictation. As she sat facing him with a steno pad in her lap, Alan would recite the contents of the letters off the top of his head.

"Now, you tell that fucking idiot that if he doesn't change that goddamned discount back to forty-six percent like he was supposed to three fucking months ago, I'm going to shove his discount up his ass. Did you get that?"

"Yes, Alan," Penny would answer coolly, unsmiling, one eyebrow raised. "Anything else?"

"Fuck, yes!" Alan would bark. "Let those morons in Mae West's office know that they're sixty days behind on their fucking bill! If they don't send us a fucking check for twelve hundred dollars by Monday, I'll rip their throats out!"

At that point, Penny would silently return to her cubicle to type the letters. The first would begin:

> *My dear Harvey,*
>
> *It's been far too long since we've met for drinks, and I hope you and your family are doing well. As I'm sure you can empathize, I've been terribly busy here at the bookstore. Please forgive me for not writing sooner!*
>
> *No doubt this was an oversight on your secretary's part, and I hate to even bother you with this, but when you have a moment can you please look into the increased discount we discussed a few weeks ago? I'd appreciate this a great deal.*
>
> *With warmest regards to you and Sylvia,*
> *Alan*

So it was that Penny tamed the young, impetuous Alan Kahn, saving him from the consequences of his unequaled command of all elements of the English language.

———

AFTER WORKING AT the bookstore for a few months, I was accepted as a junior at San Francisco State University. Earlier in the year, that had been the one item of the highest priority in my life. I'd yearned to move to a fantastic city and begin my studies. It was something I'd dreamed of for a very long time. Yet when I took the acceptance letter out of the envelope, I had a disarming epiphany: *I had changed my mind*. I no longer wanted to live in San Francisco, let alone begin work on my B.A. Instead, it became my intention to stay at the bookstore and, as my mother had predicted it might, see where it would lead me.

Pickwick had changed me. In a short span of time, I'd become an adult—with responsibilities, a job that inspired and motivated me, and new friendships with people who provided a real framework for my growing identity. My self-confidence was emerging like that of a feral child, and I felt free for the first time in my life. I wanted to stay in this brilliant environment for as long as possible. My parents and I discussed this turn of events, and they supported my decision to postpone college and remain at Pickwick instead. They realized even before I did that it was my destiny to make a career in the book business, and it gave them great pleasure.

I was standing at the first of many important crossroads in my life. In retrospect, I know this was the most profound choice I would ever make. It set the course for the rest of my life, and I have never—not for a moment—regretted it. When I finally returned to college fifteen years later and got a B.A. in psychology from Antioch University, I knew that my timing had been perfect.

In keeping with Shirley Arnold's original plan upon my hiring, I eventually became the manager of Pickwick's children's department. This occupied the entire mezzanine level of Pickwick and was the forerunner to the specialty children's bookshops that would, in later years, open for business all around the country. For the next year this was my domain, and while the books did appeal to me on an aesthetic level, the children (and many of the parents) did not. The kids crawled around, through, and over my immaculate displays, destroying in a moment what had taken me hours to create. This tested my patience to its limit. While my impulse was to throw these cretins over the ledge of the mezzanine, I had to grit my teeth and be polite instead, cleaning up after them, my resentment powering the broom that swept up their cookie crumbs.

It was a pleasure, however, to focus on the beauty of the illustrated books being published at the time. In the early 1970s, Maurice Sendak was on the rise, as were Remy Charlip and Edward Gorey. There was a revival of Arthur Rackham's work as well, and Fleur Cowles (*Tiger Flower*) and Steven Kellogg (*Can I Keep Him?*) were climbing up the best-seller lists. A small independent publisher, Harlan Quist, was producing ironic, gorgeous books such as *The Geranium On the Windowsill Just Died, But Teacher You Went Right On . . .*, a lovely story about an insensitive teacher who pays more attention to the textbooks than to the beauty that his students behold all around them.

Maurice Sendak published *In the Night Kitchen* during my tenure in the children's department, and I remember the controversy surrounding his vivid illustrations in this book. In it, a little boy called Mickey has a dream in which he falls through the night sky into a big bowl of cake batter, shedding his pajamas along the way until we see him completely naked, penis and all. This book was the first to break the mold of what for decades had been a puritanical genre.

At twenty years old, my sense of whimsy was just beginning to emerge, fed heartily by the ecstatic creativity in those children's books. Each day, I sorted through the cartons that arrived, filled with fairy tales, fantasies, and books about nightmares hiding in closets. I'd become lost in the beautiful images before me, while shelving both the new and backlist titles. Happy that I was finally allowed to do the reorder buying for my department, the only interruption would occur during one of my ongoing battles with Lou Epstein over the Classics section.

Mr. "E," as we fondly called him, had been president of the Pickwick Bookshop chain (which grew to sixteen locations in Southern California) since he opened the Hollywood store in 1938. He was deservedly known as the granddaddy of Los Angeles bookselling. From a hole-in-the-wall joint on Sixth Street in downtown L.A., where he sold used books, he built an empire of fine independent bookstores. When I met him, he was a seventy-year-old walking, breathing human library, with a great shock of white hair, bushy eyebrows, and a Cuban cigar always stuck in his mouth.

Mr. E expected more of me, perhaps, than he did from the other young sales clerks at Pickwick because he sensed that my interest in books was serious. In a brusquely paternal way he paid close attention to my job performance, and with a mixture of pride and fear I then set upon a course that made him my mentor. When he wasn't harassing me about my inability to speak Hebrew ("What kind of a Jew *are* you, Wendy?"), he was stalking me up on the mezzanine to find something that could be improved in the children's book department.

He eventually discovered that I was alphabetizing the children's classics by title, which I was more familiar with at that time, rather than author. This was deeply offensive to Mr. E. About once a month he would approach me, all six-foot-two of him, and chastise me for my lack of literary continuity. "It's the *parents* who buy these books," he barked, waving his cigar in my face, "not the kids! Parents are looking for *authors!*" He then began the tedious process of pulling each book off the shelves to alphabetize them by author. Watching this elderly millionaire in action, performing a minimum-wage task that he probably hadn't done for thirty years, was a remarkable sight. Regardless, because I both loved and feared him, I let him have his way.

When enough time had passed for him to forget about our running feud, I'd reshelve the books in order by title, from *Anne of Green Gables* to *The Wind in the Willows*. Then, having had a memory lapse a month or so later, he would reappear to harangue me about the errors of my ways, and the process would begin all over. It was our lovely running joke, although finally I acknowledged that he was right and kept the section alphabetized by author.

Mr. E would also engage me in discussions about sales in the children's department, advise me on how best to merchandise new releases, and chasten me when I overbought on a title. *"Far gelt bakumt men alts, nor nit kain saichel!!"* he'd say in Yiddish, shaking his finger at me affectionately. "Money buys everything except brains!"

Mr. E was a self-made man who grew up in a poor immigrant family. He was a brilliant businessman, though, and for those at Pickwick who showed more than just a passing interest in the industry, he gave of his wisdom freely. One of the many pearls he shared with me was that although best sellers are exciting, they come and go. It's basically a business of one's and two's when it comes to the backlist books that consistently make money for a bookstore over the long haul. More than three decades later, I believe this philosophy still holds true for independent bookstores.

There were no such things as discount book chains thirty years ago; in fact, this idea was simply unthinkable to Mr. E. "Never give anyone a discount!" he would tell us. "I don't even give my rabbi a discount!" But times were different back then, and when Crown Books burst on the scene ten years later with cut-rate prices, it was a hard reality to accept.

Ben Latting and Lloyd Harkema were two floor managers at Pickwick who left indelible impressions on me. If Ben was cut from the cloth of kindness, Lloyd was made from a burlap bag. They both maintained the quaint Pickwick formality, however, especially when it came to how we were all addressed—as Mr., Miss, or Mrs.—and in maintaining a strict dress code for the sales clerks. It required that the men wear coats and ties, and the womenfolk skirts or dresses (slacks of any kind were *verboten*). Of course this meant that our outsides never matched our insides, but it didn't matter.

Lloyd Harkema went to work at Pickwick in 1945. Born and raised in Massachusetts, he had an arrogance about him made worse by wielding a sadistic superiority over his staff. The man was a snob of the first order, and even his elegant suits couldn't hide from us the fact that he was a simple drunk. Most days, he went to Diamond Jim's restaurant across the street from Pickwick on his lunch breaks and came back sauced to the gills, his suit jacket sprinkled with cigarette ash.

And *how* he catered to the throngs of movie stars and directors that came through our doors! Behaving as though each one were

a personal friend, he greeted them as they came in with a sycophantic faux-familiarity that was embarrassing to observe.

Alfred Hitchcock was a frequent visitor at Pickwick. He would
browse quietly in the mystery section by himself as the staff
looked on in awe from a discreet distance. What a lovely moment
it was to respectfully peek at Mr. Hitchcock as his shiny bald head
could be seen over the tops of the bookcases, moving and bob-
bing from one end of the row to the other. But then Mr. Harkema
would spot him.

"Hitch!" he yelled, drawing the attention of everyone in the
store to the shy director, "*HITCH!!* How the hell are you?" He
would rush over to Mr. Hitchcock, who was not amused, and
pump his hand enthusiastically. There would be a collective groan
of humiliation from the staff, followed by an attempt to act as
though we didn't really work there.

I thanked my lucky stars every day for Mr. Latting, though, a
humane, civil, and elegant bookman who possessed a knowledge
of books that astounded me. Ben had a brisk, yet never abrupt, air
about him, and a spontaneous deadpan sense of humor that killed
me. In winter he dressed in tweed jackets and well-made slacks;
in summer, seersucker suits. Almost always wearing a bow tie, Mr.
Latting would stand behind the front counter of the bookstore
with a purposeful elegance, hawk-eyeing the sales clerks and customers simultaneously. He had thick, accentuated eyebrows, and
when he raised them for emphasis we never knew what would
come out of his mouth. I was standing next to him one quiet
afternoon when Ben answered the phone.

"Pickwick Bookshop—good afternoon!" he said with manic
glee. "Why, yes, Madame. You require a biography of Oscar

Levant? Mm-hmm. I'll put you on hold while I see what we presently have in stock. By the way, madame, are you aware that *him dead?*" Ben, always taking irreverent liberties with the English language, was incorrigible.

Besides making me laugh all through my shifts, Ben instilled in me three essential tools for the proper care and handling of books. Listen to me now, folks. One: never write on a piece of paper while using a book as a clipboard, for you will automatically leave an impression of your words on the cover. Two: use bookmarks! Don't hold your place in the book by bringing the dust jacket over to the right page, for you'll surely crease it. And three: for God's sake, don't even *think* about placing a book face down while it's open to the page you're on! The spine could easily crack, and then you're left with a warped copy of, say, your favorite biography of J. M. Barrie, or the latest John le Carré novel.

After about a year I received another promotion. The backlist buyer at Pickwick, who reordered books for the entire chain, was a woman named Joni Miller. She hired me to work as her assistant, and I responded happily to the chance for enlightenment from this idiosyncratic book guru who was in a class by herself.

Joni had long braids that reached almost to her waist, and thick wire-rim glasses. She dressed in hippie clothing and looked for all the world like Pickwick's resident Earth Mother. A few years older than I was, Joni immediately became my magical role model in the book business. She was as mad as a hatter, which was fine with me. Actually, I was no slouch in that area myself, so I knew this was bound to be a great match.

Joni was as smart as a whip, sophisticated (in a radiant, eccentric way), and had a dry, sarcastic cleverness that would send me off into peals of laughter several times a day. We sat side by side at a double desk on the main floor of the store, smack in the middle of all the action off of Hollywood Boulevard. Every nutcase that wandered into the store felt compelled to stop by and visit us.

It was our job to combine the branch orders to get the best discounts possible, place the orders with the publishers, and then have them drop-ship the books to the individual Pickwick locations in Southern California. This was an extremely efficient system that Mr. E had initiated years earlier.

Joni and I also worked closely with the publisher's reps who called on us, so I became familiar with their titles, discount schedules, return policies, and customer service departments. This was before the arrival of Barnes & Noble and Borders bookstores, mind you, and at the time Pickwick was one of the largest accounts the publishers had. We could, and did, pull our weight when need be, to get the special privileges our sales volume justified. Advertising allowances, extra discount points, and fast, personalized service were some of the perks we came to expect from the publishers.

When we needed books quickly, best sellers in particular, I would call the local wholesaler. They were able to deliver the books to us in two days, unlike the three or four weeks it took when we ordered from publishers on the east coast. Nowadays, bookstores continue to take advantage of this convenience.

The great challenge in working for Miss Miller was that, despite how bright and winsome she was, she seemed to have anxiety attacks on a daily basis. These occurrences were alternately hilarious and alarming, and being Joni's mental health consultant became part of my job. I was mindful of her panic when it came slowly rising to the surface and would excuse myself to take a break.

It was a short walk down to the drugstore on the corner of Highland and Hollywood. There I'd buy Joni a ration of cigarettes, Cadbury chocolate bars, and Choward's violet candies. By the time I returned, Joni looked like Elsa Lancaster in *The Bride of Frankenstein*, eyes bulging and sitting stiff as a board in her chair.

"Calm down, bwana," I'd say. "Look what I brought you!" With an exaggerated formality, I'd spread the treats out on her desk.

Within an hour, Joni's orange plastic ashtray was overflowing with Marlboro butts again, her blood sugar had normalized, and something that resembled well-being would return to her demeanor. I was working for a brilliant lunatic, and the on-the-job training would serve me well in the future, as people like Joni never ceased to cross my path in the book business as well as in my personal life.

The customers we waited on every day at Pickwick made up a roster of winners at the Oscars, Emmys, and Grammys in the early 1970s. The actors included Maggie Smith, Richard Burton, Sally Field, Michael Douglas, and Doris Day. Tom Brokaw (who was then an anchor for KNBC in Los Angeles) came in frequently, as did another television deity, Harriet Nelson. From the world of pop music we had customers such as Joni Mitchell (my personal spiritual goddess), David Crosby, Art Garfunkel, Linda Ronstadt, Elvis Presley, and Diana Ross. As for the literary giants, Tennessee Williams, Harlan Ellison, and Ray Bradbury were among the loyal Pickwick regulars.

I waited on Mick Jagger once when he came into the store. Surely he could see my jackhammer heart pounding in my chest.

My hands trembled, and I broke out in a cold sweat—in other words, I acted my age. For more than an hour, my good friend Mick and I walked around the store as I helped him to find biographies, novels, and music books. He was reserved but pleasant, which gradually made me calm down a notch or two. The rock star finally decided upon a dozen or so books, and his bill came to just under ninety dollars. It boggles my mind to realize that today that amount of money might buy all of three hardcover books—if you're lucky.

Good old Mick paid with a personal check, and needless to say I didn't ask him for I.D. When he left, I was tempted to keep his paper check for my scrapbook and cover his bill with my own money. However, since my weekly take-home pay was even less than Mick's bill, I had to kiss that idea good-bye.

THE BEST-SELLING BOOKS of those years help to put my job at Pickwick into both a literary context and a cultural time warp. In nonfiction, I recall *Bury My Heart at Wounded Knee* (Dee Brown), the book that put Native American issues squarely in the middle of discussions on racism; *I'm OK—You're OK* (Thomas A. Harris, M.D.), about transactional psychoanalysis; *Inside the Third Reich* (Albert Speer); *The Sensuous Woman* ("J"), with a theme about sexual freedom that piggybacked on the early feminist movement; and *Dr. Atkins' Diet Revolution*, which remains a best seller more than three decades later.

The range of fiction wasn't limited to any particular genre. Among my favorites were *Slaughterhouse Five* (Kurt Vonnegut);

The Exorcist (William Peter Blatty), the scariest book I'd ever read; *One Hundred Years of Solitude* (Gabriel García Márquez), which introduced Latin-American literature to a worldwide audience; *The French Lieutenant's Woman* (John Fowles); and *Rabbit Redux* (John Updike), a painfully astute portrait of middle-class Americans. Lest I neglect the other end of the literary gamut, *Jonathan Livingston Seagull* (Richard Bach), a poorly written, adolescent-level parable about finding spiritual satisfaction, sold more copies than any other novel that preceded it.

Just the mention of any of these books today instantly brings me back to the time and place that was Pickwick.

You can bet that, no matter the request, we almost always had the book the customer wanted. If it meant that a salesclerk had to climb a ladder to reach it on a high, dusty shelf, or crawl behind a bookcase where overstock sometimes ended up, Pickwick maintained an inventory that was superb. The clerks always knew where to find the stock that wasn't visibly on display. In many bookstores today, the proprietor either (understandably) can't afford to keep slower-moving books on hand or isn't intuitive enough to anticipate customers' needs. In our erudite fortress on Hollywood Boulevard, however, this was never the case.

So that was how it went for me at Pickwick, with equal measures of knowledge and madness in the salty soup of my life there. I doubt that any of us could have foreseen how profoundly the bookstore, our friendships, and our experiences there would affect us for the rest of our lives, and even, I dare say, change our destinies. But as the decades passed, each bringing more clarity to the one gone by, this became increasingly apparent to me.

Two days before Mr. E retired, he took Penny and me to lunch at our favorite restaurant, Musso and Frank's Grill. We had always been two of his pet employees, his "girls," and, over a plate of his "usual" at Musso's—half-spaghetti, half-ravioli—he spoke to us with great emotion. It was a lonely, difficult time for him, the conclusion of his long and exceptional career in the book business. He had played an immense role in making Los Angeles the second-biggest book market in the country. Penny and I were simply gob-smacked to be invited to spend a few hours alone with him.

"I look back on the years and have to ask myself what I took from them," he said. "I built the book business the way I wanted it to be. I made a lot of money. But the most important thing is that I learned so much, about books, about people, and that I'm still so wondrous of the things I see around me." As he spoke, he looked transcendent. I put my hand on his arm in a spontaneous gesture of love.

Lou Epstein was the person who helped me find my desire to be with books, to make the book business my career, and, finally, to love books as a way of life. This is what I told him at the end of our lunch together. He had given me a gift beyond measure, one that few receive in a lifetime, and it has never failed to serve me on my journey.

I resigned from Pickwick at the end of 1972, after working there for two and a half years. Before Mr. E retired, he had sold the chain to the B. Dalton Corporation, later to become Barnes & Noble, and with the old man gone the store began its transformation. It was time for me to move on. On my last day, a delivery van carrying B. Dalton's computerized cash registers pulled up in front of the store, and the new machines were unceremoniously dumped onto the countertops at the front desk. In a few months, the vintage neon "Mr. Pickwick" sign would be removed from the roof of the building, to be replaced with B. Dalton's generic logo.

It was the death knell for a cultured and romantic era of bookselling. Pickwick Bookshop was my genesis, the place where my heart and mind took root. It gave a deeper meaning to the rest of my career and set the course of my life.

Two

GATHERING MOSS
AT *ROLLING STONE*

Suddenly, surprisingly, I'm crying; mewing my sadness. Vanessa sits
up and puts her arms awkwardly over me. "It's OK, hey."
"What's going on, man?"
Vanessa rocks me. "Shhhh."
"Why is everyone so crazy?"
"It's not everyone."

—ALEXANDRA FULLER,

DON'T LET'S GO TO THE DOGS TONIGHT, 2001

WHEN I RESIGNED from Pickwick, I was all of twenty-
two years old. By that time, I'd moved out of my parents' house
and was living in my first apartment—with my best friend, Penny
Rose. We'd decided to be roommates and, against all odds, lived
together harmoniously for about a year. It was a bizarre meeting
of the minds, rather like pairing Jane Austen and Edie Sedgwick
in a home for wayward girls.

We found an apartment in Hollywood, a faux two-bedroom
place in a 1920s building that was big on Deco charm, though
light on the upkeep. I think the rent was $125 a month, which
Penny and I shared equally despite the fact that she took the actual
bedroom and I slept in the dining alcove. It didn't have a door, so

I made one out of a paisley Indian bedspread that hung from the archway on a cheap curtain rod. There was just enough room in there for a twin bed, a desk, and a small rattan stool.

Our makeshift couch in the living room was a mattress covered with yet another Indian bedspread (very hip in the 1970s) and a few throw pillows. After smoking a joint one afternoon and dashing off to a hardware store, we painted the bathroom black, leaving the trim and ceiling white. It was hideous, of course, but we were too lazy to ever get around to changing it. Poor as church mice, we'd buy two-pound blocks of cheddar cheese at the market, and most of our meals consisted of steamed rice mixed with grated cheese and frozen spinach.

Still, I was so happy to be in my own place that none of these household drawbacks mattered. I bought my first car. It was a little French number, a 1960 Simca that cost me eighty bucks. The passenger door only opened if it was kicked with brute force from the inside. It took ten minutes for the wipers to warm up before they'd work, inching their way across the windshield before reaching a level of speed that did any good in the rain. My beloved Simca came with a stick shift on the steering wheel and had tinfoil stuffed in the hole where the gas cap had once been. It suited me just fine.

The next bookstore I worked in was Papa Bach (a play on the word "paperback") in West Los Angeles. This was a far cry from Pickwick, but the pay was a bit higher and the store was special in its own way. The owner was a man named John Harris, a middle-aged, intellectual hippie who stocked Papa Bach with the best selection of literature I'd yet come across. There were books by South American, European, African, and Cuban writers that we ordered from small presses and obscure university publishers. The poetry section was much more extensive than Pickwick's. John was passionate about promoting both local and international poets whose books would otherwise never have found shelf space in Los Angeles. Unfortunately, poetry is a hard sell in the best of times, and many bookstores—both then and now—limit their inventory for fear of having to return most of it to the publishers.

Papa Bach stood on principle, though, and had a reputation as a place where minds could meet; debates were carried on freely among staff and customers about every liberal cause and issue. It was a radical melting pot of artistic freedoms and proletarian ideology, and I was never sure where I fit. After all, I was a closeted bourgeois pig.

Sure, I'd been politically active in high school and for the next several years as well. Being in the class of 1968, one of the most volatile years in the antiwar and civil-rights movements, my political awareness came hard and fast. It was easy to get swept up in the power of that time, when the Black Panthers were changing the course of African Americans and Lyndon Johnson was forcing our troops to slaughter innocent people in Vietnam. My boyfriend and I had been part of the demonstration at the Century Plaza Hotel the night President Johnson was there, finding ourselves in the middle of the melee that ensued, police in riot gear throwing tear gas, provoking tears of pain, rage, and fear.

Although I was politically well-intentioned, eventually I had to call my motives into question. I believed with my whole heart in peace and social justice; this was how my parents had raised me. Where my doubt came in was in my ability to create change by falling into the mass of protestors and public demonstrations that seemed to create more hostility than clarity. It seemed that the complexity of the political issues was not being served well by hysteria and resentment. When I finally retreated from that arena, it was because I came to believe, as I do today, that a just and peaceful world must begin in the consciousness of the individual.

Both the customers and my co-workers at Papa Bach were freewheeling Socialists, Marxists, and feminists. Undeniably, it was an interesting environment to work in, vastly different from the comfortable political niche I had long inhabited, and I learned more about ideologies than I ever thought possible. What inhibited me, however, was my inability to think outside the box.

As at Pickwick, I had quickly learned about a certain kind of bookselling. As one of the buyers at Papa Bach, the challenges of ordering for a small independent bookstore soon became clear. We dealt with many alternative presses, most of which I was unfamiliar with, and their minimum-order requirements made it difficult to reach the quantity for a discount we could live with (traditionally, a retailer requires a 40 percent discount off the list price of a book to meet its sales margin). At Pickwick, we were able to fill special orders within a few days, but I found myself having to wait two or three weeks before accumulating enough books to place an order for Papa Bach with many of these small presses.

A part of me missed selling the books on the *New York Times* best-seller lists. Instead of mainstream fiction, the shelves in the store were filled with dense philosophical novels by Czech and French writers. Papa Bach eschewed the popular book categories for a heady stock of literary criticism, postmodern philosophy, and political theory titles. Ironically, fifteen years later, I would begin repping publishers that specialize in these academic books, but at the time I had very little interest in or understanding of them.

Being such a writer-friendly store, Papa Bach sponsored poetry readings at least once a month. I was there for most of them because I was still writing poetry at the time and loved the wild, spontaneous nature of these events. Wine and cheese were served in abundance, and as the evenings went on they became increasingly raucous. Most performance art as we know it today has its roots in the Beat movement of the 1950s and early '60s, when poetry readings were theatrical, uninhibited, and confrontational, as the poets engaged freely with the audience.

Bukowski gave a reading at Papa Bach once, already drunk when he arrived at the store. We'd bought a case of beer especially for him that night, and he guzzled bottle after bottle while ranting from *The Days Run Away Like Wild Horses Over the Hills*. This was about a year after the folly of my visit to his apartment. When his bleary eyes skimmed over my face, I was grateful for the lack of recognition. All I wanted was to soak up the sleight-of-hand in his words. Even when he turned mean and vulgar toward the end of the reading, I could appreciate the heat of his aggressive, radiant charm.

I only lasted at Papa Bach for six months. Pickwick was an impossible act to follow, and the ambience at my new job was far too sanctimonious for my trickster mentality. I didn't get into the book business to sell posters of Che Guevara and Bobby Seale, although I respected the sentiment that readers attached to these militant icons. When the opportunity arose, I left for a better-paying job at Campbell's Bookstore in Westwood, adjoining the UCLA campus.

A true carriage-trade bookstore with an air of privilege and taste, it was the antithesis of Papa Bach. The owners, Blanche and Robert Campbell, were terribly conservative book people—very pleasant to work for, but pedantic and old-fashioned. They were an elderly couple who had owned the bookstore for decades. She wore pearls every day, he a dark suit and tie, and they both addressed me as "dear." I was happy to be back in my retail element at Campbell's, surrounded by shelves of general trade books and where the stock came close to being as broad and thoughtful 'as that of Pickwick's. Grateful to have a job in the middle of the recession of 1973, I plugged away as a salesclerk with my usual enthusiasm and humor. It was fun to hand-sell copies of my favorite books of that year, including *Sybil* (Flora R. Schreiber) and *Something Happened* (Joseph Heller). Above all, *84 Charing Cross Road* by Helene Hanff finally came out in paperback. This is one of my best-loved books of all time, and if you haven't discovered it yet I recommend it with my whole heart. Told through a series of smart and witty letters, it's the true tale of a New York bibliophile during World War II and her relationship with the owner and staff of a used bookshop in London. I placed this book in more hands while I worked at Campbell's than any other in my career.

After a year there, I realized that boredom was slapping me in the face. Compared to the histrionics at Pickwick and the intellectual, radical environment at Papa Bach, the clientele at Campbell's was so colorless as to be stifling. I sensed that retail bookselling had run its course in my life. My education had been stellar, my teachers brilliant and wise. It had exposed me to the whole range of human nature, and in the process I discovered the willingness to take risks.

I began to consider publishing as my next career move. In the spring of 1973, Campbell's was sold to the Brentano's bookstore chain. *Again* with the computerized cash registers! *Again* with the bar codes that made me dizzy! It seemed the perfect time for me to quit, so I did. Without a job, and with mixed feelings on both sides, I moved back in with my parents. They'd left my bedroom just as it had been when I'd moved out two years earlier. The orange shag carpeting and purple paint on the walls (I'd insisted on this décor after discovering LSD in 1967) were there to greet me like old, slightly irritating friends.

At first we circled one another warily, my parents and I, unaccustomed as we were to the changing roles in the household. I was a different person than before I'd moved out, with a broader sense of self and boundaries that I kept drawing closer to my mental circumference. But I was a guest in their house now and had to maintain a new regard for my parents' own boundaries, vague though they were. It didn't take long before I realized that their lifestyle hadn't changed much at all.

I woke up at three in the morning once to use the bathroom and heard voices coming from the downstairs den. Rubbing my eyes, I walked into the room. There was my father with Gallagher, the comedian who invented the Sledge-O-Matic in the 1970s and had established a large fan base after appearing on national television several times. Dad, Gallagher's mentor, was sitting in his favorite red armchair, a dopey audience of one watching the comic try out a new sketch he'd been working on. I stood there in my pajamas until they noticed me.

"Honey!" my dad said, "is everything all right?" as though something was peculiar in *my* world.

"What are you doing, Dad? It's after three in the morning. You'll wake Mom up."

"Oh, she just went to bed," he replied. "She fixed us something to snack on."

I stared at the two of them for a long beat. *You're both insane*, I thought, noting the full highball glasses on the coffee table, *and so is my mother*. "Hi, Leo," I said to Gallagher. "Good night, Leo." Then I shuffled back upstairs to the relative quiet of my bedroom and went back to sleep. Home sweet home—oh, yeah.

Working in bookstores made me take notice of new and unique publishers. Straight Arrow, the book division of *Rolling Stone*, published *Fear and Loathing on the Campaign Trail*, Hunter S. Thompson's break-out book, in 1973. Annie Leibowitz, at that time the staff photographer for the magazine, published her first collection of photos with Straight Arrow. It was called *Shooting Stars,* a portfolio of Annie's images of 1960s rock-and-roll icons. Another hit for the press was *The Big Fix*, Roger Simon's hard-boiled mystery that featured a private investigator named Moses Wine. It was one of the best American mysteries I'd read.

But it was their publication of *A Connoisseur's Guide to Marijuana*, by William Daniel Drake, that broke Straight Arrow's meter on the scale of hip controversy. This marked the first time a publisher boldly went forward with a traditional trade book that supported a recreational drug. *Marijuana* was boldly marketed— not in secrecy, or behind a veil of double-entendre—but out in the open, with ads in *Publishers Weekly* (then the book industry's only trade magazine, read by everyone in the business) and in the country's biggest newspapers. It was sent out for review with the same confidence that a big house would employ for a novel or biography. Straight Arrow brought pot out of the closet and placed it upon mainstream America's coffee tables, with style and courage.

Why would I want to work for any other publisher?

Not even knowing if there were any job openings, I went after Straight Arrow with single-minded intensity. In May 1973, the American Booksellers Association (ABA) held its annual convention in Los Angeles. Most of the publishers in the United States would be converging on the convention center to hawk their forthcoming books for the fall publishing season, pump up the advances on the lead titles and symbolically prostitute themselves (while gravely denying it) to retail customers both big and small. They all tried to outshine one another with the magnitude and glitz of their booths.

You'd think that a book convention would somehow be more urbane, less strident than those of, say, the sports, food, or electronics industries, wouldn't you? What a laugh. The product may be rather more erudite, the personalities more cerebral, but when it comes to making money the publishing industry is no different from the rest. It's all a hustle, and the ABA trade show was a shock to my preconceived notions.

I walked into a huge hall with overhead lights so bright, they made my eyes sting. Men in suits leered at me—and at every other young woman in proximity—while neon-colored banners on each aisle moved slowly in the gentle draft of air conditioners. Some booksellers walked around steering shopping carts into which they absentmindedly tossed free books, while others were weighed down with backpacks brimming with posters, buttons, bound galleys, and promotional book litter. And every few minutes I was startled by the voice of Royce Smith, the ABA's president for many years, which came over the loudspeakers to announce raffle drawings and to admonish publishers for abandoning their booths during the lunch hour.

It was like a county fair, or a vaudeville production, and at first I found it appalling. Was I at the right convention? And if I was, what the hell was I doing there? I put my cigarette out in an ashtray at the Random House booth, shook the fog from my head, and soldiered on with the brazen ignorance of a fool.

My God! I cringe to think of the unflattering gray suit and spike heels I wore that day. I teetered along with the grace of a water buffalo. Just when my poor feet were about to give out on me, I found myself standing in front of the Straight Arrow booth. There were huge blow-ups of the dust jackets of their new books on the walls, small, round conference tables stacked high with catalogs and order forms, and bound galleys of their lead titles for fall 1973 that were handed out discreetly to a few lucky booksellers and reviewers.

After a few minutes of espionage, I asked a woman wearing a Straight Arrow ABA badge around her neck who the person in charge might be. "The president of the company is Alan Rinzler," she said. "He's standing right behind you."

Turning, I saw a thin, wiry man with a salt-and-pepper Afro that was spiked up and out like Hebraic cotton candy gone mad. Nervously running his hands through his hair he looked seriously, unnervingly intense. Wire-rimmed glasses sat on his softly beaked nose. He wore a tweed suit that matched the color of his curly locks. Approaching him, I extended my hand.

"I understand you're the president of Straight Arrow Books."
Alan took my hand and held it, trying to figure out if he knew me.

"Who are you?" His eyes squinted suspiciously.

"I'm Wendy Werris—and I want to work for you," I crowed.
He was still holding my hand, the palm of which was now sweaty.

"Ah-ha!" Alan gave me a fixed look. "Are you Jewish?" he
asked. His question unnerved me; surely he was joking.

"Well, yes," I said cagily. Now *I* was the suspicious one.

"Ah-ha! Me too. What's your sign?"

"Scorpio," I muttered, annoyed now, sweat breaking out on my
brow. At least he had let go of my hand.

His face lit up. "Me too! When's your birthday?"

Then it dawned on me. This wasn't a joke: it was my *interview*,
and I knew that if I aced this last essential question I'd be hired.
I took an extremely deep breath. "It's October 26," I squeaked.

Alan slapped his hand to his forehead and cried, "OH, MY
GOD! ME TOO! When can you start?"

And with that, my life in publishing began. I'd met my ethnic,
astrological, and psychic twin. Alan Rinzler would become my
new mentor on this next, questionable part of my journey through
the book business.

I drove home that day down Olympic Boulevard in a daze, my
new car—a 1963 turquoise blue Nash Rambler—bouncing along
on its last spring and four dying spark plugs. When I walked into
the house, my parents were waiting anxiously for me. "Well?" my
mother said. "How did it go?"

"I think I'm moving to San Francisco," I told them, and before
they could respond I turned, took the stairs to my room two at a
time and went to bed at four in the afternoon.

———

IT TOOK NEARLY two months for Rinzler to create a job description for me, negotiate my salary with the CFO of *Rolling Stone*, and get them to agree to pay for my move to San Francisco. I endured a very weird summer in 1973, living with my parents on Alta Vista Boulevard and being unemployed. I waited on tenterhooks for Straight Arrow to make a commitment to me with a firm job offer. It was a time of demented turmoil in the midst of too many hours to fill. I read *The Last Temptation of Christ* by Nikos Kazantzakis for the second time, clipped cartoons from *The New Yorker,* and did crossword puzzles with my father. He was working in his home office that summer, usually with a flask of icy Smirnoff vodka on the desk next to his new-fangled electric typewriter. When he wasn't busy with freelance writing gigs (which were few and far between), he was hired for acting jobs in television shows that were popular at the time—*Chico and the Man, Gilligan's Island,* and *The Brady Bunch.* Dad was a great character actor, another benefit accrued from his years in vaudeville.

It pained me to see his writing career beginning to falter. With the incredible success of *Laugh-In,* the style of comedy was changing. For the first time in their long association, my father's writing agent was having a difficult time getting work for him because of Dad's age—and he was barely in his sixties. Young TV producers were hiring young, "hip" writers who were attuned to the youth market. Despite my father's spectacular résumé, and the many stars he had written for, he found that his talent had become passé, an afterthought, a creative relic of times past. Ageism is a cruel reality of the Hollywood caste system.

He and my mother maintained their pleasant lifestyle for as long as they could, staying in touch with and continuing to entertain their wide circle of friends in the industry. It was important to them to keep up the appearance of stability, while falling victim to a wretched charade in the process. My parents were good, decent people and deserved better. When the Writers Guild canceled my father's health insurance because his income had fallen, my cynicism about show business crystallized. The demise of my father's career was so heartbreaking that I swore always to keep my career at a safe distance from Hollywood's egomaniacal trappings.

That summer I stayed up late with my folks to watch Johnny Carson on *The Tonight Show.* One hot July night, Johnny did a sketch in which he played a man talking to the Jolly Green Giant, the animated star of a popular TV commercial for frozen corn. When the curtain opened, Johnny was standing on the stage in between two extremely tall, bright green legs made out of Styrofoam. He was looking up and having a conversation with the Giant, whose face was out of camera range. The Giant bellowed to Johnny in the low, bass "Ho, ho, ho" voice that the commercial made famous. At one point, Johnny said something that offended the Giant, who then pelted him from above with huge kernels of bright yellow fake corn. It was a funny gag and made us all laugh.

Dad's birthday was two days later. I went to the market for my mother, who was preparing a special meal for the family that night. Driving back from the store, I was in the distracted state I'd grown accustomed to all summer while waiting to hear from Straight Arrow.

As I approached the house, I could have sworn there were two fifteen-foot-tall green legs standing on our front lawn. When I got a little closer, my hallucination expanded to reveal a pile of basketball-sized kernels of bright yellow corn. It was then that I drove the car right up the curb and onto our front lawn.

I got out of the car, walked over, and knocked on the legs. I wasn't hallucinating, they were really there, and as wide around as the old eucalyptus tree on our lawn. Then I picked up one of the corn kernels, which weighed almost nothing. As I stood there holding it and staring up to see where the tops of the legs ended—a couple of feet above our roof—my mother came walking out of the house.

"What the hell is this?" I yelled, caught between a laugh and a scream. "How did this get here?"

My mother stood there in bare feet, an apron tied around her waist, herself flummoxed. "Get in the house, damn it. Move the car and bring in the groceries *right now*."

I did all three and then plopped down on the couch in the living room, my mother facing me on the love seat. "You know John Shrum, your father's friend?" she asked.

I nodded my head. John was the art director for *The Tonight Show* and had been to parties at our house many times. "Well, he found out it was Dad's birthday and had those props delivered on a truck about an hour ago. This is John's idea of a joke."

I stared at my mother, still in a daze. "When does John plan to take the Jolly Green Giant away?" We could hear the chatter and shrill laughter coming from our front lawn, where the neighbors were gathering.

"We don't know," my mother replied glumly. "Your father is very upset. He has a call in to John at the studio."

I shot up off the couch. "You don't *know*? What do you mean, you don't know? I don't believe this! Our house looks like a float in the Rose Bowl parade!" Storming out of the room, I ran upstairs to pout in my bedroom.

How had I become a member of this family? My father was nuts; my mother popped Valium every ninety minutes. Show business attracted a gang of rascals into our lives, circling our threshold like happy thieves come to steal any chance we had at being a "normal" family. Sure, there were things to be said for the insane realm of spontaneity we lived in. Sometimes I was even proud of my family for being so skewed. But having the Jolly Green Giant on our front lawn for more than three days was not one of those times. We made the nightly news, and people drove by our house to take pictures at all hours. It was embarrassing, and I wanted the spectacle and attention to go away.

More than that, *I* wanted to go away, as far away from my family as possible. When Alan Rinzler finally called with the good news that I'd been hired, I couldn't get away from Los Angeles fast enough. Within a week I was packed and had made arrangements to stay with a friend in San Francisco while I looked for my own place. My parents threw me a wonderful going-away party where I got drunk and went on a crying jag. When my departure date finally arrived, I waved good-bye to them through the window of the Rambler, hit Highway 101, and careened north toward my new life in book publishing.

Did it ever occur to me how woefully unprepared—and underqualified—I was for the job at Straight Arrow? Nah. Or if it did, my consciousness rejected the idea. I was so bloody young, a compulsive know-it-all, mesmerized by the idea of risk. Leaving L.A. for the first time, coupled with the leap from retail bookselling to publishing, didn't faze me at the time. It seemed I'd inherited my mother's nerve and my father's mental flexibility—or so I thought.

The Straight Arrow office was in the same building as *Rolling Stone* itself, in San Francisco's lower Market Street district on Third Street. It was a four-story brick structure that was right next door to the MJB Coffee factory, and on my first morning at work I was welcomed by the smell of roasting beans. Taking the elevator up to the second floor, I was met by Alan Rinzler's British secretary, a lovely young woman named Rosemary Nightingale. She took me to Alan's office, where he greeted me with a hug and introduced me to his dog, Pushkin, who was a brown standard poodle with vast amounts of bushy fur that was not unlike Alan's own mop. I scratched his head, and both he and Alan approved. Pushkin came to the office every day and had a perfect attendance record, something which I would fail to achieve.

The three of us walked affably around the bright, loftlike office as Alan introduced me to the staff. I shook hands with Straight Arrow's managing editor, art director, and production manager, all of them stylish people with an aesthetic I'd never encountered before, exuding all things exotic and cool in their friendly faces. I found them an intimidating bunch at first, but then they all succeeded in breaking through my uncharacteristically shy exterior during my first week on the job.

My position at Straight Arrow—which, inauspiciously, never did acquire a title—was primarily as the head of marketing, a loose concept that in my case included publicity, inventory control, and acting as sales liaison between Straight Arrow and its distributor, Simon & Schuster. My office was enormous, overlooking Third Street with a view of the cable car tracks below. I was given an IBM Selectric typewriter, the largest desk I'd ever seen, and four bulging file cabinets. Not one part of this environment was familiar to me.

When I first sat down at my desk and scanned the office, I was in shock. A deranged urge came over me to run into Alan's office and tell him that I'd lied about everything. "Just kidding, Rinzler!" I wanted to say. "I made it all up! I'm not a Jew—I'm Catholic! And my birthday's really in May! All I know about marketing is that my mother calls it 'food shopping!'"

What I actually told him, though, was that I would depend upon his guidance to get started, needed it, required it. Alan, bless him, then went out of his way during those first hysterical weeks to provide me with his patient support, as did everyone else in the office. I finally began to settle in and soaked up information about my job like a thirsty pup.

Here was where I went for the bimonthly sales and inventory reports. *There* was where I looked for the year-to-date spreadsheets. The weekly production schedules and sales figures kept me current on which books got priority in the area of publicity. I gradually updated and revised the Rolodex I'd inherited from the previous marketing person and began to memorize important phone numbers. The file cabinets took on an orderly, useful countenance. There was suddenly a rhythm to my work, and life at Straight Arrow became something to cautiously enjoy. Thoughts of failure had been living rent-free in my head from my first day on the job, and I was having trouble with the eviction process, though I continued acting as if everything was fine, making a difference in my overall attitude—or my outward appearance, anyway.

A month in, it was time for me to find an apartment. I'd been staying with friends, which was getting old. The place I rented was on Jones Street in San Francisco's Russian Hill area, a one-bedroom apartment on the third floor with bay windows facing the street. I loved my place, the hardwood floors, the big rooms, and the way my meager furnishings fit perfectly in them. I loved the sounds of the city that slipped through my windows. Being in the middle of the block, I heard cable cars running on either corner. At night they came tearing down Jackson Street, filled with excited tourists, their screams competing with the metallic whine of braking cables. The finest sounds of all, though, came from the ships in the bay as they came and went. Their foghorns were deep and sad and matched my homesick thoughts bellow for bellow.

Parking spaces in my neighborhood were so scarce that the old Rambler I'd driven to San Francisco became a burden. I soon got rid of it in a trade with one of the founders of Bookpeople, the venerable wholesaler in Berkeley. I got the better end of the bargain in a twelve-string Gibson guitar. Public transportation in the city made it easy for me to get around, and the bus and cable cars, not to mention the surprising—for this L.A. denizen—pleasure of walking, became my new modes of mobility. On Saturday mornings I'd stroll down to Cala Foods on Polk Street to do my weekly shopping. It was a hell of a trek up and down those hills, but the consummate way for me to claim my new territory and create a sense of belonging.

Living on Russian Hill also gave me a bizarre familiarity with the FBI. Patty Hearst had been kidnapped by the Symbionese Liberation Army earlier that year, and my neighborhood was targeted for regular searches. FBI agents appeared on my block on a weekly basis to question residents about the missing heiress, and the drama queen in me loved their visits.

Every Sunday night, I made a collect call to my parents in Los Angeles. These conversations occurred with varying degrees of satisfaction, depending on whether or not my father was drunk, and on how my mother was feeling. Two years earlier she'd had her first episode of heart failure, leaving her health in a precarious state. Not yet sixty, my mother was on the path to an early death, which I couldn't bear to consider. Life brought me a period of conflicting sensibilities that occurred as I reached my midtwenties, a singular state of mind that gathered itself around me when I lived in San Francisco. My thoughts about my parents were stuck between need and independence, and even the perspective I gained of their inner lives while apart from them didn't help me to understand what role they played in my life, and vice versa. It would be decades before clarity would settle in.

In time, there were successes at Straight Arrow. I was first involved with the publication of *The Mutant King*, David Dalton's groundbreaking biography of James Dean. We sent David out on a book tour, with interviews and appearances coordinated by yours truly. My next major assignment was for a book called *The Firesign Theatre's Big Mystery Joke Book*. The troupe consisted of four brilliant writers and comics who performed irreverent political and social satire in a series of skits and vignettes. The Firesign Theatre, whose most popular comedy album was *If You Lived Here, You'd Be Home By Now*, was a forerunner to *Saturday Night Live*, and it was my good fortune to design a publicity program for their book with Straight Arrow, including print ads that would appear upside-down.

Alan Rinzler, in the meantime, continued to amaze me. We worked well together; he was tenacious and indulgent with me, as he freely shared his shrewd discernment about book publishing. When I ran out of ideas about how to market a book, he'd come to my rescue and suggest new ways to find an angle. "Dig up something interesting about the author," he'd suggest. "Do some research into similar books. How were they marketed? What tag lines were used? Be covert—investigate. You're a Scorpio! You can do it." And, longing for his approval, I always did. But my pleasure in completing a project was always tainted with the fear that I wasn't good enough; that I would someday be revealed as the fraud I felt myself to be.

Straight Arrow had an annual "Picnic Pageant," a sort of freestyle, rambling potluck party for the office staff and whatever freelance editors happened to be in town. That fall, it was held on Angel Island in San Francisco Bay. We all piled onto a ferry to get there, Pushkin taking the starboard position. He happily barked his head off during the whole ride. Rinzler brought the dope, Rolling Stone sprang for the wine and cheese, and the rest of us brought a dish or two. Me, I made *matzoh brei*—per Alan's request.

It was a dazzling afternoon, sunlight casting out like diamonds across the bay, white gulls in repose on the periphery of our festivity. We all danced to tunes coming from Rosemary's portable stereo, strains of Stevie Wonder's *Innervisions* album and *Slow Dancer* by Boz Scaggs providing a hypnotic background for the pleasures of the day. We swapped stories and told jokes and flirted shamelessly with one another. Some of us passed out from too much of a good thing. It was the day that I finally bonded with the whole of Straight Arrow, and by the time our ferry returned to its dock I was genuinely smitten with my co-workers.

Moving to San Francisco meant that I had been separated from my family and friends for the first time, and the ensuing freedom turned me into something of a shape-shifter. My experiences there had no precedent, fueled as they were by the glamour of life under the *Rolling Stone* umbrella. Several times a day I shared the elevator or the stairs with people such as Jann Wenner, Annie Leibowitz, and Ben Fong-Torres, folks who had begun their careers at the magazine, achieving high-profile success.

Hunter Thompson used to wander into the Straight Arrow domain, parking himself in Alan's office while in one kind of stoned state or another. When I was first introduced to him, he was standing in front of Alan's desk, wearing his trademark aviator sunglasses while holding a beer can in one hand and a cigarette holder in the other. I couldn't stop staring at the gin blossoms on Hunter's nose. He gave me a dazed smile and just shrugged, holding up full hands that made it impossible for him to shake mine, too wasted to say a word. I nodded at him and walked out of the room. Hunter's oblivion was the trash compactor for his fame. My heart broke years later when he killed himself.

There was a charmingly seedy bar in North Beach called Enrico's where my co-workers and I sometimes met for drinks after work. One night, a group of us gathered there at a round table on the patio that faced Carol Doda's strip club on Broadway, her neon torso with its theatrically huge breasts flashing on and off from the pink sign. I was enjoying myself, about to order my second drink, when I saw the shape of an extremely tall man from the corner of my eye. His height felt oppressive to me, and I turned around to look up at him. I realized that it was Richard Brautigan. He looked almost comically like a life-size cutout of himself from the cover of *In Watermelon Sugar*, his current best-selling book of poetry. Someone at our table knew him and waved him over; Brautigan sat down right next to me at the table.

Even though he was sitting down, Brautigan was so tall that I still had to look up at him to see his face, framed as it was by wire-rimmed glasses almost identical to mine. His shoulder-length hair was a washed-out shade of brown and more than a little unkempt, and perched atop his head was a floppy brown hat. He was wearing a sports coat that had seen better days, and a pair of greasy Levi's that needed a good wash and were shredded where they reached the toes of his cowboy boots. He was also drunk. Instead of recoiling from him, I was enchanted. All through the '60s and '70s, Brautigan's poetry seemed to be standard reading among my friends, and it had touched and influenced my own life.

He ordered a vodka martini and, although I hadn't asked, another one for me. There was conversation going on around us, but because he had quietly slipped his arm around my shoulder I instantly fell deaf and dumb. There I was with America's poet *du jour*. He was pressing his thigh against mine and matched my stark silence moment for moment. My friends from Straight Arrow kept up the appearance of casual cocktail banter, although it suddenly felt conspiratorial to me. Brautigan and I must have looked like a couple of morons, he with an empty grin on his face and me with wild eyes darting here and there, silently asking my friends, "Help me! What should I do *now*?" As my intuition failed me, Brautigan ordered another round of drinks for the table and made ours doubles.

Finally, without ever having learned my name, he turned to me and asked where I lived. "Jones and Washington," I breathed, staring into his bloodshot eyes. It was then that I realized how unattractive he was, how nearly ugly his poor face was. Had the ruined features suddenly rearranged themselves into something approaching elegance, all the pain in his eyes would still have given the appearance of an unbearably distraught soul. He would, in fact, be dead of a self-inflicted gunshot wound to the head in a decade.

"Will you take me home with you?" he asked in a flatlined voice.

It wasn't that I had mixed feelings about this question; I had *no* feelings, I was so drunk. In the end, it was my ego that responded to Brautigan, the last thing to go when one has had too much to drink, and my brain was able to make a decision based on what it knew would be an experience later to become legendary in my life.

"Yes. Let's go. Let's get a cab," I said, taking his hand, saying a sheepish good-bye to my friends and leading Brautigan out to the street. All six-foot-five of him waved down a taxi that was headed in the direction of my apartment. We sat together in the backseat kissing like grumpy half-wits, haphazard in our groping that did not end until the cabdriver cleared his throat to get our attention. We had arrived at my front door.

After paying the fare, Brautigan and I managed to climb the two flights of stairs to my apartment. Once inside, I felt it would be the civilized thing to do to mention that I'd read all of his books and thought he was a fine poet. My words had the effect of making him stare at me dumbly and begin taking off his clothes at the foot of my bed. The sound of his belt, hitting the hardwood floor with its heavy and elaborate Western-style buckle, was his only audible response to me.

Having sex with Brautigan was more a cognitive gesture on my part than anything else. I was too conscious of having a brand name in my bed to accept anything more than just a vague idea of pleasure. Afterward, we fell asleep almost at once, his long body draped over mine in a "Z" so that he could fit on my bed. When I woke the next morning, he was gone—no note, tender or otherwise, scrawled on a piece of paper; no evidence that he'd ever been there. He left behind nothing of himself at all, and a sad stillness came over me.

Brautigan was becoming an empty vessel at that stage of his life, all the bright spirit that created his poetry sliding out of his grasp. While sipping coffee in my tiny kitchen that morning, I contemplated the perverse rite of passage in having had a one-night stand with a literary star.

When I got to work that morning, I threw my purse and briefcase on my desk and ran into Rinzler's office. "Oh, Alan!" I shouted for all the office to hear, "I slept with Richard Brautigan last night!"

"Great!" said Rinzler, absently scratching the top of Pushkin's head. "Do you think I can sign him for his next book now?"

Such was the absurdity of life at Straight Arrow. I never saw Brautigan again, and Rinzler was always disappointed that we were never able to publish him.

After six months with Straight Arrow, I was finally able to establish which part of my jumbled work description I was best at and enjoyed the most. Clearly, it was the sales angle. This part of publishing intrigued me, and in a way that made me really sit up and pay attention to what I was doing.

I had the spunk and confidence to persuade all sorts of Straight Arrow customers to participate in mutually beneficial transactions. If it was a co-op ad we wanted to run with a bookstore, I persuaded the owner to cough up part of the money. Getting our distributor to lower their fee to us? Piece of cake. And when Straight Arrow published *100 Years of Erotica*, a collection of vintage porn photography, I was able to get Alan Kahn, who had left Pickwick to become senior buyer for the B. Dalton chain, to stop worrying about potential lawsuits and order the book.

I finally got up the nerve to ask Rinzler if I could go out on a couple of sales calls with our local rep, David McCumskey. He agreed, and I got my first shot at selling our titles to the buyers at a couple of Bay Area bookstores.

We went first to City Lights in San Francisco, owned by the poet Lawrence Ferlinghetti and one of the great landmark bookstores in the country. I'd read Ferlinghetti's classic, *A Coney Island of the Mind*, when in high school, and meeting him that day was thrilling. His gentle cheerfulness put me at ease. The City Lights buyer, a wonderful guy named Paul Yamazaki, brought a lot of humor to the sales meeting and made me feel included in the buying process.

From there McCumskey and I drove to Berkeley for his appointment at Cody's Books on Telegraph Avenue. Cody's had opened in the 1940s, around the same time as Pickwick Bookshop. The owner, Fred Cody, was a contemporary of Lou Epstein's and nearly as legendary. While listening to him banter with our sales rep, it was clear that Fred was an intuitive, dedicated book man. He engaged me in the discussions about niche markets for each of the Straight Arrow books, putting ideas in my head about the different philosophies of bookselling. I knew I hadn't developed my own wisdom about this yet, but perhaps one day I might. As I observed the process of negotiation between book buyer and rep during a sales call—the different ways there are to present a title, and the ratio of schmooze to gravitas when selling books—I was furiously taking mental notes on the give and take that would later become invaluable to me.

Have you ever had a revelation? It bubbles over in your head like a brew of hops and dry ice, waking you up in a blast of mental harmonics with the force of ten semitrucks honking their horns at the same time. You know what I'm talking about. It happened to me while I was sitting at my desk one afternoon at Straight Arrow, when I realized that I hated my job. It was at odds with my evolving self-image. The press releases I churned out were substandard. Because I was born lacking the techno-math gene, inventory control made me fall asleep on my typewriter. Book distribution was about as interesting to me as Rod McKuen's poetry. Further, I felt confined and diminished by working in an office that swayed to a nine-to-five beat, regardless of the many perks that came with being an employee of *Rolling Stone*.

It became abundantly clear that I was a natural-born salesperson; a book-whore with a heart of gold. I had what it took to pack up a briefcase with catalogs and order forms and get on the road to peddle books wherever I could. From that moment on, and with the subtlety of a juvenile delinquent, I subconsciously set about to get myself fired.

Rinzler sent me to Washington, D.C., to run our exhibit booth at the ABA convention. He went as well but spent most of his time elsewhere, huddled in meetings with writers and literary agents. This left me trapped in our booth alone with my old friends Resentment and Compulsion, and the three of us had a brain pow-wow. *Hey! Let's take the train to New York and spend a few days with that old boyfriend of yours! Rinzler won't even notice you're gone!* Why, what a brilliant idea. Thanks, guys! If I hurry, I can catch the 5:10!

So I left the convention, left Washington, and disappeared into Manhattan for a lover's tryst. It was a colossally stupid, thought-less move; and when I waltzed back into the office three days later, a letter was waiting on my desk. I'd been terminated, and by July 1974 I was saying good-bye to the pressure cooker that was Straight Arrow Books.

It took me only a few weeks of seventy-dollar unemployment checks, coupled with my wounded pride and sense of shame, to decide to go home. I was lost in San Francisco, and my identity there felt indistinct. Who the hell was I? In the Bay Area, irony eluded me and hipness was my foe. Worst of all, the shockingly immature way I had abandoned Straight Arrow and disappointed Alan Rinzler was never far from my thoughts. I was so ashamed of myself that my only option was to run away.

Like it or not, my parents remained a source of great comfort and safety to me, and I couldn't wait to get back to them, my friends, and the flat landscape of Los Angeles. When I boarded the flight to the Burbank airport, my bags seemed curiously light, all the weight of my previous life having shifted to the task at hand— to find my integrity and bind up my future like the sturdy pages of a hand-sewn book.

Three

A YOUNG LADY SALESMAN

"I do not at all understand the mystery of grace—only that it meets us where we are but does not leave us where it found us."
—ANNE LAMOTT

WHEN I SNUCK back into Los Angeles in August 1974, head hanging, feet dragging, it was with the knowledge that I literally couldn't go home again.

My parents, who could no longer afford the mortgage on our house, had been forced to sell. It had finally happened: show business had kicked my father in the ass, and he was nearly broke. What a terrible time this was for my family; helpless to change the situation, desperate for redemption of any kind. The final insult lay in the timing of the sale of the house, which coincided with the deepest recession the country had known in my lifetime. My parents realized no profit at all from the sale of the Alta Vista homestead.

They moved into a duplex in the Miracle Mile area. It was close to our former neighborhood, comfortable and spacious enough for them, but it didn't have room for little ol' me. My sister Laurie came to the rescue, and I moved into the apartment in West L.A. that she shared with her then-husband. They let me stay in the spare room, where I slept on a sofa bed. It was agreed that I could stay there for one month and would pay them a token amount for room and board.

I looked for a job in a clumsy, half-hearted way. Feeling battered by the experience at Straight Arrow, my daily routine included a tendency to sleep until eleven o'clock, fix a late breakfast, and then scan the *L.A. Times* classifieds while in my pajamas. Having completed my work for the day, I'd then relax by either hitting the bargain matinee or going to the beach for a few hours. My skin had turned pale while living in the ghastly damp of San Francisco, and lying on the sand to work up a tan became the crux of my exercise regimen. Occasionally my mother would take me out to lunch, or I'd visit their place to mooch a meal at dinnertime. While living with my sister, my think tank did not exactly runneth over with ideas about my next job.

Toward the end of my third month of the good life at Laurie's, she threw me out. Who could blame her? I'd stopped paying rent, and I was a slob of the first order. My inertia and childish sense of entitlement made me a popular candidate for eviction on anyone's ticket. "Baa, baa, black sheep," I said to myself. "Get a clue. And an apartment."

A combination of unemployment benefits and a few secretarial jobs I did for a temp agency made it possible to rent a place of my own, and I moved in just before Laurie had a chance to kill me in my sleep. My new home was a large single apartment on Formosa Avenue in Hollywood, not far from my dad's former office at Paramount Studios. It was in one of those classic 1920s courtyard buildings, with a strip of lawn dividing the rows of apartments and free-form succulents growing tall near the front windows.

Things there deteriorated rapidly. I began buying half-gallon bottles of pink Gallo "wine," the thought of which now makes me want to hurl. Under the guise of being an *artiste*, I'd drink and smoke cigarettes all day long while sitting at my desk, churning out page after page of poetic drivel. Maybe this was my drunken attempt to emulate my father, the Writer; to compete with him, get back at him for his absence in the 1960s, and sanctify my conflicted relationship with him. We were alike, Snag and I, in that cerebral way that made us live in our heads more than in the world, so that to one another we seemed self-centered and greedy. What challenged our reciprocal love was our inability to acknowledge this similarity, resulting in blame and contradiction.

So I wasted my days on the mindless arrangement of words on sheets of paper that would be torn up and tossed out the next morning. My social calendar was always full, though, as it might be when one is twenty-something, and what little spare cash I had (after spending all that guzzle-money at the liquor store) went toward movies, concerts, and buying books.

But eventually life near the poverty level wore thin, and in no time at all mine had taken on a fragile transparency. Everyone could see right through me—my parents, sisters, friends, and foes. I was pissing my life away. But an innocuous ad in the *Los Angeles Times* that I happened upon one day changed all that.

A new book publisher was looking for a sales rep in Southern California. Some retail book experience was preferable, it said, and interviews would be held in Los Angeles the following week. I immediately sat down at the typewriter, not to pound out more of the crap I referred to as a "work in progress," but to compose my first résumé. With three years' experience in bookstores, and another spent working in-house for a publisher, my chances of getting hired were better than most. By the end of the day, I'd finished the résumé and cover letter and dropped them in a mailbox with a ritualistic intention. I wanted that job.

Two Continents Publishing was so named because it distributed both American and British publishers. If they brought out any books on their own, they were usually copublished with U.K. companies that included Methuen and Paddington Press. Prior to hiring their national sales force in 1974, they'd done all the sales and order fulfillment on their own. Two Continents was owned and operated by the Shatzkin family. Leonard, the patriarch, already had had a distinguished career in trade publishing with Doubleday & Company and would later write a book called *In Cold Type*. It skewered the publishing industry while at the same time providing ways to fix the very things he found at fault with it. It was published to great acclaim—and controversy—in 1983.

Eleanor, Len's wife, played an active role in their lifetime involvement with leftist politics. Mike, their son, still believed in the political movements born of the 1960s, which infiltrated his editorial decisions at the company. His sister, Nance, had been a devoted volunteer for George McGovern when he ran for president in 1972. The Shatzkin family coexisted pleasantly in a realm of progressive thinking and genuinely enjoyed being friends with one another. This was so different from the moody, unpredictable nature of my own family that our blighted relationships became even more apparent to me.

Nance interviewed me in her West L.A. apartment; she had moved west from the family home in New York a year earlier to establish the Two Continents presence on the west coast. We hit it off at once. Nance was close to my age, energetic, bright, and obviously the biggest fan of her parents' company. After making a pitch for myself and outlining the reasons she should hire me, Nance explained the philosophy that Two Continents was based on. The company was unique, she said, in the way it sold and marketed its books. Her father (whom she called "Len," which took some getting used to) had devised a new way for bookstores to maintain their stock, particularly on backlist titles.

After the initial order on new titles, Two Continents would determine how many copies of a title a store should have on hand based on their inventory "turn" (how long it takes a book to sell). The reps would then do a quarterly stock check and, based on how many copies of a title were sold in three months, write and submit a backlist order for the store. This concept made me more than a little uneasy. Traditionally, orders were—and are—generated by the buyers, not the reps. Even though Two Continents was offering a higher discount as an incentive to sign up for this plan, I thought there was plenty of room for error in the process.

Having been a book buyer myself, I knew how personal the ordering process was, unique to every store and based on an intimate knowledge of the customers and individual sales patterns. Still, I was intrigued enough by the Shatzkins' bold idea to be enthusiastic about the job possibility that would get my foot in the revolving door of repping. When Nance called the next week to say I'd been hired, I had stars in my eyes and a pocketbook that quivered at the idea of receiving some actual paychecks.

Two Continents held its maiden sales conference about a month later. The reps for all sales territories were there, having flown in from all over the country, and the six of us were meeting for the first time. The Shatzkins lived in a very grand but family-funky old house in Croton-on-Hudson, New York, with enough rooms to accommodate all of us in a fair amount of privacy. The house had been built in the early 1920s by a follower of Isadora Duncan, the avant-garde dancer, and included a performance hall with a stage. It was an enormous room, emptied of its rows of seats long before, and this was where we held our meetings during the three-day conference.

When we broke in the evenings for our communal dinner, the reps smoked an abundance of pot and got to know one another through the haze of laughter and confession. We shared a sense of purpose with the fledgling company, and a feeling that we were essential to the success of the Shatzkins' vision. For the first time since being employed by Pickwick Bookshop, I knew I was living out the right experience.

After hours of editorial presentations of the Two Continents books, discussions about the innovative sales program devised by Len and Mike, and a dispersal of information about the accounts in our individual territories, we were sent home to fend for ourselves and begin selling.

I was given only the most basic of training on how to be a book rep. Similar to my job at Straight Arrow, I had little if any idea about the exact nature of the work. The only given was that it was my responsibility to make sales calls to all of the bookstores in Southern California, and I simply jumped in headfirst. I can't fault the Shatzkins, though. There isn't an official sales rep "handbook" that adequately describes the manner in which a visit to a bookstore should unfold. No one can teach a rep how to prepare for the personality quirks inherent in the owners and buyers, the agony of rejection, or the disappointment at failing to bring in the expected advance orders on a new title. Learning to be a good book rep is based on a series of abject humiliations that must be experienced on one's own, and in a singular fashion—something I excelled at from the start.

As I drove to my very first sales appointment, I hit a boy on a bicycle while I was making a distracted right turn off of Vine Street. *Ooops.* The fender of my car gently knocked into his Schwinn, and he fell to the ground. I was more hysterical than the kid was. His injury was limited to a scraped elbow, but I could see when he stood and righted the bicycle that I'd done considerable damage to it. I never made it to the Westwood Bookstore that day but raced home instead to phone my insurance agent and sort out my liability coverage.

A few hours later, I was knocking on the door of the boy's apartment, blank check in hand. His parents were Asian immigrants who barely spoke English; they began yelling at me in Vietnamese through the screen door when I arrived. Once inside, I nearly prostrated myself on their shag carpeting to beg forgiveness. They couldn't understand me, of course, but I thought it interesting that when I showed them the check we were suddenly able to communicate.

"How much do you want for the bike?" I sputtered, looking

at their prepubescent son. He had his arms crossed over his chest and glared at me like a short he-devil.

"*Ahhhhh!*" said the papa, bowing slightly toward me and reaching for the check.

"*Ahhhhh* to you, too," I replied, whipping my hand with the check behind my back. "How much?"

Papa appraised me through squinting eyes, taking in my clean blonde hair, razor-creased silk trousers, and spit-shined heels. "*Ahhhhh-ha-ha!* You give me two hundred dollah! Ha, ha! We no call police!" It was highway robbery, but I had to fork over the money or, I feared, risk getting arrested *and* losing my brand-new job. I paid them exactly the same amount of money I'd be receiving at the end of my first week on the job.

So ended my first day as a publisher's sales rep.

My second day wasn't much better. I drove all the way to Santa Barbara to call on accounts, a ninety-minute drive on a good day. Having been too ignorant to call ahead for an appointment, I breezed in unannounced to Earthling Bookshop on State Street. Surely, I thought, this will be a snap! I mean, look at me: I made it to Santa Barbara all by myself. I have great books to sell, and a personality to match! But when I looked in the eyes of the owner of Earthling, I knew she did not share my fabulous opinion.

She was appalled by my audacity and sternly told me to leave and come back only when I had an appointment with her. Couldn't I see she was with a rep, and that I had interrupted them? When I glanced over at her desk, the rep, *Mr. Perfect With An Appointment*, looked at me smugly. I fled in tears, got back into my '68 Olds Cutlass (a hand-me-down from my parents), and drove straight back to Los Angeles. "*Shmuck!*" I berated myself while doing ninety on the Ventura Freeway. "*Putz!* You aren't fit to be alive!"

But I had never been so determined to succeed at a thing, and as the weeks and months went by, my will driving me like a turbo engine, I became more confident in myself. It's hard for me now to fathom that, aside from the initial contact to make appointments, nearly all of my bookstore visits were cold calls. I didn't know the buyers, had never stepped foot inside most of the stores, and the neighborhoods beyond Hollywood, Beverly Hills, and Santa Monica were unknown to me. The Thomas Guide became my closest friend, the Oldsmobile my living room, office, and dinette.

As a book rep, I learned the finer points of dining while driving. Unless the occasion called for taking a buyer out to lunch, on an ordinary day—while driving between appointments—I chowed down at the steering wheel. First I learned where all the fast-food joints were on my route, such as the In n' Out near Ventura off the 101 freeway, or the McDonald's between San Juan Capistrano and Camp Pendleton on the way to San Diego on I-5. My favorite, Jack in the Box, called to me on the way to downtown L.A., at the intersection of Vermont Avenue and Third Street.

It took me a few years to get the rules of personal etiquette down to a science in my car. Along the way, I spilled and slopped fast-food kibble on so many items of clothing that I hoped my dry cleaner would start giving me a discount. Occasionally I had to detour to the nearest Gap to buy a new sweater or T-shirt, rather than walk into an account with the remnants of Burger King's chicken broiler across my right breast.

The Two Continents list was modest in size, with about forty titles when I started with the company. This made it easy to become familiar with the books, and I developed my own sales handle for each one. I was selling the beautifully illustrated "Faerie" books by Cicely Mary Barker, a coffee table sports book called *The Rules of the Game*, a couple of leftist political titles— *Strike!* and *Amnesty*—and Dick Bruna's series of children's books that featured Miffy, a rabbit who teaches kids about animals, the alphabet, and colors. My favorite title was a gorgeous aerial photography book called *Grand Design: The Earth From Above*, by Georg Gerster. It's the only Two Continents book I still have in my home library.

My sales presentations became bolder ("You're only taking one copy? I think you can sell two in the first month, don't you agree?"), and my orders grew in proportion to the knowledge I acquired about both the books and the stores I called on. The rapport I had with my buyers became more comfortable as I progressed from bashful hesitancy to wisecracking charm. That first year of being a book rep was a happy time for me. Driving to places such as Palm Springs, San Diego, and La Jolla was an unfettered pleasure, the 1970s being a time of relatively calm traffic patterns in Southern California. I am lucky enough to have once enjoyed the long road trips that led me to so many incredible bookstores, most of which are now gone.

For the first time in my young life, I was working alone, with no co-workers to banter with, no office or bookstore to drive to each morning, and, unless I was in an account sitting with a book buyer, very little conversation with anyone during my work days. It was a difficult adjustment for me to make.

I missed the distraction of in-house gossip, six o'clock cocktails with co-workers at the end of the day, eavesdropping on telephone conversations, breaking into hysterics with a friend in the ladies' room over the mailroom guy who had forgotten to zip his fly. Instead, I had the top-forty station on my car radio to keep me company as I drove from store to store, and in the after-hours the clamor of my bodybuilding Israeli neighbors, who argued and dropped barbells on the floor above me. I took to drinking a vodka tonic in the evenings and singing along to my favorite Beatles albums, which I'd stack on the turntable for a few hours' pleasure of scratchy refrains. By bedtime my paperwork was finished, ready to be mailed the next day. Within a few months, I felt a shift in my interpretation of the quiet, from unnerving to obliging, and began to appreciate it. This seclusion, I realized, was my natural state of being.

I had grown up in a family of independent souls, all of us, perhaps, taking our cues from my father and his long, silent retreats into his office to write. It wasn't that solitude was encouraged or enforced, but we all seemed to acquire that tendency naturally over the course of our family life under one roof. We were all readers and usually could be found in one part of the house or another indulging in this shared but solitary pleasure. I found that a key requirement for a book rep is to resonate with the solitary life. We all spend so much time alone, feasting on the silence of this peculiar choice of careers, that there must be a willingness to wear aloneness like a cloak of honor. Fortunately, I was able to assume this inner posture easily.

I set up a little area in one corner of my single apartment on Formosa Avenue as a work space. There was a card table that I

used as a desk, a folding chair, and a wobbly file cabinet made of cardboard. I used one of my father's cast-off manual typewriters to prepare memos and sales reports. I had a little cat named Ruby, whose black and white markings made her look like she was wearing a tuxedo. Ruby slept with me on the Murphy bed that I pulled down from the east wall of my apartment each night, and sometimes there would be a boyfriend who shared that space with us. Life was a cozy expression of who I was becoming.

Traditionally, publishers' reps had always been men. It was a well-established boy's club when I first started out, so I had to become my own role model, inventing and improvising as I went along. Was I supposed to be alluring and playful when selling to male buyers, turning the then-stereotypical image of women to my advantage in that way? Would the illusion of helplessness make these men buy more books from me? And with the women, how was I to proceed without making them feel threatened by having to buy from a confident, independent young woman? Should I patronize them? Behave passively, or with aggression? In those early days, I had no idea what to paint for the outline of my identity as a book rep.

So I fell back on that old behavioral standby—humor. Thanks to my father, I was always pretty clever in that department, and by leading with laughter I somehow found a good balance for my sales persona. It unfolded gradually over the course of my first selling season, the spring of 1975. As I met each buyer for the first time, it was my self-deprecation that created a good first impression. "Hello," I'd say, "I'm the sacrificial lamb from Two Continents." The ability to poke fun at my ineptitude and myself helped to make the buyers relax. I would forget to bring something

essential to many sales calls—an order form, perhaps, or a pen—and have to borrow a writing implement from the buyer, or scribble the order on a note pad or the back of another publisher's catalog. But no matter what, I laughed aloud at myself, which in turn made the buyer take a detour from irritation to a fond reaction.

I was fortunate to have been raised by a woman who had a low tolerance for bullshit. My mother never put on airs, never pretended to be anything other than her natural self, and she absolutely knew who she was. People always knew where they stood with her. Her favorite expression was. "and you can *kisch miern tuchos!*" For the uninitiated, this is Yiddish for the friendly saying, "Kiss my ass, pal!"

This memory was music to my ears when I finally sorted out the confusion of how, as a publishers' sales rep, and a female one at that, I should behave with the multifaceted personalities of bookstore buyers. What worked best for me then, and still does now, was simply being myself. Straight up, undiluted, maddeningly candid me. For those who didn't appreciate this behavior, I certainly toned it down. However, before leaving the store I mentally turned around, bent over, and conjured up my mother's pearls of wisdom.

Although most of my buyers were good people who I easily got along with, there were exceptions. Walter Martindale, who had a wonderful store in Santa Monica called Martindale's Books, was an extremely volatile man in his late sixties. During my initial sales presentation, I unintentionally aggravated him by suggesting that he increase his order on the *Butterfly* children's book series. Mr. Martindale slammed the catalog shut and threw his pen down on the desk. "Young lady, you're way out of line," he hollered. *"It's not your job to tell me how to order!"*

My jaw dropped, and I sat up straight in my chair. He might as well have been my father at that moment, yelling at me for coming home past my curfew on a Saturday night. "I'm sorry, sir," I mumbled. "You're right. I'm sure you know what's best for your store."

When he saw tears beginning to well in my eyes, Mr. Martindale looked away, reopened the catalog, and turned to the next page. We resumed working, but my humiliation hung between us like a flag of surrender for the remainder of that visit.

There was a store in Long Beach, Dodd's Books, which was owned by a woman named Kim Browning. She was gay, as was most of her staff, and I always enjoyed calling on them for the hilarious, bitchy atmosphere in the back room where Kim's office was situated. The bookstore cats, two black beauties called Ike and Tina, always sat near me (or on my lap) during my appointment. While one hand petted them and felt the comfort of rhythmic purrs, my other hand filled out the order form and jotted down Kim's requests for review copies. This was a sales call I looked forward to, always taking Kim and one or two of her salesclerks out for a long lunch.

During my third or fourth visit to Dodd's, a clerk at the front counter buzzed Kim on her office intercom. She had a phone call waiting. Irritated by the interruption, Kim looked at the box on her desk and said, "You'll have to take a message. I'm with *a young lady salesman!"*

Huh? When had I become androgynous? At what point had Kim, an intelligent, modern woman by all accounts, failed to recognize that the world had started to change years before, and women were more integrated in the workplace? I was stunned. So *this* was how deeply the double standards reached. Even though Kim was a lesbian, her points of reference remained fixed in a time warp of tradition. Women were not supposed to be sales reps. And on the terribly rare occasion that they'd managed to slip through the cracks and assume an identity that only men were allowed to embody, these women became invisible. *I* was invisible, and the world saw right through me. Even the order forms that publishers printed each season bore this out: the header for the line where the rep's name was entered said "Salesman." It would be at least another decade before women assumed the hallmark of respectability in the book business. For the time being, though, I had to bite the bullet so often that my head hurt with the effort.

In late 1976, Two Continents and Methuen copublished *The Rutland Dirty Weekend Book*—a randy, hilarious satire about the English county of Rutland—by Eric Idle, a member of Monty Python. Eric came to Los Angeles to do publicity for the book and for three days I was his media escort, driving him to various interviews and book signings. At first I took him for a disarming, aloof man who seemed utterly bored by my presence, so I was surprised when, on his last night in L.A., he invited me to join him for dinner with some of his friends. I heartily accepted, running home to change clothes before returning at the designated time.

I met Eric in his suite at the Chateau Marmont on the Sunset Strip. While he finished a phone call and put on a casual sport coat, I sat and waited patiently on the couch in the sitting room. On our way to dinner, he stopped the elevator two floors down from his; a friend was holding a book for him and we detoured to pick it up. Eric knocked on the door and after a few moments Ronnie Wood opened it. He and Eric hugged, I was introduced, and the rock star shook my hand like we were old mates. We then entered his suite.

I was in a hotel room with *one of the Rolling Stones*, for crying out loud. Ronnie's wife and their toddler son were there as well, and while the others chatted amiably I sat frozen on the couch in silence with a bamboozled smile on my face. When Eric and I left after twenty minutes or so, I felt that I was exhaling for the first time in my life. "Nice, Eric," I said to him in the elevator. "Thanks for the warning." He burst out laughing, and suddenly the three-day layer of ice between us melted away in social warmth.

We walked right across Sunset to Oscar's Wine Bar, a quirky, fashionable English bistro in what had formerly been a private home. The cold night breeze had helped me regain my composure by the time we were seated at a large round table. Eric ordered a couple of bottles of red wine and the two of us sat companionably, truly engaged for the first time since he'd arrived in L.A. A few minutes later, two beautiful and friendly English models that Eric had invited arrived. The evening was taking shape as the four of us chatted and quickly finished the bottles of Merlot.

Buck Henry, the next guest to join us, walked in wearing a tan raincoat. A few years earlier his film, *Taking Off*, had come out and I'd seen it three times. He was an actor and writer of phenomenal talent, and I was thrilled to meet him. Tom Scott, the sax player and musical director who worked with Joni Mitchell, showed up a few minutes later.

The door kept opening, ushering in one surprise after another.

Paul Getty III, J. P.'s grandson who had recently had his ear cut off by Italian kidnappers, arrived with his wife, both looking rather jaundiced and hollow-eyed. Paul's shaggy hair discreetly cloaked the area around his ears.

By that time, an intensely wild thunderstorm had cracked open the L.A. skies, with rain so hard and persistent that it was audible, even above the din of conversation at our table and Miles Davis's *In a Silent Way* playing in the background. *How wonderful to be in the book business*, I thought randomly. And, looking around our table at the group of celebrated writers and performers that surrounded me, my next thought was, *Life doesn't get any better than this!* Only Eric seemed distracted, constantly looking from his watch to the front of the restaurant as if waiting for one last guest. I turned to him and asked if something was wrong.

"No, no. I'm fine, Wendy," Eric said kindly. "I'm just wondering where my friend George is."

A moment later, the door to Oscar's opened again, and George Harrison walked in, moseyed over to our table, and sat down right next to me.

To this day I have no idea how I was able to keep myself from sliding under the table in a dead faint. Throughout and beyond my teenage years, the Beatles had been my gods. From the moment I saw them on *The Ed Sullivan Show* in 1963, they were the source of my ecstasy and anguish, my near-psychotic adoration, my first, childish experience with unconditional love. And of the four of them, George had consistently been my favorite, with a passion that bordered on mental illness. To be sitting a foot away from him, sharing a bottle of wine and consulting with him, *George Harrison*, on whether to order steak tartare or the leg of lamb . . . this surpassed any of the thousands of fantasies I had custom-designed in my mind about him year after year after year.

Even having his wife, Olivia, sitting on the other side of him at our table couldn't detract from the state of nirvana I had reached.

It quickly became obvious that George and Eric were extremely close friends. As I watched the two of them interact, it seemed they could have been brothers—goofy, easy, relaxed siblings. I felt privy to some awesome secret in the fucked-up world of celebrity that leaves little room for the players to just be themselves, free of self-consciousness and pretense. Their authenticity moved me, drew me in at the same time it made me bashful.

Somehow I managed to not only keep my wits about me over the next three hours but also carry on snippets of conversation with George Harrison as though it was an ordinary, everyday occurrence in my life. If I appeared nonplussed, it was simply a cover for the volcano of sentiment threatening to blow at any moment. Adding to this, George was sitting in such a way that each time the lightning from the storm slid through the front window of the restaurant, it illuminated his face. The magic of the evening was almost unbearable to me.

When I finally walked into my apartment, sometime after midnight, I broke down and cried. With a profound sense of gratitude, it dawned on me that I'd been given this experience only because my life had fused to the book business. I was exactly where I belonged, with an abundant future ahead of me.

I didn't see Eric Idle again for over twenty-five years. One day while I was leaving a doctor's office in Beverly Hills, we passed each other on the stairs. My recognition of Eric hit me like a sucker punch, and I had a split second in which to make a decision. Following my instincts, I turned and looked up at him.

"Excuse me," I said.

Eric turned and looked at me with that hint of distrust I've seen so often when a celebrity is recognized and approached. Foregoing any apologies for interrupting him, I dove right in.

"When your book, *The Rutland Dirty Weekend Book*, was published, I was—"

I'd barely gotten the words out of my mouth when Eric's face lit up with a smile. He cut me off. "My God!" he said, "That must be twenty-four, twenty-five years ago!"

"Let me do the math," I offered, counting in my head. "It was actually twenty-*seven* years ago." We had both paused on the staircase, ten feet apart, one hand each on the railing. "I don't know if you remember me. My name is Wendy, and when you came to L.A. to publicize the book, I was your media escort for a few days."

Eric seemed to be running through the computer print-out of memory in his head as he searched my face. "Yes, I think I do remember you. It's been ages, though."

I just wanted to get to my finish, the part that really mattered. "On your last night here, you invited me to have dinner with you. We went to Oscar's Wine Bar on Sunset, and you introduced me to your friend George." I could almost see my words hanging in the air on that staircase; they danced in front of Eric's eyes like gems and in his face I read both poignancy and gladness. I knew that he and George Harrison had been friends until the end of George's life.

"Oh, thank you. *Thank you for remembering that,*" Eric said with gratitude, and I knew it was sincere. "God bless you." Maybe I'd given him a sliver of his dead friend's spirit that might have otherwise been lost.

I turned to leave. "Thank *you*, Eric. It was the best night of my life," I said and walked out of the building as he continued slowly up the stairs, no doubt focusing more and more on the happy details of that evening so long ago.

My Beatles moment notwithstanding, after a couple of years with Two Continents I became restless for something greater: established trade publishers with a history behind them and a depth of literature to their lists. I was hungry for editorial knowledge and the wisdom of veteran salespeople that could lead me to the next level of enlightenment in the book industry. The Shatzkin family had been incredibly good to me, allowing me entry into the arena of publisher's reps, and I was grateful to them. It was right that my first job had been with a small publisher, the micro conditions providing the basis upon which I could really build my skills.

One of the most distinctive payoffs of being a book rep is the camaraderie that one realizes in meeting others of the same ilk. It's a small world, this business of books, and sooner or later we all meet one another and form relationships unlike any others in our lives. We share an understanding of the unique aspects of our jobs, and there's a symbiosis at work on many levels. We drink together and rage together; we share gossip and rumors, and sometimes we pair off and have sex with each other. In many ways we cannot live without one another. The friends I made thirty years ago are still my comrades, bookended within a thousand pages of empathetic love.

Being one of only a few female book reps in the industry in

the 1970s, and being so young, many of the salesmen I'd met while working at Pickwick Bookshop took me under their wing. Ernie Greenspan worked for Crown Publishing, Bob Cohen for Random House, and Jack Dawley—the first African-American to become a book rep—was with Simon & Schuster. The Farrar, Straus & Giroux rep was a gorgeous man named Alan Kishbaugh who I would follow around with my tongue hanging out of my mouth. These men, many of them gone now, were all saints to me. Never was a girl so lucky as I was to have mentors like these, all of them classy, intelligent bookmen who supported, spoiled, and protected me from my own youthful foibles.

Bill McKay was part of this same generation of reps whom I'd first met at Pickwick. I bumped into him one day in a bookstore when our appointments happened to overlap, and we sat a while and chatted. Bill had been with Doubleday for years until becoming a commission rep. Instead of selling for just one publisher and being what's known as a "house rep," he was an independent contractor and sold for several different houses. Bill, one of those archetypal tall, dark, and handsome men, had brown eyes that actually twinkled when he smiled. He was also a good midwestern boy with an unpretentious manner and quick wit that I felt comfortable with.

Bill and his partner, Floyd Nourse, covered the thirteen western states for the likes of E. P. Dutton, Bobbs-Merrill, Chilton, and a few other distinctive publishers. There were four reps in their group—two in Northern California and two in the southern part of the state, where Bill was based. He pounded me with questions that day—how were things going with Two Continents? Was I happy with the job? Did the traveling agree with me?

As I answered his questions in the trustworthy way one does with a friend, apparently Bill was pleased with my responses. Little did I know that day, but Nourse-McKay Associates was looking for someone to replace the rep they'd recently fired who had shared the Los Angeles territory with Bill. After we said good-bye, I didn't give the conversation another thought.

I received a phone call from Bill about a week later. He and Floyd were interested in talking with me about coming to work for them. There was no point in trying to be blasé about this; I told Bill right away that nothing would please me more. Floyd would fly down from San Francisco the next week to meet with Bill and me for my official interview.

Over margaritas and chips at a Mexican restaurant near Bill's home, I was offered the job. Good god! Was I prepared to make my way down Testosterone Alley, where I would be the only girl in an all-male commission group? You bet I was. And I couldn't wait to strut my stuff.

Four

THE GARP CHRONICLES

> If you have a burning, restless urge to write or paint, simply eat
> something sweet and the feeling will pass.
>
> —FRAN LEBOWITZ

WHEN NOURSE-MCKAY offered me a salary of $325
a week, I accepted at once, thrilled to be earning what seemed a
fortune to me in 1976. Who knew that I was supposed to negotiate a salary, play coy, and strike a nerve in the employer's heart?
Not I, apparently. So as I held my first paycheck in trembling
hands, over the moon with gratitude, Bill and Floyd were probably laughing all the way to the bank to deposit one enormous
commission check after another. We sold for some very big publishers, after all, and in the 1970s and '80s there were at least double the number of independent bookstores and wholesalers in the
country that there are today.

No matter—the job came with a company car. Floyd, in his gravelly, nicotine-edged voice, called early on to explain the procedure to me. "Wendy, it's time to pick out your car. Use the company credit card to make the down payment, and have the monthly statement sent to me in the office." Oh, well, I said to myself, in that oh-welly kind of way, and stared at the receiver as though it had just turned into a gold-plated steering wheel.

"Why, of course, Floyd!" I dutifully replied. "I'll take care of that in the next few days." *What*—like I had something better to do than buy my first brand-new car with someone else's money? Before the receiver hit the cradle of the phone, I'd grabbed my keys and went flying out the door to Bob Smith Volkswagen in Hollywood.

Tripping the light fantastic through the VW showroom in jeans and a T-shirt, I was suddenly joined by a handsome, friendly salesman. He sidled up to me and said, "I see you're interested in the Rabbit XL, young lady!" The guy had one eyebrow raised, Groucho-style, and unfortunately reminded me of an old boyfriend who I still pined over. His nametag read "Lefty."

"Gee, how can you tell?" I offered sarcastically while sitting inside the spanking-new 1976 car, hands gripped on the steering wheel.

This made Lefty chuckle. "How about a test drive?" he said.

Five minutes later, I was driving on the Hollywood Freeway, flirting with the raffish Lefty, my hair blowing in the wind below the open sunroof. The Rabbit drove with a smooth, powerful ease. It oozed that weirdly seductive new-car smell and was painted a dashing midnight blue. I loved it. The car was "me," whoever the hell *that* was thirty years ago.

Pulling back onto the VW lot, Lefty and I got out of the car. Turning to him, I smiled and announced, "It's perfect! I'll take it."

Oh, how green was my valley. Similar to my automatic acceptance of the first salary offer Nourse-McKay made, when I sat down with Lefty and his sales manager I agreed to the first price they quoted. Having no idea that car salesmen expect the customer to protest, feign displeasure, and negotiate the price down as low as possible, my naïveté—and life-long affinity for impulsive behavior—helped Lefty make an unusually large commission that day.

I phoned Floyd Nourse that night to tell him of my fabulous purchase. "Did you get a good price on the car?" he asked expectantly.

"Of course I did, Floyd," I replied. "The salesman was awfully nice, and the first price he mentioned seemed reasonable. So I accepted his offer."

I heard a sharp intake of breath on the other end of the line. "WHAT? Are you telling me you didn't negotiate with him?" Floyd nearly screamed. "Didn't you take someone with you when you went to the VW dealer?"

In 1976, it was unheard of for a woman to venture out to buy a car without the assistance of a man. The auto industry was still embedded in the macho belief that it was a man's job to buy a car, regardless of whether it was for himself, his wife, or his daughter. This was a train of thought that I just never hopped on.

The new job expanded my territory to include not only Southern California, but Arizona and New Mexico as well. This was foreign territory to me in more ways than one. My knowledge of the American Southwest at that point was limited to the unnatural wonders of Las Vegas, where my parents had taken us on vacations at least twice a year.

The idea of camping or hiking in the wilderness for a family outing seemed completely aberrant to my parents. A week in the desert at the Tropicana Hotel, however, where my sisters and I swam in the Olympic-sized pool all day and ordered hot-fudge sundaes from room service at midnight, satisfied their obligation to teach us about mother earth. For my parents, dinner at a house table while seeing the original Rat Pack perform on stage over at the Sands Hotel, followed by gambling until four in the morning with Frank Sinatra (my father's former boss), went a long way toward contributing to the environment. Proud Brooklynites that they were, the only concept of nature that made sense to them was *human* nature, with all its venal pleasures.

My first road trip took me to Albuquerque, Santa Fe, Phoenix, and Tucson. I took a crash course in how to coordinate air travel, car rentals, hotels, and itineraries from a friend who was a seasoned business traveler, and at the age of twenty-six spread my angst-ridden wings to fly.

The prospect of having to call on forty unfamiliar bookstores *and* buyers had me in a state of near-psychosis on the day I left Los Angeles. When I stepped off the plane in Albuquerque, I was immediately struck by two sensations. The first was the thirty-degree temperature that had my teeth chattering like a marionette's, and the second was the effects of being 4,000 feet above sea level. This altitude made my head feel as though I was wearing a Stetson hat that had rocks sewn into its broad brim. Let me tell you—the light-headedness that overcame me, in contrast to the imaginary weight that settled on my head, made for an interesting physiological paradox. Try combining that with a panic attack, and you'll understand why I wanted to get right back on the plane and go home.

But I didn't. Finding my way to baggage claim, I lit a cigarette and realized that to give up then would be tantamount to career suicide. I reminded myself that this was just another one of my bouts with separation anxiety, and that a drink and a phone call to my parents might break the chain of mental events.

This malady of panic attacks had first made a comfy home in my head when I was eight or nine years old in the late 1950s. At the time, my father was writing a nightclub act for a comic named Ben Blue. Both of them had started their careers in vaudeville, and Ben became quite a comedic success in the early days of television. He was the silliest man I'd ever met; he could make me fall over with laughter just by looking at me with a straight face and raised eyebrows. In the 1950s he had a regular gig at Billy Gray's Bandbox in the Fairfax district of Los Angeles, and my father was Ben's head writer. It was during one of these engagements that my world went askew.

Dad used to get home from the club at about midnight, long after I'd gone to bed. On one such night, I woke to hear my mother crying in the kitchen. It was two in the morning. One by one, my sleepy sisters and I joined her there, where she was sitting at the dinette table smoking cigarettes and drinking coffee. She had a tissue clenched in her hand.

"I don't know where your father is," she said bitterly. "He still isn't home, and there's no answer at the nightclub. *Damn* him!"

Susie, Laurie, and I surrounded our mother protectively. "Where do you think he is?" asked Susie, at fourteen the eldest.

"Should we call the police?" She was trying to take charge of the situation, but my mother would have none of it.

"No!" she sobbed. "I just wish he would call. I'm sure he's all right. Oh, how could he do this? I'm so worried!" And with that crazy mixed message she sent us all back to bed.

When I lay down again, pulling the blanket up to my chin as though it was a body bag, utter terror settled into my mind and my body. My breath came in short, spasmodic gasps, and the pressure in my chest was on the verge of exploding. Surely I was going to die. Drawing my small body into a fetal position, I didn't move all night. Curiously, though, I couldn't cry, but perhaps my trembling was a substitute for tears. All through those frightening wee hours of the morning, I listened to my mother move furtively about the house, weeping, dialing the phone from time to time and then slamming the receiver down each time it reached a void on the other end of the line.

I finally heard my father come in sometime around dawn. My elation quickly relapsed into anxiety when I heard my mother yelling at him, my father responding in muted, pleading tones. I listened to their conversation as it shuttled back and forth in opposing volumes and was finally able to cry. The only distinguishable words in the morass of my parents' anger and contrition were *divorce . . . forgive . . . honey . . . please*. I felt the tremor of a hairline crack in the diameter of my inner world. That night, the source of my well-being and safety disappeared.

It took a few days for my parents to reconcile. During that time, a story slowly emerged. We were told that my father had gone on a drunk after the show, passed out in Ben Blue's dressing room, and didn't wake up until sunrise. I wanted to believe that. The alternative—that Dad had spent the night in the arms of another woman—was more than I could bear as a child. My parents weren't speaking to one another, and our home took on an uncharacteristically somber mood that extended my first anxiety attack. The feeling of doom took away my appetite and fed my insomnia at the same time. Being too ashamed to express these feelings to anyone in my family, this was a terrifying experience for me. No one seemed to realize that something was terribly wrong with me, which made my isolation even more dreadful.

Eventually my mother forgave her errant husband, and the incident was never discussed again, swept, as it were, under the rug of my family's soul. But I was never the same after that. An innocuous experience such as going to a friend's house for a sleepover would turn into a panic attack shortly after we went to bed. In the middle of the day at school, I'd be overcome with the certainty that if I didn't get home as quickly as possible, I would literally die. My mother would be called and I'd moan to her over the phone that I had a "stomachache." "You have to come and get me! Please!"

She would arrive, dressed in a housecoat and slippers, gripping my arm until I was in the car. "What's the matter with you?" she'd snipe, filled with resentment. *"You make me so ashamed!"*

Besides my weird meringue of chemical imbalance, these panic attacks were clearly symptomatic of separation anxiety. As a kid, I couldn't handle being separated from my mother (angry, menopausal woman that she was), my comfortable niche at home, or the security of my family. Four decades later, I realized that it was my sense of separation *from myself* that made me anxious. During those moments, when I thought that the very worst could and *would* happen to me, all sense of balance and reality succumbed to fear. But what parent in the 1950s had any understanding of this? And what little girl has the cognitive means to explain or self-diagnose her feelings? My parents and I simply developed our own cycle of misunderstanding among ourselves. I panicked and cried; they yelled at me for being foolish. It was a shared delusion that fairly wrecked my childhood, but in the ensuing years I came to forgive my parents as well as myself for this unintentional heartache.

But while driving from the Albuquerque airport to my hotel, that revelation was still decades away. Frantically smoking Tareytons, hyperventilating with a pounding heart, it was all I could do to arrive at the Hilton in one piece.

After leaving my bags in my room on the seventh floor, I went down to the bar to drink vodka and sodas. I was the only woman by herself in the dark, smoky room, and the men who were giving me the once-over hastened my move to a corner, eyes averted and more than a little fearful. While I drank, I pondered the insane heroics that brought me to Albuquerque. I knew that there were almost no female business travelers in the 1970s, but I also acknowledged that if anyone could forge the trail for those to come later, it was probably me. This thought came and went without a trace of vanity. I was simply different, and I'd always known it.

Sitting with my back to the room, I finished my second drink and calmly walked out of the bar to the relative safety of my room upstairs. My parents were glad to hear from me when I rang them in Los Angeles, and simply hearing their voices took the edge off my panic. Before getting into bed, I double-locked the door, placed a chair under the knob, and kept the bathroom light on for comfort.

Albuquerque is an easy town to navigate. Central Avenue became my compass, and I found the bookstores easily. There was a place called The Living Batch (or "The Batch," as the locals called it) that was a vast bookstore carrying both alternative and commercial presses. The buyer was a guy named Gus Blaisdell, an older hippie intellectual with a penchant for women that had him on his fourth marriage when I met him. The bookstore at the University of New Mexico carried a large stock of academic titles, but also had a fairly good trade selection in its bright, airy space. Patricia Nelson was the buyer, and we struck up an instant rapport. I had dinner at her apartment the night after meeting her, which was a welcome respite from the food at the Hilton.

Patricia also introduced me to Ione Graves, who was the sales rep for Oxford University Press. We were in Albuquerque at the same time during one of my sales trips there, and both of us were invited to have dinner in Patricia's home. It was August 16, 1977. I drove down Central Avenue to get there, listening to a local AM radio station on the way. Suddenly the disk jockey interrupted the program to announce that Elvis Presley had died. It was only by the grace of God that I didn't plow into the car ahead of me: the news was so shocking, so weirdly thrilling, that for a moment I actually lost control of the rental car. Elvis—dead! It was too bizarre to comprehend, and by the time I got to Patricia's house I felt like Chicken Little when I shared the news with her and Ione, whom I'd never met before.

I shook Ione's hand, taking in her elegant height and beautiful

African jewelry, and said, "It's wonderful to meet you. Patricia has told me so much about you, and by the way did you know that *Elvis Presley died a few hours ago*? Can you believe it? I just heard it on the radio and almost got into an accident! The King is Dead!"

The two women stared at me, mouths agape, and didn't say a word. I stood there like a pallbearer on acid, waiting for them to react, and then all three of us burst into hysterics at the same time. The laughter went on for at least two minutes, and finally I fell into one of Patricia's mission-style armchairs.

"Well, it's nice to meet you, too, Wendy!" Ione finally said, and that marked the beginning of our friendship. Since then, we call each other every year on the anniversary of Elvis's death, honoring our long-time bond that was ignited by one of the stranger events in American history. This passing so captivated the country and broke so many fans' hearts that it invariably features in the news as each anniversary comes and goes.

After a few days, I continued on to Santa Fe, New Mexico. A beautiful hour's drive from Albuquerque through the Sandia mountain range, I eventually found myself in an authentic Southwestern enclave built around a central plaza. The hotel I stayed in, La Fonda, was a four-story adobe building, right off the plaza, with fireplaces in each of the rooms and pounded metal mirrors on the walls. It was charming. I'd never been in a place so steeped in a specific culture before, and after selling each day I'd wander around the plaza to visit each of the Native American craft stalls. At 7,000 feet, the altitude in Santa Fe was even higher than Albuquerque's. My spending abilities, though, were clearly unaffected and perhaps even amplified; I went on one of my very first shopping binges there.

The amount of handmade turquoise and mother-of-pearl jewelry was astonishing, the pottery and rugs eye candy. I spent an absurd amount of money on these trinkets, which took on a completely different appearance, it seemed, when I laid them all out in my apartment in Hollywood upon returning home. Nothing fit in with my design scheme, such as it was in those days, and gradually I gave everything away to friends.

There were some great independent bookstores in Santa Fe— Collected Works, Los Llanos Books, Santa Fe Bookseller—and, as in Albuquerque, I had to be mindful of what I was presenting to the buyers. Books on Hollywood or celebrities, for instance, weren't popular in the Southwest, and many of my political and social theory titles didn't belong there either. So I concentrated on what *did* sell and pushed titles about the Southwest, Native Americans, and local travel guides. Only novelists with a proven track record had a chance in this part of my territory, or books by local authors, so I always presented these as well. I was still growing into my job, becoming more discerning about what books were appropriate in which stores. This required concentration and attention, but the result was that I was selling more books in more strategic ways.

After five days in New Mexico and a briefcase filled with orders, I felt like I had the monopoly on kick-ass book trafficking. However, during my first sales call in Tucson, at the Book Mark, this delusion was quickly dispelled. It was the best bookstore in town: an institution, in fact, throughout all of Arizona. It was a huge, barnlike place, which, had they only been able to discount, might have forestalled the advent of future chain bookstores. Arriving there directly from the Tucson airport, I first introduced myself to the owner of the store, Ed Eggars. Ed was about sixty years old and a kindly soul from Missouri. He'd been in a wheelchair since his boyhood when, rumor had it, he was bitten by a cow on his family farm and suffered a viral infection that left him a paraplegic.

Ed and I chatted amiably for a while. I could tell he was a real book man, with a passion for the printed word and a level of knowledge about bookselling that I could only hope to attain some day. Eventually I pulled my briefcase out—one of those old "salesman's" cases that you hardly see any more, a clunky, boxy thing made out of vinyl that had flaps on top of it that opened up flat, almost like a hardcover book. It was filled with my master catalogs (marked up with my notes from the sales conferences), order forms, samples from the illustrated books I was selling that season, folded and gathered sheets (F&G's) from the children's books, book jackets, and discount schedules. "Shall we begin?" I asked Ed.

"The way we like to do it at the Book Mark, Wendy, is to have the rep first take an inventory," Ed replied. "That way, our buy on the new books is more accurate."

When a book goes from hardback to paper, a publisher will often retain the rights to the paper edition rather than sell them to another house. But regardless of who brings out the new edition, a book buyer will use the hardcover sales on a title to determine how many copies to buy in paper. Naturally, those titles needed to be inventoried by hand—in those days before computerized inventory control—and so did every other title that a store carried for the sake of restocking backlist books. Unless, on a rare occasion, a clerk in the store had done the inventory before the rep arrived, it was left to the reps to perform this task. I'd done this many times before, of course, but never in a store the size of the Book Mark.

Oh, my *god*. When I started in the fiction section, I realized that *each shelf of books had another row behind it.* Then, while wiping my brow in exasperation, I noticed the two shelves of overstock at the very top of each bookcase. The Book Mark was in Tucson, in the middle of the Mojave Desert, so you can imagine the thin film of dust that covered the surface of every book in the store.

There I stood, backlist order forms in hand, pen poised, eyes beginning to glaze. Then Ed was at my side in his wheelchair. "The ladders are at the end of each row," he said. "You can use them for the shelves you can't reach." Spoken like a true gentleman, I thought. In the meantime, I was cursing the ground he wheeled upon.

It took me an hour and a half to finish the fiction section, and I was thirty minutes into the nature section when I stopped to use the rest room. I had to wash my hands twice to get the grime and dust out from under my nails, and my blouse was sticking to my back with sweat. On the way back to my artless task, a tiny woman who introduced herself as Anne Underhill, the backlist buyer for the store, stopped me in my tracks.

"You look like you could use a break right about now," she chuckled. "Why don't we go out to lunch?"

Although I'd heard and read about people who suffered from anorexia, until that moment I'd never encountered anyone with the disease. It was appalling for me to see the state that Anne was in. A middle-aged woman with thin, graying hair, she couldn't have weighed more than seventy pounds. When I took her offered hand to shake it, it felt like a child's glove filled with twigs, so thin and brittle that I was afraid to apply any pressure to it. Her arms and legs reminded me of the circumference of beach-umbrella poles, and her face looked like one of the dried and shrunken heads one views in anthropology books. It was only the animation in Anne's features that made her face seem alive. She was one step removed from being a corpse, and I was grief-stricken. What, I wondered, would she possibly have for lunch?

We got into my rental car and drove to a nearby restaurant. Anne was chatty on the way there; in fact, she wouldn't shut up. She talked in an incessant way that was designed to distract and control, as though her intelligent banter would make her seem as ordinary as the next person—which, of course, she was not, and she and I both knew it.

We settled into our booth at the restaurant and ordered lunch. Anne kept up a steady stream of chatter, telling me about her recently married daughter, how she came to live in Tucson, how much she loved working at the bookstore, and on and on ad nauseam. I was trying to stay focused on Anne's face but was so fascinated by her emaciated body that I couldn't help but stare at the spindly arms and hands, the transparency of the skin on her pitiful neck. Our food finally arrived, and I welcomed the diversion.

Anne had ordered a tuna sandwich and a Coke. As I dug into my hamburger, she continued talking, rarely taking her eyes from me. She was telling me about her years spent as a librarian when I suddenly noticed that more than half the food on her plate was gone, and I hadn't seen her take a single bite. It was intriguing me to the core. What the hell was she doing with her food? I began to pay closer attention.

The first time I saw her tear part of the sandwich off and then watched it disappear into her lap, I thought I'd imagined it. But she did it again, with such finesse and studied movement that it would have seemed impressive were it not for the toxicity of this very action. Anne was punishing herself; she was starving herself to death. I had never encountered such self-loathing in my life and realized that her conversational monologue was designed to keep people from looking at the wreckage of her body. By keeping the attention focused elsewhere, she was blatantly warning people that her anorexia was never to be mentioned or discussed.

When we got up to leave, I glanced down into her lap. There, hastily wrapped in a napkin, was most of Anne's lunch. In one swift move she shoved it into her handbag, snapped it shut, and rose to leave. As we walked out of the restaurant she turned to me, patted her stomach, and said: "That was good! Thank you." It would be the only time Anne and I would "share" a meal together. Until she died fifteen years later, I avoided taking her out when I was in Tucson and selling to the Book Mark.

It took me six hours to finish taking that first inventory at the store. I had to phone the Haunted Bookshop, where I had an appointment that afternoon, to reschedule them for the next day. By the time Ed and I had finished doing the new book buy, and Anne had written the backlist orders for me, it was nearly seven o'clock. I collapsed when I got to my room at the Aztec Inn on Speedway. After taking a long, hot shower, I called downstairs to room service and ordered a bowl of soup and a glass of wine. Even though my orders from the Book Mark alone had already paid for my Southwest trip in full—so good was that account— I still had four days to go before I could go home. When I returned to Los Angeles after my first road trip, I was a veteran book rep.

The dowry I brought to Nourse-McKay was one of hard work, book smarts, and a burning desire to succeed. I did an exceptional job for them from the start, and to their credit they often acknowledged and thanked me for it. But it didn't take long for me to realize that the two partners had an appalling relationship, bordering on the juvenile and filled with mutual contempt.

Bill and Floyd would both phone me late at night to complain about one another. Accusations of lying and arrogance eventually gave way to juicy character assassinations ("He's a goddamn drunk!" or "Did you hear the load of crap he told the sales manager today?" or "I can't stand how he patronizes!"), and before I knew it my job had taken on a kind of conspiratorial bent. I was as judicious as I knew how to be at that stage in my life, though, playing both sides of the fence confidentially while looking out for myself at the same time.

I *so* wanted to make a good impression on the folks at E. P. Dutton, by far the most significant line in the Nourse-McKay line-up of publisher clients. It was the first important trade house I'd be repping for, and Floyd and Bill were counting on me to strengthen their already excellent relationship with the publisher. Besides being the exclusive American publisher for all of A. A. Milne's *Pooh* books, Dutton's author stable was literary and prestigious. It included Wilfred Sheed, Edmund White, Lawrence Durrell, Stanley Elkin, and Jayne Anne Phillips. Dutton published Alice Hoffman's breakout book, *The Drowning Season*. Their children's publishing division was considered one of the finest in the industry, with authors such as Fred Gwynne (*Chocolate Moose for Dinner*) and Jan Pienkowski (*The Haunted House*, one of the very first pop-up books). Their distinguished *oeuvre* was awe-inspiring to me, the pup on the sales force.

Walking into the Dutton offices on Park Avenue South for my first sales conference, I was struck dumb when I looked at the glass case in the reception area. It held the original stuffed animal that first belonged to A. A. Milne's son, Christopher, a faded and raggedy little yellow bear that would become the inspiration for *Winnie the Pooh*. There was something so vulnerable about its re-sewn seams and aging button eyes that I had to stop myself from crying on the spot. That fragile, wee bear might well have been the Holy Grail of my childhood.

As Floyd and Bill walked me through the offices, I was introduced to most of the people in the sales department. We wandered through the cubicles filled with friendly people who were obviously fond of my bosses. I began to feel at home. We finally arrived at the corner office of the sales manager, Frank Heidelberger, the man who I soon began referring to as "Uncle Frank" and from whom I would learn more about selling books than anyone else who came before or after him.

Frank was a tall, slender man of about sixty, with wavy white hair and a soft Bronx accent. Dressed in the suit and tie that, in those days, was standard attire for businessmen in Manhattan, he took my hand in a warm grasp and greeted me with a grin that was both devilish and formal.

"So," Frank said warmly, "you've gone to work for these two knuckleheads? I hope you know what you're getting yourself into!"

I laughed, delighted with this man already. "Oh, is there something you'd like to tell me before I sign the contract?"

"Not before I've had a martini, young lady! Shall we go? I made a reservation at Paul and Jimmy's." Frank reached for his hat on the coat rack behind him and put it on his head in one debonair move. This completed his ensemble, and I was charmed by the style that I never got to see in Los Angeles, and that would become outmoded when the 1980s arrived. With Bill and Floyd leading the way, we all walked out of Frank's office. He kept his hand gently on my back, guiding me protectively all the way to the restaurant on Eighteenth Street.

It was December 1976, a time when it was socially acceptable to have cocktails at lunch. The men ordered vodka martinis, while I demurred in favor of a "ladylike" screwdriver. I was still between a rock and a hard place when it came to knowing my place in the business world, and any attempt at being on a par with the men would have been premature and surely met with much resistance by my male colleagues.

So I let Frank light my cigarettes *and* suggest what I should order for lunch at Paul and Jimmy's; I sat quietly and paid attention while the men chattered away; I didn't flinch when all three of them rose from their chairs as I excused myself to go to the ladies' room. These were men of a certain generation; they had fought in World War II or, at the least, the Korean War, and, sharing a similar old-fashioned principle about women's roles, were not yet aware of the fact that gender models were changing.

I felt no resentment toward any of this, mind you. In fact, I took a kind of benign pleasure from the protective nature of these mannerisms. I hadn't embraced any of the first-wave feminist platforms; I didn't see the sense in hating men and never would. It was always in my nature to be independent and brave. I could deal with the "chauvinism" of those early days in my career, perhaps because I had the good fortune to not take it personally. As Bill, Floyd, and I got to know one another better, and as Frank Heidelberger became a close and important mentor and friend, I learned the rules of their world. The first time Frank saw me wearing a pair of jeans, at an informal dinner during a sales conference, he made it clear that he found it inappropriate. He also hated seeing women get drunk. And Bill and Floyd were emphatic about how I should conduct myself during editorial presentations at the Dutton meetings: I was to be a good listener and speak only when spoken to until I became familiar with the staff and the publishing philosophy of the company.

So I acquiesced to all of these gender-specific regulations, be they innuendos or direct instructions, and rarely felt that by doing so I was chipping away at my own soul. It was fairly easy for me to distinguish between what was business and what wasn't. My self-image was personal, and all the rest fell into place after that. Playing the gender game, ever-changing though it was, came fairly easily to me in the book business. Perhaps I was lucky that way. My intention was to keep climbing the wobbly ladder, because if I lost my inner balance the fall would be brutal. So, keeping my identity fairly intact, I did what I was told by the men in charge.

Sounds lofty, doesn't it? Naturally, then, on the first day of my first Dutton sales conference I blew it. Thomas Congdon was an editor at Dutton who had his own self-named imprint. Bill and Floyd had given me a heads-up about Tom; he was a powerful editor at the company and would later be remembered most for publishing the now notorious David Irving's *Trail of the Fox* on Edwin Rommel. He was also A. Scott Berg's editor on one of my favorite books, *Max Perkins: Editor of Genius.*

That morning, Tom was presenting a frivolous title about dysfunctional behavior in household pets. It seemed that every rep in the room except me saw it for what it was—a remainder (excess stock of a title that sells poorly and is marked down by half its cover price)-in-waiting. When Tom finished his pitch, he announced a projected sales advance of 7,500 copies. At most, it would probably sell about 2,000 copies, and come out in paperback in less than a year, but I didn't realize this at the time.

Completely ignoring what Bill and Floyd had told me about keeping my mouth shut at the sales conference, and feeling a deviant fondness for the book, my hand flew up and I said, with great confidence, "Tom, I think the advance is too low!"

"Well, I think so, too, Wendy," Tom proclaimed, "and I'm going to raise the advance to ten thousand copies!"

Within seconds I could feel the deep freeze set in, and a dozen pair of reps' eyes glaring at me, wondering if my head zipped up the back. I hung my head in shame for the rest of the day, but that was how I learned the First Commandment of sales meetings: never, ever tell an editor to increase the print run of a book. If you really believe in the book, discuss it with the sales manager privately!

As the days passed in the conference room of the Gramercy Park Hotel, I was introduced to the rest of the power players at Dutton. Jack MacRae was the president of the company, a dashing, urbane fellow who bummed cigarettes from me during the many cocktail hours we guzzled our way through during both lunch and dinner all week. Henry Robbins was the editor-in-chief who informed, above all, my grasp on excellent writing. Ralph Bolson, the Ed Norton of the company, was Frank Heidelberger's second in command and spoke through the side of his mouth with a rapid Brooklyn cadence. Jane Pasanen, with her Breck-shampooed, shiny blonde hair, was the publicity director, and Lois Shapiro—everyone's favorite *yiddishe mama*—ran the advertising department. This was the stellar generation of publishing figures that I first learned from, stood in awe of, and through whom my fortunate pedigree could later be traced.

In December 1977, a scant ten days before the next Dutton sales conference, the reps were sent bound galleys of a book by an author none of us had heard of before. His name was John Irving, and the book had an unusual title: *The World According to Garp*. The galleys arrived with an urgent note from Irving's editor, Henry Robbins.

"You *must* read this book," it said, "before we meet. It is our lead title for spring 1978, and we'll be discussing it in depth at the sales conference. Regards, HR."

Both the memo and the book, which at first seemed so inconsequential, baffled me. It was by an unknown author and had a most peculiar title, and I put off starting it until a couple of days before I had to fly to New York. I finished *Garp* on the plane going east, and by the time we touched down at JFK I knew that something extraordinary was about to occur in the publishing world. The book was unique, daring, and brilliant and would go on to be a phenomenal success.

What was left out of the story, though, was the challenge that faced the Dutton sales reps in having to hard-sell and explain the unusual plot of Irving's novel to the booksellers. We had so little to go on, and, again, John Irving was an unknown back then. The "tip sheet"—a one-page summary of each new book, with marketing, author, and comparison information that's given out at sales conferences—included the following sales handle:

A wonderfully affectionate portrait of the life and times of a famous mother and her equally famous son—a novel so outrageously imaginative and funny and touching and profound that critics and readers alike will love it.

But *Garp* was infused with so many wonderful elements—a transsexual football star, a boy named "Egg," prostitution in Vienna, feminists who amputate their tongues—that after my first couple of tongue-tied efforts to encapsulate them for a book buyer, I gave up altogether. Instead, I begged.

"Look," I'd say sternly, "anything I tell you about this book won't do it justice. You'll just look at me as though I've gone mental on you. *Garp* is going to fly off the shelves. The reviews are going to be fantastic, and Dutton is offering a one [copy]-free-with-ten [copies] on it. If the book doesn't sell, you can return it—and I will personally pay for the return freight. But that's not going to happen. Trust me."

Sometimes a book rep has to humiliate herself for the sake of a book she's fallen in love with. This is what I did, and the results were stunning. I got those damned orders.

Dutton mailed bound galleys of *Garp* to several book buyers about a month before it was published. How smug I felt as my phone began to ring with calls from my accounts. "I just finished reading the book. Damn, it's good! It's the best thing I've read in years. Go ahead and double my order—I'm worried I didn't order enough copies," they all said.

It was all I could do to stop myself from saying "I *told* you so!" Within two weeks of *Garp's* release date in April, it grabbed the number-one position on all the best-seller lists across the country and stayed there for months. I was ecstatic! I was vindicated. My first experience with a best-selling book was a heady one indeed.

Henry Robbins was on a roll. Fran Lebowitz had recently joined the ranks of his acclaimed author list, and *Metropolitan Life* was a huge success. Robert Tannenbaum's very first book, *Badge of the Assassin*, was rising up the best-seller lists, and *True Confessions* by John Gregory Dunne was about to go into its fourth printing. There were so many "HR" gems in release in 1978 and 1979 that I could have made Henry a charm bracelet beaded with his accomplishments. The *New York Times* and *Newsweek* were clamoring for interviews with him. It was thrilling to be working for E. P. Dutton at a time when both Tom Congdon and Henry Robbins were headlining its editorial achievements.

I worshipped Henry. We would ring one another up almost every week to chat on the phone about book sales and industry gossip, and our conversations were always warm, funny, and confidential. At sales conferences, I'd sidle up to him, hanging on his every word. What I learned from Henry and his singular, distinctive vision of books and writing took me to a deeper level of literary understanding than I'd ever thought possible. He was an elegant, smart, and gentle soul.

But Henry died that summer, a few short months after *Garp* reached the best-seller lists. On his way to work during one of the hottest days on record in Manhattan, he had a massive heart attack in the Fourteenth Street subway station. Pronounced dead at the scene, Henry was only fifty-one years old.

It was a shattering event for all of us in the E. P. Dutton family, and my profound grief dictated that I fly to New York to attend the memorial service a few days later. George Carroll, who would later become my business partner (since Pickwick, he and I had worked for all the same publishers), was the Dutton sales rep in Northern California at the time. He agreed to join me at the service, and we flew to New York together in early August.

The *New York Times* obituary, dated August 1, 1979, said: "In discussing his editing technique, Mr. Robbins [once said], 'I'm an under-editor. I try to find soft spots—the places where things don't quite work—and point them out to a writer. I try to avoid imposing my ideas as to what should happen in a book. I wouldn't dream of suggesting new characters or changing the sex of characters, for example, as I've heard other editors doing. . . .'"

The occasion of Henry's memorial service brought together most of the publishing luminaries in New York. It was held at the venerable Ethical Culture Society on Central Park West, and I was honored to be one of the designated ushers.

The eulogies were poignant and moving. John Gregory Dunne, Robert Giroux, Donald Barthelme, and others each spoke before the deeply emotional gathering. It was John Irving's reflections, however, that wrung every last bit of sorrow out of me. He said, in part:

> About five years ago, I began a novel with this sentence: "In the world according to Garp, we are all terminal cases." That sentence didn't sit well with me, and I kept moving it ahead, and it became the last line of the fourth chapter, and so on. And after

three or four years, I couldn't get that sentence far enough away from me, so I let it be the last line of the novel. In the world according to Garp, we are all terminal cases. But it still didn't sit well with me, so I asked Henry what he thought. He told me that it reminded him of the helplessly unsatisfying condolences we always try to offer people who have lost people they love. "But it's the only thing there is to say," Henry said. "And that's the point, isn't it?" he asked me. I agreed that it was. "And you believe it, don't you, that we are all terminal cases?" Yes, I said, I believed it. "Then don't worry how it sits with you," Henry said. "Leave the line where it is." So I did. I always trusted him, and he never disappointed me. So long, Henry.

John Gregory Dunne, who attended with his wife, Joan Didion, said, from the podium:

For a writer, Henry was the quintessential editor because he was a listener; he didn't try to impose his personality on you. You trusted him. He would say something didn't work, or it was a little soft, but he wouldn't say how it was soft, and you would start to say "No, it's not soft," and then you would talk to him, and you would work your way through the problem yourself. And that, I think, was his genius as an editor.

And novelist Donald Barthelme, one of Henry's writers when he was at Farrar, Straus & Giroux, recalled:

Writers of necessity depend upon their editors for a certain amount of confidence, both before and after the book is published.

Henry supplied this with surpassing generosity and tact. His perceptions were acute, and he trusted them and acted on them to the permanent enrichment of our literary life. He was a rare man, and he will be sorely missed.

After the service, a large group gathered in the apartment of Henry's widow, Evelyn, for the sustenance of hard liquor, soft miniquiches, and smoked salmon. It was the first time I'd been to the Dakota apartments, and I spent more time gaping at the architectural wonders there than I did in conversation with the other guests. I was out of my league among such an elite crowd. I knew I was welcomed there, and that my presence was meaningful to many, but I felt terribly shy nonetheless. I'm sure I drank too much and ended up downstairs circling the beautiful courtyard of the Dakota with George as the summer heat made the sky turn violet at the end of that sorrowful day.

George and I flew back to California in the morning. We sat in coach, of course, that being the midpoint of our salad days, and our seats were in the very last row of the 747. It was a long flight. At one point, having fortified myself with a couple of minibottles of vodka, I took a stroll up the aisle for a bit of exercise and distraction. To my great pleasure, John Gregory Dunne and Joan Didion were on board, sitting in first class in the very first row of the plane.

"Speak of the devil!" I said to the literary "It" couple of the moment. "How nice to see you two on this flight."

John got up to hug me. "Hell of a day, wasn't it?" he said, and I agreed and thanked him for the marvelous eulogy he'd given Henry, who had been John's editor on *True Confessions*, which

Dutton published earlier that year. I waved to Joan, who smiled at me in her sweet, fragile way.

"Where are you sitting? We'll come back and visit," John said, as the flight attendant placed her palm on my back and gently pushed me in the direction of where I belonged. Talking to John over my shoulder, I told him where George and I could be found and returned to my seat.

A few minutes later, John and Joan were standing in the aisle next to us in the back of the plane. "Ironic, isn't it," George uttered, "that Wendy and I are sitting in the very last row, and you're in the very first. Where's the justice in that?" We all shared in the laugh that followed, although I was uneasy about the possibility that George had just made a faux pas. This was, after all, a very important couple he was teasing.

But John graciously saved the moment. "You know," he said, "it's not easy for us to be at a social gathering—if one could call it that—having cocktails with an army of New York literati."

"You're kidding!" I said, genuinely surprised at this disclosure. "Why do you say such a thing?"

John put his arm around Joan's slim waist and looked at her with an ironic lovingness. "Oh, you know what they say about us, don't you?" he asked. "Ever since our success with *Play It As It Lays*, and we both became 'difficult' to work with?" George and I were now craning our necks like circus freaks, waiting for John's answer. "They say 'He's an arrogant bastard, but that Joan—well, *she's* just impossible!'" With that, they collapsed in hysterics, and so did we.

It was startling, to say the least, to hear the *auteur* demean himself with such ease and flair. I felt so pleased to be at the receiving end of this frank admission.

Henry Robbins's death opened my eyes to the fickle nature of publishing; for within months of his demise, his authors began leaving E. P. Dutton in droves. Looking for more prestigious editors and higher advances, their agents led them in the direction of other publishers. My naïveté at the time caused me to take things like this rather personally. Having grown up with an internal resistance to change, each instance of an author leaving Dutton was cause for upset. My first experience with this occurred with Fran Lebowitz in 1982.

When Dutton published Fran's first book, *Metropolitan Life*, it became a sensation, and deservedly so, for she had a hilarious wit and was soon being compared to Robert Benchley and Dorothy Parker. I read the book twice and drove my friends mad by phoning them in hysterics to read, out loud, snippets such as "Food is an important part of a balanced diet." Or "RIP, an acronym for rest in pleasure, is an organization for those deceased who feel for one reason or another that they are just not getting enough out of death."

About a year after Henry died, the mass-market edition of *Metropolitan Life* was published, and Fran flew to Los Angeles to do publicity for the book. She and I had already met at the Dutton office in New York. We'd also spent a wonderful evening together with George Carroll and Jane Rosenman at Bill Whitehead's apartment in the Chelsea Hotel (Bill and Jane were both senior editors at Dutton). I rang Fran up before she flew out to L.A., and we made plans to get together. The only time slot available was on the last day of her visit, when I would meet her for breakfast and drive her to the airport.

She was staying at the Beverly Hills Hotel. I always loved the steep ascent from Sunset Boulevard up the drive to the entrance of my favorite Los Angeles hotel, and that morning was no different. I brought my little VW Rabbit to a screeching halt, tossed my keys to the handsome young valet, and bounded up the green-and-pink-carpeted steps to the lobby.

I knocked on the door of Fran's room, heard her yell out "I'll be right there, Wendy!" and then proceeded to wait for a good five minutes. When Fran answered the door, she was wearing her mandatory blue jeans, white button-down man's shirt, and white socks. She didn't have shoes on. Her hair was wet, and she was rubbing a towel through it with one hand while lighting a cigarette with the other. She gave me a big hug and welcomed me in.

"Sorry I made you wait—I just got out of the shower. Then I had to put out the fire I started. I left a cigarette going near the curtain in the bathroom."

"Jesus, Fran," I shouted, "are you nuts? Did you set off the smoke alarm?" I realized then that the room was very smoky, which had nothing to do with the pile of cigarette butts in the ashtray on the end table.

"I don't know. This is supposed to be such a great hotel! Why don't they hang fireproof curtains?" She was sincerely indignant, which made me burst out laughing.

"Hey! You hungry?" Fran said between drags on her Marlboro. "Let's call room service. I'm starving." I took off my shoes and sank cross-legged into one of the plush armchairs in the living room of the suite. Fran picked up the phone, asked me what I wanted for breakfast (a bagel and coffee), and then proceeded to order enough food for an army. I took a cigarette out of her pack and lit it.

"How's the tour going?" I asked. "Oh, and before I forget— we have to leave for the airport in an hour." As much as I hated driving to LAX, this was the only way I'd be able to have some extra time with Fran—and a free meal at the Beverly Hills Hotel.

She sat on the couch across from me, her feet up on the mahogany coffee table. "The trip's been decent. I did a couple of interviews and a signing at B. Dalton in Hollywood, the one that used to be Pickwick Bookshop. But I hate book tours. I hate having to leave New York!" Fran lit another Marlboro and checked her watch, which made me look at my own. We were doing all right for time.

"I brought the proofs of the new book with me and was able to read through half of them on the plane," Fran said. "I'll finish the rest on my way back. It's called *Social Studies*."

This was news to me. Fran's second book hadn't been mentioned in any of Dutton's interoffice memos or my phone conversations with Uncle Frank. "Fantastic!" I said, "I guess Dutton's going to have it on the fall '81 list, because I haven't heard a word about it. You know, I'll bet they make the first printing twice as big as they did for *Metropolitan Life*."

There was a knock at the door, and a room-service waiter wheeled in a trolley that had two coffee pots and a half-dozen covered plates on it. Fran signed the bill and the two of us lifted the stainless steel domes that were concealing omelets, pancakes, fried potatoes, Canadian bacon, and a basket of bagels. We filled our plates, poured steaming cups of coffee, and brought the feast back over to the coffee table. We ate in silence for a few minutes, and finally Fran cleared her throat and put her fork down.

"I guess you haven't heard," she said.

I swallowed a forkful of pancakes. "Heard what?"

"Uh . . . I've left Dutton. I'm doing *Social Studies* with Random House. They offered me a much better deal and a terrific editor, so I signed with them. They're publishing the book early next year."

Like the adolescent whose father had just gotten on an Eastern Airlines plane bound for Miami to work for Jackie Gleason, I immediately felt the pain of abandonment. "No! How could you do this to me?" was my mature and polite response. "I can't believe this is happening!" I threw my napkin on the plate, lit a cigarette, and crossed my arms over my chest. "And why didn't you tell me?" Naturally, this event was all about me, me, *me*.

Fran looked at me with an indulgent smile. "Listen to you! What's the matter with you? This is a great opportunity for me! I thought you'd be happy about it. How could I stay at Dutton if Henry's not around any more? It just didn't make any sense."

I immediately apologized. I realized that my outburst had been rude and childish, and that Fran's defection from Dutton was simply a matter of good business sense on her part. It had nothing to do with me, or the work I'd put into the success of her first book, nor should it have any bearing at all on our friendship. This event provided an invaluable lesson about the hard choices we all have to make in our business lives. It also served as a wake-up call for me, reminding me of how much work I still had to do regarding a troubled interior life that so easily tended to interpret events as rejection and abandonment.

The awkward moment having resolved itself and passed, it was suddenly time to leave for the airport. We called for a bellhop and, before he arrived, made a clean sweep of the room: Beverly Hills Hotel notepads, soaps, ashtrays, and toiletries all fit neatly into either Fran's carry-on bag or my purse. There was a knock on the door. We piled everything into my car and headed west on Sunset Boulevard toward the airport. Fran had the window rolled down on the passenger side and also opened the sun roof, enjoying the breeze on a beautiful afternoon.

The radio was tuned to KMET, the first FM station in L.A. to feature alternative rock music in Los Angeles, and I cranked it up when *While You See a Chance*, the new Steve Winwood song, came on. Fran and I sang along, sounding completely off-key.

When we were about halfway to LAX, Fran asked me if she could drive. I'd been in her car in New York—she owned an old black Checker cab that was an undeniable treat to ride in, with fold-down seats in the back and a roomy interior. "Sure," I told her, "let me just pull over at the next light."

"I've never driven in L.A. before. It's gotta be easier than maneuvering around Manhattan," Fran said with confidence. We switched places, and when the light turned green Fran accelerated with a jolt.

"Hey!" I yelled, "Slow down, you maniac!"

"Are you kidding? I *am* driving slowly. Hey, what's that Deco building over there? It's gorgeous!"

Fran was rubbernecking with a scary, distracted nonchalance. "Watch where you're going!" I shrieked. "There's a truck right in front of us!" She slammed on the brakes and stopped driving like a rube, promising to get us to the airport safely. We proceeded south on Sepulveda Boulevard. When we reached the next intersection, Fran stopped dutifully at the red light. I told her to make a left turn.

The traffic signal had a left-turn arrow on it, which was red at the time. Before I realized what was happening, Fran was slowly pulling the Rabbit out into the middle of the intersection. She looked both ways and proceeded to turn left on the red arrow, narrowly missing a car that was coming toward us.

"Aaaaaaaaaaaahhhhh!" I screamed, putting my hands over my eyes. "What the fuck are you doing? You almost killed us!"

Fran glanced at me innocently. "Can't you turn left on red lights in California?"

"NO!" I moaned. "What made you think that was legal?"

Pouting, and then taking a drag off of her cigarette, Fran said, "Well . . . it's illegal to turn right on a red in New York. And I know that it's legal to do that here. So I just figured it was also legal to turn *left* on a red light."

I wisely kept my opinion of this theory to myself, and Fran's driving became much more subdued. In fact, she was now driving so slowly that people behind us were either honking their horns or passing us and shouting obscenities. She was a bipolar driver, for god's sake—either speeding or crawling on the road, with very little area in between.

I nearly wept with joy when we finally pulled up, still alive, in front of the United terminal. We took Fran's luggage out of the trunk of my car, embraced warmly, and waved good-bye to each other as she followed the skycap into the terminal. Fran couldn't wait to get back to New York, and I couldn't wait to be home, recovering from my near-brush with death at the hands of Fran Lebowitz.

I bought a copy of *Social Studies* the day it came out, turning immediately to the dedication page. It read, appropriately, "In memory of Henry Robbins."

Five

WISE WOMEN, CHEAP BOOKS

"I don't see anything," I said that first time.
"Watch closely," she said, "and hush."
But I felt them before I saw them, small warm sparks along my
arms. Then there they were, fireflies lighting up and expanding in
howls and swirls as they abandoned human flesh.
"Like snowflakes," Franny said, "none of them the same and yet
each one, from where we stand, exactly like the one before."
—ALICE SEBOLD, *THE LOVELY BONES*, 2002

It was never boring being the daughter of the Queen
of Brooklyn. My mother Charlotte was the kind of person who
freely belched at the dinner table and then spurned our looks of
disgust by saying, in her Flatbush Avenue accent, "Well! Par-
dawnay mwah!" She never apologized for who she was and walked
on this earth with not a crumb of self-consciousness. Because I
didn't have enough time with my mother, my understanding of
her is based mostly on speculation. We were both too young when
she left this world's orbit. I was twenty-seven, and Charlotte was
sixty-three. But as my father's old joke tells it, you're only young
once in a while.

I had read magazines before I had read books, learning the alphabet from their glossy color covers. When the mail arrived, it usually brought copies of the rags that were so diverse that I still, to this day, enjoy the pleasures of dueling journalistic sensibilities. My father received *The New Yorker* every week, while my mother relished her subscriptions to *Photoplay, Silver Screen,* and *Good Housekeeping.* The neutral publication, *Daily Variety*, was read by everyone in the house. We were raised on show business, as well as Charlotte's love of gossip, scandal, and the larger-than-life drama of movie stars' lives.

Because I pored over *Variety* every day from the moment I could read, I never thought it peculiar that some of the first words I learned were "flix" (movies), "tix" (movie tickets), and "boffo" (a positive movie review)—the language of Hollywood. And I was probably the only kid in eighth grade who knew *both* meanings of the word "residual," the significant one relating to the checks my father would receive in the mail from time to time when reruns of shows he'd written were aired on TV. They made Charlotte extremely happy.

My mother was an early riser, up before any of us during the week to putter around the kitchen. This room was her domain, and she relished the solitude it offered in the early mornings. The first thing she did when she woke up was to make a cup of coffee, brewed in the style she had learned from her Romanian mother. She'd take the small, beat-up pot from the dish drain next to the sink and place it on a burner on the stove. To this she added a couple of tablespoons of ground coffee and enough water from the tap to equal a generous cup.

When the water-caffeine brew came to a full boil, Charlotte

would turn off the flame and pour the coffee through a tiny strainer right into her favorite chipped cup. After adding a few drops of milk, just enough to change the pH balance, she'd sit down at the dinette table, prop up her bare feet, and light her first Chesterfield of the day. Maybe this was my mother's form of meditation. Maybe one of our tortoiseshell cats, Bagels or Lox, would poke her head around the kitchen corner and, seeing that it was only Charlotte, return to her natural sleeping position on the white carpeting that my mother always regretted buying. This may have been the only time in the whole day that Charlotte experienced peace of mind.

There at the kitchen table, dotted with salt and pepper shakers, a napkin holder, and the ever-present pen and pad of paper, Charlotte sat surrounded by handwritten notes that we wrote to one another, or to ourselves. There was a shopping list (milk, vodka, cat food, aspirin, lamb chops); a scrawl from my father ("Char," he would write, "please do NOT wake me! I was up writing until 5:00 A.M. and had to take *four* Seconals so I could sleep! ILU, Snag"); and maybe a jab at one of my sisters ("Laurie! Don't forget the thank-you note to Aunt Estelle for your Christmas gifts. Love, Ma"). There she'd sit in her housecoat, the first sip of coffee touching her mouth in the still of the morning savored like a kiss.

In my heart, I believe my mother was always sorry that she'd had to leave Brooklyn. On the surface, there was nothing wrong with her life in Los Angeles. She had the best of friends, a generous allowance from my father, a lovely home, and an active social life. But her family was in New York. She was very close to her sisters, Hattie and Estelle. She adored her youngest brother, Uncle

Jack. There were also old and dear friends there who gave her the comfort of personal history and a shared sense of the past. So despite my mother's wry observations on everything around her, and the gaminerie she exuded most of the time, there seemed an unfulfilled longing in her that appeared in her face when she thought no one was watching.

When we were still living on Alfred Street, my father got a job writing for Abbott and Costello, who were playing a theater in Vancouver, B.C. It was a long run—three weeks or so—and by the second week of his absence, my mother began to show signs of distress. Although I was pretty young—ten or eleven years old—my sensitivity toward others' emotions was already fairly well developed. One night on my way to bed, I walked past my parents' bedroom and heard my mother softly crying. She was lying on her back in their bed, one arm flung over her forehead, the other across her stomach, with her hand holding a lit cigarette.

I quietly walked into the room, and she turned to look at me. There were tears softly falling down her cheeks, and I felt so small.

"What's wrong, Mom?" I asked her. "I don't like to see you cry."

My mother put a brave smile on her face for me. "Oh, nothing," she murmured, "I just have the blues." She reached out and touched the sleeve of my pajama top, which I took as a sign that nothing more would be said. Then I kissed her and quietly walked to my room.

This incident gave me pause then and continues to affect me today. I witnessed my mother's raw turmoil at an age when most children have no idea that their parents are just as human as they are, with complicated emotional lives and painful experiences. This was a moment between my mother and myself that I paid attention to, as if recalling its occurrence would later serve to help me justify my own sorrowful feelings.

What I saw in my mother's face that night in 1961 was loneliness and trepidation as she announced *"I just have the blues."* Her husband had been out of town for two weeks, taking with him the anchor of belonging that Charlotte had naturally come to rely upon. I knew she felt very much alone, longing for the comfort that my father brought to our home and her everyday existence.

—∞—

MY MOTHER WAS a social, freewheeling animal who had a wide circle of female friends all her life. One group of women included fellow mothers she'd first met in the PTA at Rosewood Avenue School in West Hollywood, which my sisters and I all attended. They were all bright, energetic, and raucous ladies and met on a regular basis to work on the craft projects that my mother initiated.

Walking up to the front door of our house after school, I would hear them before I saw them. "Oh, go on! She's a horse's ass!" someone would yell, followed by the unmistakable chatter of female voices responding all at once to this opinionated statement. There would be the clatter of scissors being dropped on a table, and spoons knocking against ceramic cups while milk was stirred in coffee, and I knew that my mother's "group" was in the house. Always trying to time my entrance to come right after the latest explosion of laughter, when I walked into our dining room through the foyer, I'd be greeted warmly by the half-dozen or so middle-aged gals.

"Howaaaya?" they'd ask; "Dwahlling, you look so pretty!"

they'd croon, until, flushed with embarrassment, I'd beat a hasty retreat to the kitchen to grab a snack. Stopping long enough to read the front page of *Variety* and Army Archerd's gossip column in the middle, I'd eventually end up back in the dining room.

The group would be up to their usual tricks. If they were working on their decorative address books, our dining-room table would be covered with pots of glue, pinking shears, pieces of felt-like velvet in assorted colors, rhinestones, and small plastic flowers. On the beaded-flower days, I'd absently sift through the plastic trays that were filled with tiny ceramic beads. These were arranged by color, and then by hues within their range, and I'd sit in awe as the women's fingers ably threaded the beads onto wire as thin as dental floss until, like magic, they came to resemble roses and daffodils.

The other group consisted of the wives of the comedy writers whom my father either worked with or had met in the small, insular world of Hollywood wordsmiths. These friends were slightly more sophisticated than the PTA women, received a bigger "allowance" from their husbands than the others, and lived in better neighborhoods. My mother treated them no differently than her PTA buddies. During my parents' dinner parties, when both the men and the women drank to jolly excess, Charlotte would corral these girlfriends into the kitchen and make them help with the cooking and serving. Like our dining room on PTA afternoons, the kitchen in our house would be hazy with the smoke of cigarettes burning continuously, either in ashtrays or between the Revlon-crimsoned lips of the various women. While my father played bartender in the den where the men gathered to get drunk, their voices rising as the evening went on, and the "can-you-top-this" shticks and jokes growing more and more raunchy, my mother and her friends chain-smoked while deveining shrimp and sipping rye in the kitchen.

Charlotte referred to all of these women as "the girls." Most of them were Brooklynites who, like her, had moved west with their husbands, all at about the same time in the 1950s. It was reassuring to me to observe her with her friends and take in the happy pleasure on her face. Although during my mean-spirited, self-centered teenage years I rarely elicited this from her, at least I knew there were others in her world who could bring her good spirits to the surface.

Over the years, my mother had three or four "best" friends that I knew of, women who alternated between claiming this role depending on how recently they'd had a wicked row with Charlotte that could take months to patch up. In the complex fabric of these friendships, it was sometimes hard for me to distinguish the current pecking order. There was one woman, however, who remained a constant companion in my mother's life. Her name was Nellie Collins, and she worked for our family as our housekeeper for over twenty years.

Nellie was in our lives from the time I was a chubby four-year-old, running around in my underpants and gathering my first memories in the haystack that was my developing brain. She was at our house every single Friday, from early in the morning until we sat down to supper, bringing order to our chaotic house and cleaning in her measured, intentional way. Nellie was tall, solidly built, and big-boned without being heavy. Her skin was the color of rich chocolate milk, and, incongruously, there was a sprinkling of freckles across her lovely face.

When I was little, I drove Nellie nuts. My days were extremely busy, after all, and I was forever running out the front door to draw chalk flowers on the driveway, or sing at the top of my lungs to our black cat, Spotty. Just as impulsively, I'd remember some essential piece of business to be tended to back inside the house— checking to see whether the half-eaten peach I'd left on the kitchen counter was still there, or who my mother was talking to on the phone. Then it would dawn on me that I hadn't been on the swing set in our back yard in at least eight minutes and would fly back out through the front door again.

This was the rhythm of my daily young life, but Fridays were special because that's when Nellie was at our house. Every time I ran outside, I'd slam the screen door shut, making it stick to the frame. When I wanted to get back into the house (approximately five minutes later), it was impossible, at the age of four or five, to either get the screen door open or speak properly. In frustration, I would shout: "Neddie! Neddie! Open de' do'!"

Nellie would come to the screen door and stand before me, hand on hip, glaring down at my little blonde head. "How many more times you gonna have me runnin' to this damn door today, *Miss* Wendeh?" she'd say with disdain, making an opening just big enough for me to come tearing through. Each time I ran past her, I heard her chuckle in that soprano way of hers, and I knew I was forgiven. By the end of the day, though, my mother would be screaming at me to stop bothering Nellie, with a conspicuous absence of irony in her voice.

As I grew older, I began to pay more attention to the unique relationship between Nellie and my mother. They were about the same age but came from backgrounds so different that my comprehension of their close bond was a slow and very gradual event. While Charlotte had always lived a very comfortable existence, Nellie's life was a painful struggle to survive.

She and her family barely got by on the lower-income crumbs that the world had thrown them. Her husband worked for the railroad all his life, until he was disabled by a serious stroke. Nellie took care of him as best she could in their small house in south-central L.A. but had to pay for nursing care when she was out at work. A few years after this, their only daughter died of heart disease at a young age, leaving Nellie and her husband to care for their granddaughter. She had a deep religious faith that, despite all her troubles, kept her good spirit intact and her sense of humor alive and kicking ass at all times. We loved her.

Later, when I entered adolescence in the 1960s, I still looked forward to seeing Nellie. On Friday afternoons when I got home from school, I'd walk into the house, throw my book bag and purse on the floor of the foyer, and continue into the little dinette off the kitchen. Nellie and my mother would always be there, barefoot, deep in conversation at the octagonal table, cups of coffee in front of them, smoking nonfiltered Chesterfields. Their voices were soft and easy; their posture relaxed. After so many years of seeing this familiar tableau, I barely noticed it as I stuck my head in the refrigerator and looked for something to eat.

"Hi," I'd yell to them. If someone had walked by at that moment, it would have seemed that I was talking to the packaged ham on the bottom shelf of the fridge. "What's going on?"

"We're talking," my mother responded. "We're having a private conversation."

I was being snubbed.

"Okay. I can take a hint, you guys!" I said to the jar of Hell-man's mayonnaise in the door of the white Maytag. "There's nothing to eat anyway!" I slammed the door shut and walked into the dinette.

Nellie would be sitting with one leg tucked beneath her on the chair, she and my mother leaning into one another as they talked. "Why can't I listen?" I pouted, being the sixteen-year-old mess that I was, overweight, resentful, a full-fledged member of an imaginary rock band called The Raging Hormones.

My mother picked a speck of loose tobacco from her tongue before glaring at me. "Because you can't. Now leave us alone!"

I turned on my heel imperiously and entered the solace of my bedroom upstairs. Decorated as I had requested, in shades of bright orange and deep purple, I had the perfect digs in which to write my churlish poetry, come down from acid trips, read Beat poetry, and log in to my daily journal. It was the same thing every Friday afternoon. My mother and our cleaning lady had one another's full attention in those late-afternoon female caucuses that, although they didn't include me, later served as my guide for how to be a friend. What was it they were talking about? In hindsight, I know it must have been the same things that my girlfriends and I discuss now—men, money, menopause; the joys and the mysteries of being alive.

I came to recognize that this is what women do—confide and trust deeply in one another, and proceed on the assumption that they will be understood and interpreted on the basis of their very word. In this unlikely friendship between Nellie Collins and my mother lay the seeds for the sort of people I would attract as friends, and the architecture of these bonds.

My FRIENDSHIP WITH Miriam "Micky" Bass, book woman extraordinaire, was fashioned in part on these role models of my adolescence. Miriam's family lived around the corner from mine in the 1960s when we lived on Alta Vista. She was a couple of years older than I, and although initially I was very close with her younger sister, who was in my class at Fairfax High School, in a few years' time Miriam and I would bond like nobody's business. Quite independently of one another, we had both started to work in the book business at the same time.

In the early 1970s, while I was mesmerized by my job at Pickwick Bookshop, Miriam began working at Hunter's Bookshop in Beverly Hills. At the time, these were the two finest bookstores in Southern California, but they catered to completely different clienteles. Being right on Hollywood Boulevard, Pickwick attracted every nut, crank, and borderline personality that lived in and around the neighborhood. The large number of celebrity customers melded into this mix with little if any confusion, making Pickwick a Mecca of eccentricity and charisma. I felt right at home there because of this.

Hunter's, on the other hand, was on Rodeo Drive in Beverly Hills. As if by some strange metaphysical broom, vagrants and schizophrenic people were swept away from the streets around the bookstore on a daily basis so that Hunter's never had to face the drooling masses of book fiends I'd grown accustomed to at Pickwick. The customers Miriam waited on at Hunter's were primarily white Jewish professionals who came from old California money, or the upper echelon of show business *machers* and aging, authentic movie stars of the 1940s and '50s.

This is not to say that Miriam didn't have her hands full with difficult customers, as the ratio of ego to civility in Beverly Hills was considerably higher than in neighboring Hollywood. The two bookstores were only about three miles apart, but the neighborhoods were as foreign to one another as Boyle Heights and Hancock Park.

Where Miriam and I each ended up working at the start of our book careers was also emblematic of our family backgrounds. While her parents were Socialist Zionists, mine were Democratic Mutts. The Bass family was upper-middle class; the Werrises were *nouveau*-middle class. Miriam's mother, Rose, was actively involved with Hadassah and other Zionist organizations; Charlotte went shopping or stayed up all night in Pasadena to watch the floats in the Rose Bowl Parade.

It was our mutual love of books that drew us together like iron filings on an Etch-a-Sketch surface. When Miriam left Hunter's, where she started in the advertising department and went on to become assistant manager of the store, it was around the same time that I began repping. The first time we actually worked together as peers was when she became the buyer for Vroman's Bookstore in Pasadena, and I was her rep for the publishers I carried through Nourse-McKay.

Micky (as I called her, this being the family nickname that I first knew her by) was nothing short of a brilliant book person. Although she hadn't been at Vroman's for very long, she was already acutely aware of who its customers were and what markets her buying should focus on. Vroman's was and is a fine independent bookstore, carrying a full line of books in a beautiful carriage-trade atmosphere. Although my style of selling was amiable and respectful from the time I began peddling books, Micky was an especially easy "sell." Her years at Hunter's had made her so familiar with authors, backlist treasures, and book categories—particularly those titles that could be shelved in more than one area of a store—that I barely had to pitch the new books to her.

Initially, this unnerved me—until I realized that her numbers were invariably close to the suggested order I had in mind for each title, based on what I knew about the books and their publishers' plans for them. I was awestruck by her innate ability to buy correctly for Vroman's, including books on religious studies, for instance, that my other stores would have passed on but which Micky knew would sell to her conservative clientele in Pasadena. Her mind was a vivid memory bank of previous sales figures as well, so that if I was selling her a new edition of a dictionary, she remembered what the last edition had sold and then bought accordingly.

Micky never editorialized when she bought books, either. Barbara Cartland, the enormously popular romance writer of the late 1970s and early '80s, wrote at least two books a year that were dreadful, mawkish tomes of sentimental crap. Her publisher happened to be E. P. Dutton, so I had the dubious honor of presenting these books to my buyers on a regular basis. Micky and I never failed to get hysterical when we came to Dame Cartland's pages in the catalog. With bizarre titles like *Rainbow in the Spray* and *Two Hearts in Hungary*, we howled with laughter at Micky's desk in a discreet corner of the bookstore.

These were books that she knew were both hideously written

and warped in their emphasis on the weakness of women, yet Micky dutifully stocked up on them because she knew they would sell and Vroman's customers expected to find them on the shelves. Her opinion of individual books never interfered with how she did her job. She was first and foremost a businesswoman and didn't apply value judgments to her buying.

Micky's health was always a source of great concern to me. From the time we first met as teenagers, she grappled with an insidious weight problem. The obesity that prevailed over her body gave her the gait and sway of a beautiful, lumbering bear, and when we were together I was mindful to slow my typically hurried walk to a kind of stroll so that we'd be synchronized in step. Micky was tall, about five-foot-eight, and had a gorgeous head of curly brunette hair. Her lovely brown eyes and the girlish little gap between her two front teeth gave her face an open and eager appearance that never failed to make me feel happy.

In Micky's later years, I lost count of how many times she would phone me to excitedly explain the new diet she was on. Never in denial about her weight problem, she tried every diet from Atkins to Suzanne Somers to *The Zone*. Each time she began a new regimen, it was with the conviction and certainty of a woman who wanted only to be healthy. She failed at every turn, however, and would soon be back on the dangerously overweight journey.

Micky left Vroman's in 1980 to work for a new company called Crown Books, the first retailer to discount massively. "Books cost too much!" crowed Robert Haft in the now infamous commercials that marked the first and only time a book retailer advertised on television; "You'll never have to pay full price again when you shop at Crown!" As the buyer and merchandise manager for this growing, threatening chain, Micky was castigated by the independent bookselling community in California. People who had championed her swift, much-deserved rise in the book business suddenly resented her for being part of a shift in the industry that presented a grave peril to their survival. Discounts given by publishers on orders were based on quantity (a practice that has since changed to be more uniform and inclusive), and where the independent bookstores received an average 42 percent discount, the chains, which would regularly order over a thousand books at a time, received a discount of about 47 percent—or more. The same bottom-line economics that allowed the chains to offer discounts on books prevented the mom-and-pop stores from doing the same, which drove many of their customers away.

Micky was aware of this and sensitive toward those who felt that she had betrayed them, but in typical fashion she moved forward and didn't look back. She had more integrity than most people I've ever known and knew exactly who she was. This career move was a milestone for her, the difference between having a comfortable, mediocre-paying job and being on the executive track to a challenging, creative position. Micky was an incredibly thoughtful and caring woman, but she also had a measure of self-esteem that always propelled her forward into a better direction no matter the effect on the world around her. When it came to business, she didn't believe in taking anything personally.

Crown Books—and Micky's visionary role in making the company a success for more than a decade—were first credited with, and then vilified for, initiating a jolting change in an industry that had followed an unvarying business paradigm for more than a century. Over time, booksellers with varying strategems were forced to adopt the policy of discounting the price of books. Those with the tenacity to take on this challenge survived. Tragically, many others—independent, neighborhood-friendly bookstores—were driven out of business. Because of the rush of imitators, it was difficult to point the finger of blame at one particular book retailer, and Micky's personal vilification was brief.

The allure of buying for over forty stores under the Crown Books umbrella was a source of great satisfaction for Miriam. When she first joined the company in 1982, there were about ten locations in Southern California, but over time Crown expanded into Washington state, Texas, Chicago, and Northern California. I loved calling on Miriam in those days. She worked out of a big, anonymous warehouse in Orange County, in an office filled with the kitschy souvenirs and collectibles that reflected her unique taste and idiosyncrasies. When I'd walk in for my bimonthly appointments, I'd usually be yelping in aesthetic pain at her latest acquisitions. "That's hideous!" were frequently the first words out of my mouth, as I'd notice a ceramic dinosaur that she'd picked up in Fresno, or a book poster signed by Jackie Collins.

At some point, Miriam developed an obsession with Catholic icons and paraphernalia and began collecting statues of nuns. This would have been a matter of perfect propriety were it not for the fact that the woman was a Jew, for God's sake, and a culturally dedicated one at that. Miriam spoke, gestured, and thought like the very embodiment of the quintessential Jewish American Princess. She didn't know how to use a vacuum cleaner, wouldn't be caught dead in a Target store, and had never taken a city bus in her life. She supported many Jewish organizations. Yet, later in her life,

Miriam found a kinship with cheap plastic figurines of nuns and queer effigies of the Virgin Mary. Walking into her office at Crown was like entering a Judaic interpretation of Catholicism at its kitschiest, a priceless bit of entertainment.

Miriam ordered books in huge quantities because of the number of stores she was buying for; she was a commission rep's delight, and we were all financially rewarded by her orders. Her objectivity, however, had followed her from Vroman's. When I'd present her with a title on Judaism—a collection of Jewish folk tales, for instance, or a new memoir about the Holocaust—she would buy it for only half of the Crown stores.

"How can you buy so few of these?" I'd squeal, in my best I'm-not-really-begging voice. "We're putting the author on tour!"

Miriam wouldn't even look up, skipping over to the next page of the catalog. "Nah," she'd say with authority, "we don't sell Jew books in the suburbs." I was quickly reminded that our close friendship did not exist on her side of the office door. She never allowed her emotions to interfere with business.

On my fortieth birthday in 1990, Miriam flew me up to the Napa Valley in Northern California for a night at a luxury resort followed by an early-morning ride in a hot air balloon the next day. It seemed like a terrific idea to me at the time—a weekend with one of my best friends that would culminate in floating above the beautiful vineyards of Napa. I looked forward to it for weeks.

We arrived at the inn on a Saturday afternoon, had a gourmet dinner in the restaurant, and went back to our room fairly early. The following morning, we would have to be up by six o'clock to meet the balloon on time. We watched a bit of television, and within fifteen minutes I looked over to Miriam's bed to find her snoring happily, already in a deep sleep. Turning out the light on the nightstand between our beds, I closed my eyes.

Out of nowhere, an anxiety attack struck me like a tire iron. After my eyes flew open, the attack dutifully traveled from my mind into my entire body, and I began the sweaty toss-and-turn panic dance. Sleep was impossible. I tried my best not to disturb Miriam, using mental tricks I'd learned from a former therapist to talk some sense to myself. Still, the brutal thoughts of dread won out. At the time, I was in a psycho-relationship with a guy who was about as good for me as a glass of Drano. He was married and alcoholic, and he lived very far away. The more I thought of N. and how powerless I felt with him, the more hysterical I became.

"Miriam!" I whispered, as subtly as a bullhorn. "I'm calling room service to bring me a glass of milk! I can't sleep!"

She woke up immediately. "What's the matter? Are you okay?"

"No! I am not okay!" I yelled. "I'm having an anxiety attack, and I can't stop thinking about N. And I've just realized that I'm terrified to go up in that balloon tomorrow! Forget it! I'm not going!"

Miriam, in her big nightshirt that came down to her calves, sat on the edge of the bed and looked at me like I was insane. "Oh, *please*. Everything is fine. Forget about that shmuck! The balloon ride is going to be a blast!" Here was the voice of reason that my panic had annihilated in me. "I'll wait up with you until room service comes, and then we'll go back to sleep."

She always made everything seem so effortless and sensible. That night, though, I just couldn't catch up to her calm outlook, and I didn't fall asleep until about three in the morning. With the worst anxiety hangover of my life the next day, I found myself up

Mom and Dad on their honeymoon, 1938 (self-portrait).

Dad with his girls: Laurie, Wendy, and Susie on Alfred Street, 1953 (Charlotte Werris).

The Jolly Green Giant set from the previous night's *Tonight Show*—an unwanted birthday gift for my father delivered to our front lawn by Johnny Carson's art director. Los Angeles, 1970 (unknown).

Dad at his office on the Paramount Studios lot, Los Angeles, 1948 (unknown).

Mom and Dad on New Year's Eve, 1970 (unknown).

Louis Epstein in his office at Pickwick Bookshop, Hollywood, 1969 (unknown).

Pickwick Bookshop, Hollywood c.1950 (unknown).

Adam Rinzler and Alan Kahn, Minneapolis, 1973 (Kathy Mack).

"Uncle" Frank Heidelberger, E. P. Dutton Sales Director, treasured mentor, and friend. New York, 1980 (Wendy Werris).

With Henry Robbins at the ABA convention in Los Angeles, 1979 (unknown).

Dad on stage with "The Great One" during a taping of *The Jackie Gleason Show* in Miami Beach, 1965 (unknown).

Questionable behavior with George at the ABA in New Orleans, 1986 (unknown).

A somber shot of I-5 Associates—George Carroll (left) and Jack O'Leary —at the ABA in Las Vegas, 1990 (unknown).

With Jonathan Weiss (left) and George at an Oxford University Press sales conference, New York, 1993 (unknown).

I was gob-smacked to meet Art Carney, Dad's old friend, at a tribute to Jackie Gleason held by the Museum of Television & Radio, New York, 1987 (Steve Roven).

September, 1970
6743 Hollywood Boulevard

September, 2000
6743 Hollywood Boulevard!!

Penny Rose and I celebrated our fiftieth birthdays together in 2000. Both shots were taken in front of Pickwick Bookshop, thirty years apart, and were used on our party invitation (John Smart).

With the beloved Miriam Bass while she awaited her kidney transplant, Los Angeles, 1999 (Linda Bass).

Ben Latting at the Pickwick Bookshop reunion, Los Angeles, 2005 (Wendy Werris).

Hugh Callens at the reunion (Wendy Werris).

An original Pickwick Bookshop bookmark with the address of the Hollywood store. In later years, the addresses of the branch locations would be added.

My Pickwick nametag, which I refer to as my "Rosebud." I'll always treasure it.

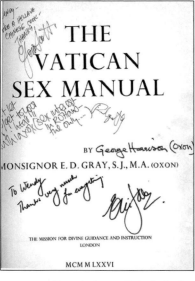

Frontispiece of *The Rutland Dirty Weekend Book*, signed to me by Tom Scott, Paul Getty III, George Harrison, and Eric Idle.

in the sky in a fucking hot air balloon with Miriam Bass. During one of the few moments when I didn't have my eyes squeezed shut, when I looked at her I saw an expression of perfect joy and contentment on her face. Miriam stood upright with the temerity of a prizefighter, palms pressed lightly on the edge of the basket, looking out and down to the fields of gentle color we floated above.

On the other hand, I gripped one of the inner poles so tightly that I left fingernail marks on my hands and only looked over my shoulder once or twice during the ride to see where we were. My beloved, fearless friend lived in the moment, while my own terror had me thinking ahead to the departure gate at the Oakland airport back on terra firma. Micky's spontaneous trust in, and love of, life was always the sand that made me want to turn my anxious thoughts into pearls.

In May 1997, I was in New York for sales conferences. Calling home one night to pick up my voice mail, I was shattered to hear a message from Micky's sister Linda. In a tearful voice, she explained that Micky was in the hospital in Los Angeles, gravely ill from kidney failure. I returned Linda's call immediately. Micky had flown home for a short vacation from Bethesda, where she was then living and working for a book distributor called National Book Network. When Linda and the rest of the Bass family had seen the weak, disoriented state she arrived in, they rushed Micky to the hospital. By the time she was admitted, both of her kidneys had stopped functioning.

My next phone call was to Micky at Cedars-Sinai Medical Center. "I'm sick—really sick," she said with an effort. "I don't know what to do. The doctors told me that I need a kidney transplant." Every breath sounded difficult for Micky, and our conversation ended quickly with my assurance that I'd see her in the hospital the minute I got home from New York.

There are snap decisions that we make all through the course of our days. Sometimes we instantly regret them. Other times, we're in awe at how we were able to reach a state of absolute certainty in the time it takes to blink. I'd experienced both of these moments, of course, many times in my life. Yet there was another level of realization that had evaded my understanding until that night when I was on the phone with Micky, a juncture the mind reaches where grace meets pure intention. For me, it was the instantaneous knowledge that love has no limits, and that we each embody that idea to the best of our awareness of it. My mind grabbed hold of this truth with knowingness.

I picked up the phone and got Micky back on the line. "Let me be your kidney donor," I heard myself saying to her. "I know this is the right thing to do, and I've made up my mind to do it."

There was silence on the other end of the phone. In the next beat or two, I understood that Micky was crying and waited patiently for her response.

"Are you sure?" she finally gasped. "Is this really what you want to do?"

"Micky, I've never been so certain of anything in my life. You've been like family to me for almost forty years. The only thing that concerns me is that we might not share the same blood type, because I know mine is extremely rare."

Micky took a deep breath, exhaled, and announced: "I'm B-Positive."

"So am I, sister," I screamed, "so am I! It must be our Eastern-European Jew-genes that brought this on!"

The first major hurdle was out of the way, and about a month later I began the long process of compatibility testing with one physical exam after another. Micky had been so sick that her hospital stay extended to four weeks. Once she was stabilized and it became clear that she could withstand transplant surgery, I became an official donor candidate. Enduring with gladness the myriad of peculiar tests, prodding and poking, collection of various specimens, and drawing of so much blood that I began calling the doctor "Dracula," it was finally determined that I was one healthy chick. Count Dracula gave the okay for Micky and me to enter into the tissue-typing phase of the process.

We had to wait an agonizing week for the results of this crucial lab work. Like our blood type, would our genetic tissue make for a good match? We were dealing with very long odds, and if the match failed I knew I couldn't donate a kidney to Micky. She had already started thrice-weekly dialysis treatments, and a healthy organ now would mean she would be hooked up to the dreaded machine for only a few months, rather than two or three years— the average waiting time for a cadaver kidney. Micky was a wreck that week, and so was I. Finally, six days later, we got the phone call from her nephrology doctor.

We were a perfect match!

The hallelujah chorus gave a deafening roar, and Micky and I, her family and friends, and our associates in the book business began to celebrate the incredible good fortune this journey had brought us to. Bouquets of flowers and notes of congratulation began to pour in. The surgery was scheduled for July 17 in Los Angeles, just a few weeks away.

Micky continued the leave of absence from her job in Maryland

and stayed with her sister while we awaited the transplant surgery. Because she only had a minimum of kidney function at that point, she was on a very restrictive diet and began effortlessly to lose the weight that would make surgery less dangerous for her. A Micky that none of us had ever imagined began to appear. She lost eighty pounds and four dress sizes and looked positively dazzling.

As for me, I would be lying if I said I didn't lose a lot of sleep during those last weeks. As much as I wanted to help save my friend's life, I was afraid—about the surgery, the recovery, and, frankly, life with only one kidney. A friend of mine had recently donated a kidney to her sister, and I made many phone calls to her in an effort to assuage some of my fear. It was a profoundly introspective time for me as I searched for the balance between self-doubt and giving the gift of prolonged life to Micky. In the end, though, my love for her helped me to release all apprehension. I was ready.

There was one final test for me to take, about ten days before the surgery. To determine which of my kidneys would be removed and transplanted into Micky, the doctor ordered me to undergo an arteriogram. Although it was a fairly simple procedure, I would be given anesthesia and had to be admitted to Cedars-Sinai as an outpatient that morning. Micky would come and take me home in her car at about four in the afternoon.

After the arteriogram, I had to lie completely still in a hospital bed for several hours. Stoned as I still was on the lingering anesthesia, a great sense of joy settled within me during that time. I'd crossed the final threshold, and the transplant was only days away. Micky would have kidney function again, and her dependence on a dialysis machine would reach a blessed end. When the surgeon walked into my room, I turned my head toward him with a dopey smile on my face. "Hey! What's up, Doc?" I said to him.

He walked over to my bed and pulled a chair up close. "I'm afraid I don't have good news," he said grimly. "We found an irregularity in your arteriogram. You have a kidney disorder, and it won't be possible to go ahead with the transplant."

I was struck dumb. It seemed that my mind did a clean sweep of the whole universe, seeking something akin to logic. All I could do was stare at the doctor with my mouth open as wide as a fist.

"You have a genetic disorder called medullary Sponge Kidney," he continued. "You were born with it. Typically it begins to affect the kidneys during childhood; but since you've never had any problems, it's doubtful that you ever will."

I began to stammer. "Then why can't I donate a kidney to Micky?" My face collapsed into a cartoonlike grimace of despair. I grabbed the doctor's arm.

"The AMA has strict guidelines on this sort of thing. Given that there's a small chance that you may need both your kidneys one day, it would be against the law for me to perform the transplant. I'm terribly sorry." The doctor seemed genuinely distraught. It would now be his regrettable job to break the news to Micky, who was waiting outside in the hall, unaware of what was happening.

"I have to be with you when you tell her. I insist on this," I said, already trying to wipe the tears from my face and get a goddamn grip on myself. I was slipping into a rage of frustration at the prospect of sharing this news with Micky. I had the doctor walk me out to the hall, and she was standing there with an expectant, glorious smile on her face. The doctor and I greeted her, and he explained that we would have a short meeting in an office a few doors down. Micky and I followed him into the room and took our seats side by side.

"There's no easy way to tell you this, Miriam," the doctor began. "We've discovered that Wendy has a kidney disorder, and she won't be able to be your donor."

Micky and I both broke down. We put our arms around each other and bawled like babies, while the doctor discreetly took his leave to give us some privacy. This was the biggest disappointment of my life, and I felt that I had utterly failed my friend. At the same time, it was gradually dawning on Micky that her future looked bleak. She would have to go on the national kidney donor waiting list, a long and circuitous road with an uncertain ending. After several painful moments, we were able to compose ourselves and leave the hospital. During the drive to my house, the mutual reassurances went on and on, as I told Micky I knew she would be all right and survive this, and she told me sternly that I had absolutely nothing to feel guilty about; I had done nothing wrong, and everything right. It would take months before I could believe that.

Micky returned to Maryland and her position at National Book Network. For the next two and a half years, she underwent dialysis treatments three times a week for three hours at a stretch. She never complained and pragmatically arranged her personal and business lives around the treatments. If she had to travel for business, she called ahead to make an appointment at the dialysis center in this city or that. All during the interminable wait for a kidney, she was allowed to drink only four ounces of water a day. If she suffered because of any of this, we never heard about it. She simply went on being Micky—brave, strong, funny, and hopeful as ever.

In January 2001, during a visit home to Los Angeles, the beeper she wore twenty-four hours a day finally went off. A kidney had been found for her in Pennsylvania, donated by the family of a young man killed in a motorcycle accident. Micky took a red-eye flight to the east coast. One day later she underwent a successful transplant; and because the surgery took place in Pittsburgh, she named the kidney "Steeler"—the beloved last laugh.

After the transplant, Micky lived a dialysis-free life for two more years. She spent every one of these days experiencing great happiness and enjoyed a thousand blessings. Life had become so precious to Micky that she even put her career on the line to move back to Los Angeles, where her loved ones were. National Book Network, however, refused to accept her resignation. She was so loved by her bosses that they agreed to let her work for them out of a Los Angeles office that Micky ultimately created.

While the medical community might say that Micky's kidney transplant improved her life, her family and friends feel that the potent toxicity of the antirejection drugs could have actually killed her. Whatever the case may be, when Micky died of heart failure in 2003, the whole book industry mourned.

The Miriam Hope Bass Award for Excellence in Small Press Publishing was established shortly after her death. Each year an independent press receives this prize, a most fitting memorial to an extraordinary woman. On her memorial plaque at the cemetery where she's interred, one of Micky's most beloved expressions has become her epitaph in bronze. It reads: *"You won't believe what happened to me on my way here."*

Six

DON'T GET UP, GENTLEMEN . . .

She even had a kind of special position among men; she was an exception, she fitted none of the categories they commonly used when talking about girls; she wasn't a cock-teaser, a cold fish, an easy lay or a sneaky bitch; she was an honorary person.

—MARGARET ATWOOD

IT'S 1990. I'm walking out of the Doral Hotel in Manhattan with George Carroll, whom I've known since the time we both worked for Pickwick Bookshop in 1970. George and I have been business partners in a commission rep group for several years at this point, and today he's a little irritated with me. The Doral is a fleabag when compared to the nice hotels we were used to staying in on these trips back east for sales conferences. But I'm in the first of a series of financial dead zones that will beckon to me with alarming regularity in the years to come. My grasp on money, which I find so much fun to spend, is slipping away from me with the speed of a lit cigarette falling from a tenth floor window of the Plaza Hotel.

George tolerates this lowering of hotel standards, though, because he tolerates me. We're like a cashmere twin set, always worn together, but in colors that clash. Turquoise blue and lime green; that sort of thing. Our history is already awash with colorful, slightly depraved shared experiences. Actually, George and I first met on the phone. I was working, as mentioned extensively in Chapter 1, at the Hollywood branch of Pickwick; he managed the store in Fresno. George phoned one day when I was working for Joni Miller at the reorder desk, and as soon as I heard that voice (dark honey dripping in slow-mo, on the midrange Barry White scale) I knew we were intended to meet in person.

What I didn't know was that, in the turbulent annals of the book business, George and I would become a legendary posse of two.

As we leave the seen-better-days hotel on that lovely spring day, free of briefcases and pressing appointments, our intention is to grab a bite to eat at the Cosmo Deli on Fifty-first and then return to our rooms for naps. We walk briskly through the lobby and then out to the street at exactly the same moment that Kurt Vonnegut is walking past the taxi stand in front of the Doral. George and I recognize him instantly. We glance at one another and then, reading each other's radar, turn south instead of north: away from the direction of the deli. Falling into step a couple of people behind the famous writer, George and I have apparently decided to stalk Mr. Vonnegut.

We cannot help ourselves. As if on a tail in a Harry Bosch case, we stay only close enough to keep our subject in sight. As usual, Lexington Avenue is crowded with people on this weekday afternoon, and Vonnegut seems to disappear into the throngs. Is it possible that no one else recognizes him? In the people walking past me, I'm not aware that any heads are turning to look back at the tall, curly-headed, mustachioed man in the trench coat. But George and I trundle along in pursuit.

After five blocks, I turn to my partner and say: "What the hell are we doing? We can't just keep following him."

George, taking my elbow to guide me around a couple in front of us who are walking too slowly, replies out of the corner of his mouth: "I don't know what we're doing, but we can't stop now."

All is well.

Our mission takes us past Forty-second Street and still we march on, Vonnegut's trench coat flapping in the breeze ahead of us. It's become the Holy Grail, a chalice filled with literary radiance and the fulfillment of . . . what? What are we hoping to accomplish? Where is Vonnegut going? Whatever his ultimate destination, George and I are determined to reach it with him. We've crossed Thirty-fourth Street now, when suddenly the trench coat turns left on Thirty-third. Eastward we go, walking a bit faster now to stalk with greater intention. It's official: George and I have completely lost our minds. Third Avenue comes and goes, and now we're right on Vonnegut's tail. I could reach out and almost touch his back.

So when Vonnegut stops to sit down on a bench, George, taken aback, comes to a halt and I plow right into him. The writer takes this opportunity to look up at us just then. His expression is utterly indifferent as he glances back and forth between George and me, and I realize that we're making fools of ourselves. The only way out of this is to begin speaking; but when I finally do, it seems that my voice has taken on the timbre of a twelve-year-old girl's. Who is this person talking, I wonder, as the words fly out of my mouth?

"Oh, Mr. Vonnegut! We're such *fans* of yours!" I sputter, sensing George's own uneasy presence right next to me.

The writer looks me in the eye and mumbles, "Well, it's very nice of you to say that. Very, very nice." He has a crooked smile on his face, and then his eyes glaze over.

"You know," I say, feeling encouraged, "we're in the *book business*!! So it's not as though you're being stalked by a couple of *ordinary, nutty admirers*! My friend and I . . ." and here I look proudly at the horrified George, ". . . we're *publisher's reps*!"

Vonnegut leans unsteadily to one side and grins. "Is that right! And who're you workin' for these days?"

It's possible the man's been drinking or is in a strange mental state of some sort. Perhaps it's the madness, so common in writers, that erupts in bursts of creativity, producing books like *Welcome to the Monkey House* and *Slaughterhouse Five*. The state that Vonnegut appears to be in doesn't intimidate or frighten me; I am, instead, pleased by it. And now George seems to be as well.

I pull out a small notepad from the bottom of my purse and ask the writer for his autograph. He obliges; we shake hands all around and say good-bye, leaving him alone on a little bench on Thirty-third Street. George and I walk back uptown to the deli, feeling silly and spent by the experience. Stalkers? A couple of morons? I'm still not sure.

Through a fateful serendipity and an unusual set of circumstances—availability, the impulsive decisions made by publishers, and the geography of the western United States—in 1983 I became a partner in a commission sales group with two unique gentlemen, George being one and Jack O'Leary the other. At that time in my life, the idea of teaming up in a sales group with men seemed no stranger than anything else I'd welcomed in my peculiar lifestyle.

As I approached my midthirties, my requirements for a comfortable life included the protection of men. My unusual sense of independence at that time was easily mistaken for great self-confidence, but in truth the way I perceived myself was almost shameful. Although I had survived a violent physical assault in the recent past, it would be many years before the emotional damage was repaired. My interior life was still shot full of holes from a painful adolescence, when my father left us for months at a time to write for Jackie Gleason. Mistakenly labeling Dad's actions as "abandonment," the secret that I sat on was that I was not a worthy person. If I had been, I believed, then my father would never have bestowed nearly a decade of absence on me in the 1960s.

The result of this kind of thinking was to habitually attract men who, on the surface, seemed to care for and support me but in the end rejected the pedestal I would unfairly put them on. I'm sure it made them uncomfortable. None of these men were sociopaths; none the sort that required a worshipful girl. Their foibles fell within the range of "normal," conflicted chauvinism, and only much later did I realize that the one who put a hex on these relationships was myself. When my business partnership began with George and Jack, I was still the sort of woman who looked to others to give me a sense of who I was; a value, a distraction from the rowdy messages in my head that told me I was undesirable. I suppose I milked this insanity for as long as I needed to, until I began to change.

Jack O'Leary had been the Simon & Schuster sales rep in the Bay Area for almost twenty years when I met him. He had recently quit in protest over the corporate hoops he was expected to jump through at Simon, shouting "Fuck you!" to his boss at the conclusion of his annual performance review and storming out of the office in New York. I always loved this story and made an idol out of Jack for expressing the strength of his convictions in this way. He was irreverent like me, fed up with having to answer to convention, and ready to become his own boss as an independent commission rep. Well, so was I. And so was George.

We needed someone to take on the Northern California territory, and Jack—with his knowledge of the area and his built-in relationships with the book buyers there—was the obvious choice. George cleverly thought of a name for our group. We called ourselves I-5 Associates, because of the interstate highway that ran through all of our territories, and the tag stuck.

Jack, a few years older than George and I, was a veteran of both the U.S. Navy and a 12-Step group, as well as being a card-carrying member of the National Rifle Association and a devout Catholic. He'd been sober for several years when George and I first welcomed him into our group, an aspect about Jack that I felt very comfortable with. Just the year before, I'd finally realized that my "fondness" for cocaine was actually a brutal addiction that I had to confront. Going to 12-Step meetings played a big part in how I was able to walk away from a grim era in my life that began in the 1970s.

Because George had lived and repped in San Francisco at one time, he and Jack already knew one another and had established a mutual comfort level long before we all became partners. Everything worked in our favor when our business first came together. Different though the three of us were, our personalities meshed and we had the uncanny ability to bring out the best in one another. By the second time we met in New York for sales conferences, we knew one another well enough to share a newspaper over breakfast at our hotel in the following way. George would come to the table with the *New York Times*. Without saying a word, he'd hand Jack the business section, place the sports section next to his own coffee cup, and finally present me with Living & Arts. This was the indicator of our individual lifestyles and remained so for many years.

We also looked good standing in a row. I was the shortest, at five-foot-five. Next came Jack at about five-foot-ten. George, the tallest at six-foot-two, provided the rest of the balance to the image we presented to the world. We had a good symmetry about us. It didn't take long for the three of us, when we were together during sales conferences, to become one big personality that we could divvy up for this purpose or that. George was dry and cynical, Jack was as friendly and engaging as a bartender, and I alternated between being the deadpan commentator on both of them and a '50s-style political wife—demure and seductive at the same time.

Everybody seemed to love I-5 Associates. When we walked into a sales conference, we received a warm, affectionate greeting. The sales manager would hover around me solicitously before taking my coat and then would pound George and Jack on their backs with a frenetic male enthusiasm.

I never noticed my partners' deferential behavior more than when we grabbed a taxi in Manhattan. One of the guys would always climb into the backseat first, motion for me to sit down next to him, and then the other would plop down to my right.

With me crammed in the middle of these two big lugs, our briefcases and, in the winter, coats and umbrellas stuffed between and around us, it was frequently the case that I was either sitting *on* them or they on me. Despite my whining *("George, would you move your big butt over so I can breathe?"),* I felt so cared-for and protected by these men that my life seemed perfect. Once back at our hotel, I'd take their order for the sandwiches we referred to as "gut-bombs" and run down to one of the corner delis. I'd return laden with tuna on rye for George, a club sandwich on toasted white for Jack, and turkey on a Kaiser roll for myself. Added to this were a pint of chocolate fudge ice cream for the guys, and a black-and-white cookie for me—my favorite New York dessert.

Those rare nights when we didn't have a dinner meeting to attend were my favorites. The deli run being a fait accompli, we'd all meet in my room to chow down. George would lie on the floor with his back against the bed. The armchair was Jack's perch. Me, I always sprawled out on the bed in sweat pants and a T-shirt, finally sprung from the pantyhose and spike heels that had cramped my style all day long. There we'd lounge in silence, all eyes turned to CNN so George and I could catch the news and Jack could freely scan the ticker tape at the bottom of the screen that displayed the stock market numbers he watched like a hawk. He invested heavily and well. Jack was determined to take an early retirement, while George and I, in the mid-1980s, had yet to catch up with this idea.

During the decade or so that the three of us worked together, we never achieved the status of having a traditional best seller under our sales belt, one that hit the *New York Times* weekly list. This wasn't a reflection on our sales efforts, but a matter of disparity between the publishers who used house (salaried) reps and those who took on commission groups like I-5. Big trade houses like Random House, Simon & Schuster, and Harper-Collins always hire field sales reps who work exclusively for them. It makes sense. With publishers this enormous, commission reps would make more money than the director of sales at these houses. House reps are less expensive, even though their publishers pay for their health insurance, car and travel expenses, and all other sundry items such as office supplies and postage. These reps give their publishers a hundred percent of their time and effort.

Commission reps, on the other hand, often carry more than thirty lines in their bags. They're contracted by small- to medium-sized houses that can't afford their own field reps. These publishers only have to pay the reps a commission on what they actually sell, which spares them all of the other expenses. There's no limit on how much a commission rep can earn, because they're free to sell for as many publishers as they can get away with. Unfortunate though it may be, some small house will invariably fall through the cracks in the overwhelming amount of paperwork involved in repping more than a reasonable amount of lines.

George, Jack, and I were lucky. We always managed to have a solid, dependable group of publishers that brought in so much money that we never had to carry more than about fifteen lines at any one time. This kept the dreaded trips to New York for biannual sales meetings down to about eight days at a stretch, while our friends in other commission groups carrying more lines usually had to stay there for at least two weeks. Our travel expenses, although still astronomical, ran about 50 percent less than the others.

Our lines were maniacally varied, ranging from publishers that specialized in sports books and remainders, to film and theater books and business. Hands down, though, our most lucrative publisher was Microsoft Press. Microsoft hired us in 1985 upon their launching of the line, and we remained their reps for the next fifteen-plus years.

Microsoft Press seemed to grow at the same rate as Microsoft Corporation during the long period when that golden nugget was in our briefcases. I remember the first sales meeting well. It was held in a small conference room at the Hotel Nikko in San Francisco during the book convention of 1985. The meeting location was pleasant enough, but it was a no-frills conference nonetheless with, I believe, only coffee and tea for refreshments. There were only two people there from the Press, the remainder of the attendees being the brand-spanking-new sales force.

Larry Levitsky was the first sales manager of Microsoft Press. He was a die-hard New Jersey fellow who had transplanted himself to Seattle for this job, and he had some serious street smarts—and attitude. George and I knew him as a fellow rep from our days at E. P. Dutton, which was how we acquired the line. Larry stood at the front of the small room and discussed the books on the first list, a whopping five titles about the latest in computer operating systems—MS-DOS. His presentations stopped just short of having "dese" and "dose" in them. They went something like this:

"Okay. Mzzz Doss. It's an operating system. Awriiiight?? Okay. Now. The operating system makes the computer work. Awriiiight?" We all looked at him blankly. "Awriight. Any questions?"

I doubt that a single rep in that room owned a computer then, nor were any of us even contemplating this plunge into the techno-world. We were book reps, after all; our literary acumen and urbane high-mindedness made the very idea of operating such a thing far beneath us.

We were there because the Microsoft books were expensive, and that equated to commission dollars too good to pass up.

So out we went to sell these mysterious books that, much to our mercenary delight, sold like crazy that first season. And the next, and the one after that. Microsoft's list began to grow exponentially, as the market for home computer users started spreading like a San Fernando Valley housing complex. For the first couple of years, we were selling books on various versions and updates on DOS, and then in the late 1980s we heard about something called "Windows" that would be the next breakthrough in operating systems. What *were* these windows, I pondered? I considered the idea that computer users would be able to look through their monitors into a universe of loveliness and enchantment. I wanted a window like that! But first I wanted to make all that money off the books and live a better life, ignorance of technology be damned. Up to that point in my career, I'd been a good improvisational rep, managing to squeak through those moments in a sales call when I hadn't a clue what a book was about.

I hadn't anticipated the challenge in selling computer books, though, especially as PC technology became more and more advanced and specialized. Worse yet was that when I finally bought my first computer, in 1987, I chose a Macintosh—an operating system that was the antithesis of the technology driving Microsoft.

On one of my many vacations in the Pacific Northwest to visit George and his then-wife, Linda, we stopped by the Microsoft

Press office for a visit with the sales staff. By that time, Levitsky had been replaced by the much more engaging Jim Brown, another former Dutton rep who George and I were close friends with. The Press was still considered the bastard child of the Corporation, and their office wasn't yet on the renowned Microsoft "campus" in Redmond. After having lunch with Jim at a little diner near his nondescript office, we stood in the parking lot to chat before saying good-bye.

George and Jim, both baseball fanatics, were yammering away about the playoffs and their favorite pitchers, batters, and the like. My eyes began to glaze over as I fell out of the conversation altogether. I was standing in the midst of a typical macho dialogue and felt left out—in fact, I was being ignored. "*This is bullshit,*" I thought and decided to jump in at an appropriate pause and show off my technological savvy.

"Hey, Jim," I said brightly, "do you make the hardware here, or is that done on Campus?"

I watched as Jim caught George's eye. A smirk began to spread on their faces, and Jim didn't reply.

My defiance bubbled to the surface, and I crossed my arms over my chest. "I'm talking about the actual computers. Where does Microsoft make the computers?"

George looked down at something quite fascinating on his shoes.

"Uh . . .," Jim said reluctantly, "Microsoft makes software and designs operating systems, Wendy. We don't make computers. Companies like IBM and Toshiba make the computers, Wendy."

This wasn't the "window" I had in mind when I'd fantasized about looking at a wonder-world through a computer monitor.

Instead, I knew in that moment that George and Jim had a bird's-eye view into my stupid mind. I couldn't have asked a more imbecilic question if I'd tried. Standing before these two men like a vapid bovine, I looked off into a distance that was reserved for the brain-dead and felt my face turn beet-red. "Oh, of course," I sputtered. "That would make sense, wouldn't it?"

We all shuffled our feet in silence until, thank *god*, George got his keys out of his pocket and told Jim we had to get going before Linda started wondering where we were. After saying an agonized good-bye to Jim, George and I jumped into his Volvo and drove away, screaming with a wild laughter all the way back to his house. But I was aware that he and I were laughing for entirely different reasons, George because he cared for me no matter how much of an idiot I was, and I to cover my complete and utter humiliation. On the other hand, I figured that as soon as George had dropped me off at the airport the next morning, he'd phone Jim so that, together, they could have the last laugh on me. Here was a tricky, convoluted maze of loyalties that I would have to cope with as long as my partners were men. I was not, nor would I ever be, one of the lads—and eventually I started to question why I would ever want to become one.

Within five years of that first austere Microsoft Press sales meeting, the company was renting out enormous conference rooms at New York hotels like the Plaza, the Ritz-Carlton, and the Peninsula. We sat in environments that were lush with the excesses of the eighties and early nineties, executive armchairs with leather cushions and, during the breaks, sterling platters and coffee pots for the fresh pastries and French-roast brew served with great ostentation. Meeting attendance grew from twenty to about fifty, as Microsoft kept adding different tiers of middle management to the Press. We found ourselves repping for a company that gloated with self-importance and the kind of power that can gradually turn both executives and peons into paranoid cranks. Each Christmas, our holiday gifts became more and more posh. The reps were given Krups coffee-makers, Montblanc pens, and beautiful lap blankets. George, Jack, and I began earning monthly commissions that surpassed anything in our wildest dreams.

And I was still running a Macintosh.

The Microsoft Press list grew to a couple of hundred titles. During this time I developed a rather interesting mental block about these books and their increasingly complicated contents. I still didn't know the difference between Windows 3.1 and the latest version of Excel. As at all of our other meetings, George and I always sat together at the Microsoft conferences. For the first few years with the Press, my sales numbers exceeded the expected advances, and management was very pleased with my work. This, as well as the luster of being the only woman on the sales force at that point, led me confidently to my next Microsoft blunder.

In keeping with the extravagant nature of the sales conferences, one time we convened at the world-famous Windows on the World restaurant at the top of the World Trade Center. Our meeting was up first on the agenda, to be followed by dinner in the beautiful and dramatic setting. By that time, Jim Brown had been promoted to a vice-presidency at the Press, and an ambitious young woman named A. became the sales manager. She was cool, distant, and a good ten years younger than I. The first time we met, I sussed out her competitive nature. She seemed to be a man's woman, and she rejected my warm welcome to her in a subtle way that only women can detect. My concern about this relationship was instantaneous.

During the meeting at the World Trade Center, I impulsively decided to show this woman up. I'd already been selling Microsoft books for several years, while A. was still relatively new to the Press. Following her presentation of a series of titles about a major Windows upgrade, I raised my hand. A. looked my way and barely nodded at me to ask my question.

"Thank you, A. I'm impressed with all the new features on this version of Windows," I said, with professional intonations in my voice. "But you're leaving out an important issue, which I know my buyers will ask me about. So tell me—will Microsoft be launching a Macintosh version of this Windows software upgrade?"

George, ever at my side, had apparently been holding his breath as I asked the question that, from that point on, had me on probation with the Press. When I finished my brilliant interrogation of A., the only sound in the room was George, exhaling in a way that sounded like his last breath on earth. Okay, it was more a groan than a breath. Oblivious to the mental illness that my question implied, I looked up defiantly at the imperious A. and awaited her reply.

She stared at me with a triumphant smirk on her face, began to tap her foot, and then actually put her hands on her hips. "Wendy," she said, "perhaps George can answer that question for you when the meeting is over. Frankly, I don't quite know how to respond to it."

With that, A. moved on to the next title to present and seemed to slightly levitate with the assurance that she had just shamed me into dust. George frantically scribbled a note on a piece of paper and thrust it at me under the table.

"*Owie!*" I whispered to him. "You hurt my knee!"

George spoke out of the side of his mouth and muttered, "Just shut up and read it."

The note said, "*Idiot!* Windows and Macintosh are both operating systems. A computer runs one system or the other. AND WINDOWS ISN'T A SOFTWARE APPLICATION."

Incredibly, Microsoft didn't fire me after this debacle. That would come several years later. Being George's partner had everything in the world to do with this stay of execution, because he was their top rep and number one corporate ass-kisser. Maybe A. and Jim Brown were lenient with me because they saw me as an appendage of George, who was much loved by them. Maybe I was simply an object of their pity, or they may have just enjoyed having me around for laughs.

You have to understand that Microsoft was similar to a religious denomination. In the early 1990s, we started having sales meetings on their renowned "Campus" in Redmond. This was my chance to finally get a close-up of the environment created by Bill Gates, and by the end of that first day I was looking over my shoulder with the paranoia of an outsider. We took a bus ride around the property, dozens of acres of rolling lawns, Aspen trees, and uniform white, unmarked buildings. These had only small, discreet numbers stenciled on their front doors and security entries, which required photo-ID pass cards to open.

The driver of our bus, which was vibrating with the raucous levity of twenty out-of-control sales reps, patiently explained the layout of the Microsoft land to us. Some of the buildings housed programmers, designers, and analysts. Others were for graphic artists and tech support. They all looked alike to me as we rolled past the glass-and-chrome white structures; they all looked like empty vessels for the weird soul of technology. What business did I have in this wilderness of computers and operating systems? Was Bill Gates even aware that he had a publishing division, and that I was making money for him?

These were the questions that rolled through my head as we approached a large body of water in the middle of campus. "Is that a fucking mirage, or does Microsoft have its own lake?" my seat partner, Ted Wedel, asked me incredulously. The two of us stared out the window with our mouths agape.

The bus driver proudly told us that this "awesome, man-made lake" had been built on campus five years earlier, and it was the centerpiece of the entire property. This was where Microsoft had picnics in the summer and miniconferences in autumn; it took up an acre and a half of land and looked to me like an outsized Beverly Hills swimming pool in the midst of a forest of Frank Gehry rejects.

Ted, a close friend and commission book rep in the Mid-Atlantic territory, spoke up to the driver. "Hey—does the lake have a name?"

"It sure does!" said the bus driver. "It's called *Lake Bill!*"

Death by drowning, in Lake Bill! I added it to my little list of suicidal methodologies and in that moment promised myself to always honor the Macintosh in each of us.

More than a dozen Microsoft sales meetings were to follow that one at the World Trade Center, but none more memorable than on that day when I annihilated my self-esteem. After some time had passed, I felt the need to comment on something during an editorial presentation as a way to earn back my stripes. Each time I began to raise my hand, though, George would be there to grasp my arm and stop me. *"Don't do it don't do it don't do it,"* he'd mutter under his breath, saving me from the potential of further humiliation.

As the price of Microsoft's stock continued to rise at a phenomenal rate, most of the people we reported to in the sales division of the Press became more and more odd. Too young to be as wealthy as they suddenly were, they took themselves as seriously as heart attacks.

Cheerleading became mandatory for the reps at the start of each meeting, as A. or one of the other sales coaches standing at the front of the room would shout, *"Whaddawe want? SALES! Whaddawe want? SALES! I can't hear you! Again!"* I would mouth the words, mortified, flinching when the next round began: *"Whaddawe love? WINDOWS! Whaddawe love? WINDOWS!! Gooooooo Windows—yaaaaay!"*

It was embarrassing as hell, I tell you, and my resentment toward these spoiled, enthusiastic staffers finally began to interfere with my work habits. Whatever ability I had had in the past for kissing ass utterly dissolved in light of my realization about the nature of Microsoft. In my puritan's mind, what they published were products—not books. I didn't respect the corporation; rather, I was appalled by it. My integrity was screaming to be released from a situation that brought out the worst in me, and I deliberately began slacking off on the job. This involved *not* calling on accounts that I was responsible for, being a no-show (for the first time) at a sales conference, and not responding to e-mails from the sales director.

I finally got what I asked for when Microsoft abruptly fired me in the year of our Lord 2000, *amen*.

International Polygonics was one of our small publishers that provided tangible proof that I really was in the book business, and not just a pawn of Bill Gates. They published trade paperback mysteries; reprints, mostly, of old titles that had fallen out of print but were still popular and usually sold a few thousand copies out the door. IPL featured an impressive list of dead authors in its fold. These included Ngaio Marsh, John Dickson Carr, and Paul Gallico, mystery writers who had published their first books in the 1930s and '40s. The owner of the company dug deep to locate titles that had either fallen into the public domain, or whose rights were inexpensive to acquire.

The owner was a fellow named Hugh Abramson, who started the company around 1983 in New York. When George, Jack, and I became his reps in the mid-'80s, I had already met dozens of book people who walked that fine line between eccentricity and madness, and I'd grown accustomed to the personality type. In fact, I knew that in some ways I embodied it myself. When I met Hugh Abramson, I could tell he was a member of the same tribe, and I was very much at ease with him.

He was tall—at least six-foot-five—and had a completely bald head. Hugh's skin was so smooth and unlined that his face resembled a cartoon sketch of adulthood. With big eyes that bulged with enthusiasm and a slightly pigeon-toed gait, Hugh could easily have passed for the prototype of the animated character Baby Huey.

We all liked Hugh. He was ever gracious and accommodating, and we could even tolerate his often long-winded editorial presentations that invariably turned into cynical, gossipy repartees about either the dead author or his dead literary agent. Hugh was a font of information of this kind; most of the sales meetings were spent laughing hysterically as he dissed people to kingdom come. And how he loved to go on! In those pre–Caller ID days, if Hugh was on the other end of the line when I answered my phone, I had to gird my brain for a conversation that lasted no less than an hour, but provided me with the time to balance my checkbook or look for a new salmon recipe in *The Silver Palate Cookbook*.

We never made much money from selling IPL, but Hugh gave me a priceless gift when he introduced me to George Baxt, the only living writer who he published. In his former life, Baxt had written extensively for film, stage, and television. He had been a theatrical agent and publicist and became well-known as a hilarious satirist and historian of all things Hollywood. In 1968, his first mystery, *A Queer Kind of Death*, had been published to great acclaim; it was followed by two more titles in the trilogy of Pharaoh Love mysteries. Thus began his career as an Edgar-winning novelist, and it was at this stage of his life that I was blessed to become one of his friends.

Hugh was very fond of my partners and me and often took us out to lunch when we were in New York. In the spring of 1986, he invited Baxt to join us at Pete's Tavern near Gramercy Park. Baxt was a rather small man in his midsixties, plump yet graceful and with thinning gray hair. Although I was friends with several gay men at that time, I had never met such a flamboyant queen as he. If you can imagine a swish, fey, and girlish Phil Silvers, you'll have a picture of George Baxt. He was hilarious and irreverent. He batted his eyelashes to make a point when telling a dirty joke. His Brooklyn accent was delicious, and he had stories to tell about every star from the Golden Age of Hollywood and beyond. You had never heard dirt dished until you heard it from the mouth of George Baxt.

Jack and George were as taken with him as I was. As the meal went on, we unconsciously moved our chairs closer to him until, by the time dessert was served, we were in a tight scrum around this marvelous little man. When Baxt told us a story about Sal Mineo, the guys read between the lines of his sexual innuendos and commented that they didn't realize the actor had been gay.

Baxt picked up a corkscrew that our waiter had left on the table, waved it in the air, and announced: "My darlings, this *corkscrew* is straighter than Sal Mineo!" We all burst out laughing and could barely go on.

When the conversation turned to films, Jack began to fantasize about different stories and plots he'd like to see come to the big screen. "Wouldn't it be wild," he said, "to see a movie called *Apocalypse Now—The Musical*?"

Just at that moment an eerie hush fell on the restaurant, and it became absolutely silent in the moment that Baxt shouted, "Well, *I* just want to see a movie called *GIDGET GIVES HEAD!*"

Everyone in the restaurant turned to look at our table. While the rest of us all stared at our plates, aghast, and solemnly moved our silverware around, Baxt scanned the room and happily took in all of the attention that came his way. I peeked at him and grinned. He grinned back. Our friendship had begun.

We stayed in touch regularly after that. St. Martin's was to publish his new books in hardcover, and over the years George's "Murder Case" series focused on movie stars he could spin a gossipy mystery around. These included Alfred Hitchcock, Tallulah

Bankhead, Carole Lombard, and Clark Gable. These titles were formulaic, light reads that sold well in both the gay and mystery markets. Still, George complained to me every time we spoke on the phone about his consistently late royalty payments, as well as the copyeditors at the Press.

One of his mysteries had a subplot that involved Alfred Lunt, the Broadway producer and director who had become famous in the 1930s and '40s for his hit plays. One day the phone rang in George's apartment on West Fifty-fifth Street in New York. It was a young woman from St. Martin's who was proofreading his new book before it went to press. She was inquiring about a supposed misspelling in George's manuscript.

"Mr. Baxt," she trilled, "*Lunt* is not a word. I'm sure you meant to type either 'lint' or 'lent.' Which one should I use?"

George exploded. "It's LUNT, you moron. Haven't you ever heard of Alfred Lunt?"

"No, sir, I haven't," said the terrified copyeditor. "But how is it spelled?"

"It's spelled like CUNT, dwahling," George yelled. "C-U-N-T." With that, he slammed the phone down.

Loyalty to and appreciation of me aside, what made me love this little Jewish man more than anything else was that he reminded me of my father—and he knew who my father was. Because of George's years in television and the theater, Snag's writing work was very familiar to him, and he praised it to the heavens. These two talented men had started out in show business at about the same time, in the days of burlesque and radio. Such was my attachment to Baxt that, similar to my relationships with my partners, he quickly became my queer paternal figure.

By the mid-1980s, I-5 Associates was well established, and the three of us regularly traveled through the thirteen Western states that defined our group's territory. When I agreed to take on what I later realized was more than I could handle—Southern California, Arizona, New Mexico, Colorado, *and* Utah—it meant that I'd be living out of a suitcase for about three months a year. The money was good, and initially the travel through uncharted territory was interesting and amusing to me.

The first time I stayed at the Lodge On the Desert in Tucson, I was charmed to find a working fireplace in my room, kindling at the ready in the grate, and a basket of logs on the lovely tiled area that surrounded it in a half-circle. The beds were covered with chenille spreads, and large oval-shaped handmade rugs that were vibrant with color were scattered generously throughout the room. The hotel even had a library in its lounge, the shelves lined with worn copies of mass-market paperbacks and hardcover books missing their dust jackets. Still, the selection was good enough to soothe any traveler's homesickness.

In Salt Lake City, the overwhelming Mormon influence was, at first, fascinating to my skeptical way of thinking about religion in those days. The lobby of my hotel had a display rack of literature about the religion, dozens of little pamphlets that described how to best observe, experience, and pay homage to the spiritual brainchild of Joseph Smith. When I opened the drawer of the nightstand in my room to find a place to stash my pot, there was a Book of Mormon staring me in the face. I slammed the drawer shut and found a different place to hide my drugs.

And don't get me started on Utah's provincial drinking laws, which dictate that restaurants can only serve setups for alcoholic drinks—club soda, ice, orange juice, etc.—but not the liquor. That has to be bought in liquor stores, available in airline-sized bottles that can then be consumed in dining establishments. The whole process seemed absurd to me.

For about two years, I lived a weird gypsy life, of being home for three weeks and then going on the road for one, before finally cracking. How lonely it all became to me! Each time I checked into a hotel, I'd shove open the door to my room with my shoulder as I carried my bags with a growing resentment. Every time I had to fly on a plane, I felt that a little part of me died after each take-off and landing. My ruminations while on the road became bizarre, as I began to consider the breadth and parameters of my soul. If parts of me died from air travel, how many more were biting the dust each time I turned the key in a strange rental car, or laid my head on a lumpy, hypoallergenic pillow that was not my own?

Arriving in Salt Lake City on a snowy, frigid afternoon in February, I drove my Hertz car directly to my first appointment. For a few hours, I sold books to a conservative, humorless man who was the buyer for Deseret Book Company, a chain of Mormon-owned bookstores in Utah. By the time I checked in to my hotel, I was so depressed that the Book of Mormon started to look pretty good to me. The only thing that would make me snap out of my comfortable place on the mental pity-pot was talking to a pal, so I picked up the phone and rang my friend Penny Rose in Los Angeles. Since meeting as co-workers at Pickwick Bookshop in 1970, we had continued to be as close as sisters.

"*Kemosabe,*" I said to myself, "*please pick up the phone.*" It rang a few times while I pictured Penny's tiny garret in the Hollywood

Hills, her home in the early 1980s, filled with the pressed-flower collages she made and her books of a metaphysical nature neatly lined on shelves above a small desk. I'd spent hundreds of hours there with her, smoking cigarettes, drinking icy vodka, and discussing the nature of our lives. How I longed to be there with my best friend instead of in a dreary, antiseptic hotel room!

Penny, sounding out of breath, finally answered the phone. "Hi, Wen," she said. "Where are you this time?"

"In Salt Lake City, and, I might add, not feeling very salty." I lay down on the enormous bed that I already despised simply because it was not *my bed*. Lighting a cigarette, I threw my arm over my head and tried to relax. "Sounds like you're in a hurry."

"Sorry, lovey. I'm meeting James for dinner, and I'm running late." I could hear Penny's shoes on the hardwood floor of her apartment as she walked around gathering purse and keys. "Hey," she said, suddenly alert and focused on me. "You don't sound right. What's the matter?"

I let out a pathetic sigh, the only utterance I could manage.

"Wen?" Penny coaxed. "What is it?"

What I said were the only words that rang true to me. "It's nothing. *I just have the blues.*" This was immediately followed by a staggering déjà vu, as I realized that I was lying on the bed exactly the same way my mother had, the night I'd wandered into her room when she was crying over my father's absence. This confirmed that those wily blues had found their way into the center of my being, and I finally understood as an adult what my mother had felt twenty years earlier. We shared a continuing refrain of sadness in our lives that became the foremost quality we had in common.

Staring out the window as the sun went down in a violet sky, I knew that I was on the brink of a revelation. What troubled me was that I couldn't find clarity amidst my gloomy, cartwheeling thoughts. When the sky outside grew dark, I grabbed my copy of Raymond Carver's new book of short stories, *Cathedral,* stuffed it into my purse, and took the elevator down to the lobby. From there, I walked to a café a couple of blocks away, had a solitary dinner, and lost myself in the brilliance of Carver's words. By the time I dropped off to sleep in my rent-a-bed, his writing had distracted me from the wild rhythm of my earlier thoughts.

In the morning I slurped coffee like a heathen, and my mouth savored the flavor of brown sugar as it melted in my bowl of oatmeal. Before I left my room, I tidied the bathroom and straightened the bedspread, a habit of mine that I could not break even though a hotel maid would be cleaning the room after I'd gone. I walked to my rental car in the parking area and found, to my dismay, that the key would not turn in the doorlock. I tried to open it every which way and each time was met with resistance. Damn!

Returning to my room, I got on the phone with Hertz and pleaded with them to get to my hotel as soon as possible with a locksmith in tow. I waited by my white rental car, pacing in the parking lot for about fifteen minutes. When the Hertz van arrived, I wildly flagged it down. The customer service rep walked toward me with my rental contract in his hand, eyeballing the car I was standing next to.

"You know why the key won't fit in the lock, don't you?" he said, grinning broadly at me.

I crossed my arms over my chest and glared at him. "I'm not

in the mood for jokes this morning. I give up. Why doesn't the key fit?"

"Because this isn't your car, honey," he laughed. "It *looks* like your car, but that white Chevy Impala over there is yours." He pointed to a spot a couple of rows over from where we stood. Crooking his finger at me, he said, "Come with me."

So I followed this smart-ass over to the other car, put the key in the lock, and easily opened the door. I was beet-red with humiliation. "I feel like an idiot. I'm so sorry that you had to come all the way out here!" I said, sheepishly.

"Happens all the time. No need to apologize. You must travel a lot," Mr. Hertz said to me and waved good-bye as he walked to his van.

Everything about my road trips was blending into one vague perspective. The rental cars all looked alike to me. So did the hotel rooms, the cheap coffee-makers on top of the minibars that brewed nothing more than brown water, and the airline logos. My life was becoming one big seat-assignment after another, with anonymity crushing my spirit. I sat in the Chevy and rested my forehead on the steering wheel. *Let me just make it through one more day*, I begged to a source that still had no name in my life.

Arriving forty-five minutes late at the University of Utah, I rushed to the bookstore and the buyer who was waiting for me. "Susan!" I almost screamed. "I'm so sorry I'm late. You won't believe what happened to me this morning!"

"Let's go into my office and you can tell me about it." Good, kind Susan, my favorite buyer in all of Utah, a very lapsed Mormon, took my hand and settled me into a chair near her desk. "What's wrong, Wendy? You look terrible."

And with those magic words, I burst into tears—noisy, sloppy, gloppy tears. My reckoning had finally come, and—hallelujah!—the truth would be revealed in this safe, friendly environment in the back room of a bookstore. Susan found some tissues in her purse, stuffed them in my hand, and moved her chair closer to mine.

"I can't do this any more! I can't take being on the road so much," I sputtered. "This is the loneliest I've ever been in my life, Susan. There's no comfort in it!"

Susan sat quietly while I continued to weep, knowing better than to say a word while I was so vulnerable. After a few minutes, I began to calm myself, and she put her hand on my arm and gently stroked it. I blew my nose loudly, the signal that the worst of my outburst was over.

"Maybe," she said, "it's time for you to find a rep to take over for you. I actually know a couple of people who work the Rocky Mountains territory who might be interested." Susan cleared her throat. "Is it really worth it to you to make the extra money but lose your mind in the process?" Then she settled back in her chair and waited patiently for me to gather my unruly thoughts.

"You're right. Of course you're right!" I said with growing certainty. "We'll find someone to replace me here, and then I'll only be covering Southern California and Arizona. I can easily handle that." Smiling at Susan, I said, "Less money, but more peace of mind." I gave her a hug. "Thanks for putting up with me today."

It was, indeed, the last time I went to Utah. Or Colorado, or New Mexico. George, Jack, and I decided to invite Henry Hubert into our group, and he gladly accepted. Based in Denver, Henry was a survivor of Simon & Schuster and a former cohort of Jack's. He'd been their rep in the Rockies for almost twenty years before his intolerance for the corporate world wore him down to the point of quitting. Like the rest of us, he wanted to work in an atmosphere of his own creation, risky though commission sales might be. I was ecstatic that he agreed to take over a big chunk of my territory.

But I was not thinking ahead, to what the loss of income would eventually mean to me. Like my mother, I had become a compulsive spender, with no thought to the consequences of having a financial outlook that bordered on burlesque. To me, IRS actually stood for "Informal Random Spending." My recklessness when it came to money only served to fuel the crazy drama of working for myself.

As a commission sales rep, one's income varies from month to month. The highs and the lows, the heart-pounding surprise of the amount of a check and the constant uncertainty (*will I make enough money to survive this month?*) were tantamount to a drug for me. Even my former expensive cocaine habit couldn't hold a candle to the rush I got from gambling on my income.

My business relationships with George and Jack were especially informed by the insecurity that I stepped into every day, like a pair of boots lined with barbed wire. When I started out with them, the anxiety I felt led me to behave in a slightly over-deferential manner; if Jack's opinions were sterling, George's were platinum. In our discussions about publishers—which ones to continue selling, which to drop, and which to consider when they were offered to us—I usually let the men make the decisions. Naturally, I had a say in these matters, but in those days my input was often based on a sheer emotional reaction rather than on professional logic.

"We have to drop So-and-So Press! Their sales meetings are too long, and boring as hell!" I'd whine to George and Jack.

"You think so?" George would patiently reply. "I made a lot of money off them last year."

Then, thinking myself a selfish child, I'd say, "You're right. Bad idea—never mind."

When I-5 Associates first took form in 1983, I had agreed to (and lauded) the financial structure of our group. The three of us decided that we would be paid individually for exactly what each of us sold in our respective territories. George, Jack, and I would remain fiscally autonomous. This utterly contradicted the paradigm adopted by commission groups decades before we came along. In every group but ours, all the commissions received from the publishers were divided equally among the partners, regardless of geographical origin. In the Midwest, for instance, the partner who sold to bookstores in Illinois and Indiana was paid a portion of the commissions generated everywhere else in the cumulative territory equal to the share of the Kansas/Nebraska rep, no more, no less.

I remained blindly amenable to I-5's unorthodox system for at least a decade, until I realized that I had gradually taken on a position of servitude in favor of pleasing George and Jack. By the early 1990s, my territory was being decimated. Dozens of the bookstores I'd called on for years had either closed or would do so eventually; they simply could not compete with the unusually large number of chain stores that opened in Southern California and Arizona.

Independent bookstores all over the country were shutting down because of these trends, but my territory was particularly hard hit. Although George and Jack had suffered similar losses, their areas of Northern California and the Pacific Northwest remained extremely profitable. It's not an exaggeration to say that they had twice as many book accounts as I had remaining, and our incomes became increasingly uneven. The fear that developed about my future as a book rep manifested itself as misplaced resentment toward the same men I had once glorified. It festered slowly but surely.

In truth, George, Jack, and I weren't partners at all—we were members of a coalition that had come together for self-serving purposes. The three of us created a sales trinity wherein Jack was the father, George the son—and I had only the holy ghost of a chance. To make matters worse, we began to argue over what I perceived as financial discrepancies.

The tender history George and I had nurtured for twenty years saved us from falling into a fatally bitter snare; our mutual affection was stronger than that. But it was a different story with Jack. Always unpredictable, his personality became sharp and volatile. Our practical joker—who had once convinced the sales manager of Warner juvenile books that George had gotten into the book business after a long stint as a hairdresser in San Francisco—seemed to have lost his sense of humor.

As my financial situation became increasingly dire, commission money couldn't land in my mailbox quickly enough. It seemed that I'd inherited one more aspect of my father, by agreeing to a career that was financially chaotic.

Jack was responsible for breaking down some of our monthly checks by territory and account before sending George and me our portions. I couldn't afford to wait the extra days it sometimes took for the money to reach me and was on the phone to Jack about this with a frequency that I'm sure was annoying at best. Still, I didn't deserve the verbal abuse that he delivered to me on more than one occasion. It was a brutal form of communication that left me reeling between guilt and self-righteousness.

In 1993, Jack imploded. Unbeknownst to George and myself, he faxed letters to all our publishers to inform them of his decision to quit I-5 Associates and "go it solo as an independent rep." The damage to our group was almost irreparable.

It was George who took care of damage control, because I was the last person Jack wanted to hear from—his fury would have knocked me on my ass. George's patience and diplomacy not only saved us from being dropped by most of our publishers, but he also managed to convince Jack that quitting was not in his best interest. Our group was a viable, successful organization that would continue to serve him well. Furthermore, we arranged with our publishers to begin sending Jack his own individual checks. This relieved both him and me of the conundrum implicit in our financial dealings with one another. I mailed Jack a letter of apology for any undue stress I'd caused him. His forgiveness allowed the three of us to continue our alliance.

But before too long the peace was broken again. Jack resumed his criticisms of me and his mistrust in our publishers. His perception of the entire arena of I-5 was out of synch. No one was out to get Jack. The publishers admired his work ethic, and we appreciated the fine job he did selling books in Northern California. Over the years, he had made us look good in many ways. However, as Jack gradually became capricious once again, baiting us with the possibility of his retirement, our tolerance was slipping away.

In May 1995, we were all in Chicago to attend the national book convention. Opting out of our usual routine of all staying at the same hotel, Jack and his wife, Rebecca, chose to separate themselves from George and myself by booking a room at a place a few blocks away. At the time, we were representing a now-defunct business publisher called Probus. Their office was in Champaign, Illinois, a two-hour drive from Chicago, and the company treated us to limousine service to and from their sales conference.

During a coffee break at the meeting, I overheard Jack telling the Probus sales manager that he was going to retire soon. He mentioned this casually in their conversation and described the home in the Lake Tahoe area that he and Rebecca looked forward to buying.

It makes sense that publishers require a sense of commitment and stability in their sales reps, and Jack's words would likely give way to an uneasy concern in the mind of the sales manager. Once again, Jack was placing George and myself in an awkward situation, possibly subjecting the whole group to undue scrutiny. I was furious. My relationship with Jack, which had become tiresome at best, had to end. I was finished with it.

The four of us piled into the back of the limousine for the drive back to Chicago, George and I in the seats facing the O'Learys. For a while, we sat in silence, the smooth lull of the highway beneath the limo enveloping us. Finally, though, I opened my mouth to release my seething thoughts.

"How dare you talk about your retirement to Probus tonight, Jack? How dare you? Now they'll be wondering how the hell I-5 can do the job for them with no rep in the Bay Area!"

Jack pointed a finger at me. "Hey, lady! This is none of your business. I'll do whatever I damn well please. And I don't like your tone of voice!"

Without giving it a second's thought, I yelled: "You know what, Jack? *Fuck you!*"

No one said a word after that. The limo dropped Jack and Rebecca at their hotel, and then George and me at ours. Laughing nervously, George said, "Way to go, Wendy! I have no idea what you just triggered, but we'll find out soon enough!"

I felt no need to apologize.

There were still two days remaining of the book convention. In the morning, George and I walked a couple of blocks away to buy fresh orange juice from a street vendor. Nearing Jack's hotel on the way back, we spotted him and Rebecca getting into a cab with all their luggage in tow. It was a stunning moment and stopped us dead in our tracks.

"Hey, O'Leary!" George called out. "Where're you going?"

Jack turned, smiled, and put up his hand to wave to us. "We're going to the airport. *I quit!*" He sat down in the backseat and slammed the door as the cab drove away. Jack had literally left George and me in the dust.

We found a rep to replace Jack in the Bay Area and moved on from a devastating farewell. George and I spoke to Jack a few times after that; he and his wife had realized their dream, taking an early retirement and moving to a house in the mountains near Lake Tahoe. I lamented my remaining conversations with Jack, which were contrived and awkward. Eventually I stopped returning his phone calls and we disappeared from one another's lives. I still become sad when I think of him, though, the way one does when the door of friendship accidentally locks itself upon closing.

Seven

NO REPS FOR THE WICKED

> From the moment I picked up your book until I laid it down, I was convulsed with laughter. Some day I intend reading it.
> —GROUCHO MARX

I GOT A nice Valentine today from Larry Todd. He sent me a little Hallmark card with warm, fuzzy animal illustrations on the front, and the sentiment *I Love Our Friendship* inside. Go figure.

Larry had been the buyer and general manager of Hunter's Books in Beverly Hills for almost twenty years, before it shut its doors in 1987.

Hunter's, where Miriam Bass had once worked, was an elegant independent bookstore chain with over a dozen branch stores in Southern California and two in Arizona. The flagship store, on Rodeo Drive, was where Hunter's corporate offices were maintained. It was at this location that the reps met with Larry Todd each season, once in the spring and again in the fall. It was here that we showed up to meet our murky fate, determined by what mood Mr. Todd was in on that day.

In those days, Larry was by turns charming or belligerent, patient or terse, good-humored or enraged. Those of us who knew better always booked our appointments for the afternoon, after Larry had eaten lunch and consumed a couple of martinis, though a two o'clock P.M. appointment didn't guarantee one's chances of a pleasant sales meeting. It was a crapshoot, not for the faint-hearted, and certainly not for a young woman like me who used to wither under anyone's ill will.

I always "dressed" for my appointments at Hunter's Books. It was, after all, in Beverly Hills and therefore required a bit of fashion sense. Besides, the taut confinement of pantyhose and three-inch heels somehow fortified me for the challenges I might face once inside the store. I dressed with severity, as though my life depended on it.

To walk into Hunter's was to enter the rarefied atmosphere of old Beverly Hills money and sophistication. The window displays were always harmoniously arranged, little art exhibitions of books. The scent of Joy perfume and Cohiba cigars emanated from the browsing customers, and book clerks bustled about with the air of maids and butlers as they assisted the upscale clientele.

In the center of the main floor, long Formica desks faced one another, charmingly strewn with the working tools of a good bookstore. Rolodexes held a thousand cards with house account information on them. Six volumes of the current edition of Bowker's *Books In Print* (since replaced by a computer Web site) leaned against one another, balanced precariously between bookends a bit too fragile to hold their hefty weight. Clumsy boxes of short slips, first cousins to those we used at Pickwick Bookshop, lay about for the salesclerks to use to mark inventory numbers on titles sold the previous day. A mismatched assortment of pens, pencils, and notepads, mingled with several rotary telephones, were the final comforting touches at the center of activity at Hunter's.

Larry's desk was in the midst of this scene of controlled chaos. He was always dressed in a jacket and tie, the latter normally pulled a bit loose by the time I arrived in the afternoon. Sitting down next to him, I'd shyly say hello, neatly arrange all my catalogs on the desk, and light a cigarette. Because of Larry's exalted position in the book business and my own sense of insignificance, I always felt that I'd just swallowed a pill that had made me very small when I was face to face with him. As I vetted his mood for (a) insolence, (b) humor, (c) low blood sugar, or (d) wrath, the intimidation rose and fell. My sales pitches to Larry were like the Song of Solomon. I tried lovingly to coax him into buying certain titles in a way that would please rather than irritate him. But to insinuate that perhaps I knew more than he about a certain author, or the merits of a book's strong marketing plan, would usually put me in the hot seat.

"*I know what I'm doing, Wendy,*" he'd say stridently. "Don't question me about this."

When something like that happened, my brains turned into poached eggs. Once I dropped a lit cigarette in my lap. My hands frantically tried to put out the burning embers, but while doing so I let fly the master catalog that rested on my thighs. I became Buster Keaton on steroids, my heart thumping with fear while

Larry sat back and smiled indulgently, but not kindly. On another occasion, when my pen fell from my hands while I was making notes about his co-op advertising requests, my nerves overshot my grasp and I accidentally kicked Larry in the shins. He sat in silence, coldly accepting my frantic apologies with what seemed like a superior sneer. Where the hell was Xanax in the 1980s, I ask you?

Always using a felt-tip pen with brown ink, Larry would write his orders directly on the catalog pages. Starting with the Beverly Hills store, the numbers that followed represented the branch locations and were listed, as Larry said, "as the crow flies." For a big book, the numbers might look like this:

$$50 - 10 - 5 - 20 - 5 - 10 - 3 - 30 - 3 - 5 - 10 - 3;$$

while for a secondary, or specialized title, the quantities might show this progression:

$$3 - 0 - 0 - 2 - 0 - 12 - 0 - 0 - 2 - 0 - 0 - 0 - 6 - 2.$$

Larry Todd remains the best book buyer I've ever worked with. He had an intuition for what would and wouldn't sell that was uncanny and repeatedly astonished me. The titles that my publishers relegated to a "midlist" status were often the ones that Larry would buy with the knowledge that they'd become blockbusters. Of an author's second novel about a family in the Midwest, for instance, he once said: "Her first book didn't sell well, but as I recall it got excellent reviews. I just have a feeling about this new one." Far be it from me to try and change his mind. I knew that nine times out of ten, Larry would be right.

The physical work would begin when I got home from a sales call at Hunter's. Laying a dozen order forms out on my living-room floor, I'd gird myself to write up the orders. First I'd write in the ship-to address of each Hunter's location, following Larry's sequence in the catalog. Then I'd retire to the kitchen and make my first screwdriver.

Once bolstered with drink, I'd place Larry's opened catalog on the floor and, on my hands and knees, shuffle from one order form to another, writing in the quantity for each title. I had to double-check all the numbers. If I made a mistake and the Sherman Oaks store received twenty-five copies of a title rather than the designated three, Larry's wrath was inevitable.

On my next break, I'd make myself another screwdriver, mindful to leave out the orange juice this time. Having further fortified myself, I'd collect the order forms from the floor and sit at my desk. There I wrote in the Hunter's bill-to address in Beverly Hills more than a dozen times. Finally, I'd separate the three-part order forms, put the white copies in an envelope to be mailed to the publisher, the pink copies in the Hunter's file in my filing cabinet, and the goldenrod copies for Larry in a stack to be added to when I repeated the process for the next publisher.

When you multiply a dozen or more Hunter's locations by the number of publishers I sold for during those years—which ranged from ten to sixteen—the carpal tunnel surgery I later required in both hands makes perfect sense. Happily, though, beginning around 2000, the digital revolution made all this triplicate paperwork either obsolete or optional.

There was a large, cavernous basement at Hunter's Beverly Hills with low ceilings and narrow aisles between bookcases crammed with overstock books. In those precomputerized days, reps were required to take manual inventories at their book accounts. Moreover, if we wanted to stay on Larry's good side, we simultaneously pulled returns for Hunter's, which extended our time in the Hunter's dungeon by a couple of hours.

Because that basement triggered my phobic claustrophobia, and Larry seemed to enjoy confronting me about the accuracy of my counting, I dreaded these biannual ordeals. One day, it dawned on me that recreational drugs might make for a more pleasurable experience while I was incarcerated there.

K., the Harper & Row (now HarperCollins) rep, met me at my apartment on the day we'd both scheduled inventory appointments at Hunter's. He brought over some pot of the highest quality, and we sat together at my kitchen table smoking a joint, drinking coffee, and schmoozing until it was time to leave for Beverly Hills. K. offered to drive, and off we went.

As soon as I walked into Hunter's, I knew I'd made a mistake. Paranoia set in as I crept across the sales floor to the stairs that led to the basement, and I thanked my lucky stars that Larry was nowhere in sight. K. and I stumbled down the stairs to the comparative safety of the quiet stockroom and began working; his books were shelved fairly close to mine in the same aisle. There we stood with our clipboards and order forms, reviewing the stock at hand. Actually, that's all we were doing, standing like dumb blocks of flesh, staring at rows of books with heavy, red-rimmed eyes, neither of us writing anything down.

It was simply impossible to count anything beyond the number three. I was so stoned that my brain would not cooperate, and the only concept I could grasp was that I was high, too high to do more than look at the book spines with a great sense of awe. Books! What magnificent objects!

After what seemed like an hour, I turned to K.

"How are you doing?" I said earnestly.

After a very long pause, he finally looked at me.

"Oh, fine," he said. "You?"

"Well, I'm . . . I'm . . . heh heh heh! Ha ha ha! *HAW, HAW, HAW* . . ." and before I knew it I was bent over, screaming with laughter, choking on it, and so was K. There was no stopping it. It took a few moments before we realized that Larry had come down to the basement and was standing behind us. All laughter stopped.

"What's so funny?" he said with rancor. "I really need these inventories today so I can start doing returns."

It was obvious that Larry hadn't had his two-martini lunch yet, which meant that his sense of humor was still in a coma. *Shit!* What dreadful timing. If he'd offered me a stack of hundred-dollar bills at that moment, I still couldn't have uttered one word that made sense. Thank God for K. He was able to rouse himself just in time.

"Hi, Larry! How are you?" he said smoothly. "We were just laughing over a dirty joke Wendy told me. She's so *naughty!*"

"Well, keep it down! We can hear you all the way upstairs," Larry barked before returning to the sales floor above us.

K. and I looked at each other and grinned like mental patients before returning to the task at hand. It was excruciating. Although Larry's admonishment had sobered me up a bit, it still took all my energy to concentrate on counting the books. As I went along each shelf, I pulled out the titles that were either too old or too slow-selling to remain in stock, turning them spine-down for easy access when the returns were pulled. K. and I worked at about the same pace, and before we knew it lunchtime had passed. Just as we were about to take a break for chow, Larry came downstairs again.

"Hi, you two! How's it going?" he chortled, having slipped into a mellow mood after imbibing at lunch. "I wish this basement was decorated like the lounge at the Beverly Wilshire Hotel, don't you?"

"Yes, but then your reps would never get *anything* done," I said. "We'd just lay around all day on the chaises and make each other drinks."

Larry broke into a big smile. "Well, there's nothing wrong with *that*, is there?" he said playfully.

K. and I stood there and just looked at him, unsure of where this was leading or how far we could carry an authentically friendly conversation with Larry before he'd think us presumptuous and get mad. This could happen in an instant, as I knew only too well. The eggshells I walked on in his presence had been crushed long before that day.

"I'll just get out of your way, then, and let you finish your work," Larry remarked and moved toward the stairs. "*Toodles!*"

K. and I were glued in place. "Why can't he be like that when I'm selling him goddamn books, for Christ's sake?" I muttered.

"Why can't pigs fly, Wendy?" K. said. "Let's go eat. I'm starving." We trundled around the corner to the Bagel Nosh, a cheap alternative to the Café Swiss, where Larry dined luxuriously nearly every day for lunch.

His longtime companion, Ken, worked at the Beverly Hills

store as manager of the paperback department. The term "code-pendent" might have found its genesis in this relationship. Ken and Larry operated as a single unit. Ken wasn't as serious a book person, but he had come on board at Hunter's when Larry was hired so they could merge their personal and professional relationships. He acted as Larry's eyes and ears, reporting any whispered affronts about his partner overheard when clerks—or reps—were within his shadowy range. Ken was civil to me in our few encounters, but each one gave me the sensation of taking a bath in a tub of cold water. No doubt Ken had a warm and loving nature, but apparently it was all reserved for Larry, whom he made it difficult for any of the reps to befriend. Any insinuation of a social relationship with Larry was apparently threatening to Ken, and so most of us remained in our appropriate professional place with Larry during all the years Hunter's was a force to be reckoned with in the book business.

Eventually the Beverly Hills store lost its honey of a lease and was forced to move to a smaller location on Beverly Drive. It was the kiss of death, and by 1987 the entire chain had closed. Larry and Ken left Los Angeles for a new life in Palm Desert, opened a small bookstore there, and I heard little of them again until after many years passed. One day in late 2000, I received a letter from Larry. He wrote to ask me for help with the memoir he was writing about his years at Hunter's Books, and to ask if I could refer him to an editor or literary agent to move him toward a publishing contract.

This communication, coming out of the deep blue, staggered me. I picked up the phone and called Miriam Bass to tell her about it.

"You won't believe this," she said, "but I heard from him, too!"

It seemed that Larry Todd was actually reaching out to a few of us whom he'd left behind so abruptly more than a decade before. After mulling this over for a few days, I decided to answer Larry's letter. We began a correspondence that was frank, warm, and revelatory. No longer a fragile little pickle, I was free to be myself with the man I once so deeply feared. Larry responded to my candor with his own honest reflections. It seemed that his self-imposed "exile" in Palm Desert had given him the time to become an introspective man.

He knew he'd been a challenge to work with at Hunter's, and that some people had been hurt by his behavior. So, too, did Larry still feel the sting of certain affronts. We began sharing long phone conversations. Gradually I began to accept Larry as a friend rather than an adversary and was rewarded with a warmth and compassion I had never known him capable of.

In 2001, Ken became quite ill. He had an inoperable brain tumor, and Larry nursed him for several months before Ken finally died. They had been together for over thirty-five years, and Larry was left adrift. My heart went out to him, and Miriam and I decided to drive to the desert to see Larry for the first time since 1988. We had a wonderful visit. He looked better than he ever had, was uproariously funny and affectionate in a way that completely endeared him to me. Ken's death and the passing of time had changed him utterly, and since then Larry and I have shared a loving friendship.

Twenty-five years ago, Larry inspired only dread in my guts each time I had to go to Hunter's to sell him books. The idea that he and I might someday become friends would have made me go diving for cover, similar to the air raid drills we had when I was a kid in the 1950s. Some unknown bit of nuclear Jell-O could have made its way to kill or maim me, for God's sake! One could never be too safe, either from Larry Todd or *the Russians*. Nor can one can ever be too grateful for a Valentine's Day card from a beloved friend, like the one I got from Larry in 2004.

✸

As GLAM, IMPERIOUS, and opulent as Hunter's Books was, Anne Chiquoine Books in Ventura, California was the size of a closet and dusty with stacks of books everywhere that threatened to topple over if anyone sneezed.

I don't know how such a woman as Anne Chiquoine ended up in the sleepy beach town of Ventura, halfway between Los Angeles and Santa Barbara. She was from the east coast, graduated from the University of Pennsylvania, and was a Max Factor model in Manhattan before marrying her first wealthy husband. Anne was erudite and irreverent. She didn't give a damn what people thought of her and lived life on her own terms. When I met her, she was in her early sixties and widowed for the third time by yet another prosperous spouse. Anne was petite and beautiful; she had short auburn hair and wore some of the most exquisite jewelry I'd ever seen in my life. The elegant diamond rings that adorned her hands were indicative of the kind of men she'd attracted in her lifetime.

Her tiny bookshop was on the ground floor of the local Elks Lodge on Main Street. It was the size of an indoor newsstand, the kind where you'd go to buy a magazine, a pack of Camels, and a

Mars bar. At the most, it was fifteen feet long and eight feet wide. Anne specialized in university press books. Much of her business came from the professors at Ventura College, the handful of town intellectuals who savored pithy philosophical and theoretical books.

The first time I called Anne for an appointment, a man's voice answered the phone.

"Anne Chiquoine Books," he said. "How may I help you?"

"Hello!" I said brightly. "May I speak to Anne, please?"

"This is Anne," the voice said. "May I help you?"

I took a moment to recover. Anne Chiquoine had a voice like a Rolls Royce engine in need of an oil change. It had a deep, low-throttle octave that made her sound like a man, albeit a highly cultured one.

We proceeded to find a date and time that worked for both of us and got off the phone. For a while I walked around my apartment trying to imitate her voice, making myself laugh like a damned fool.

When I walked into the wee bookshop, more a crawl space than a retail establishment, Anne greeted me with a degree of reserve and formality. She was wearing a gray cashmere sweater, elegant tweed trousers, and a perfect strand of pearls with matching earrings. The persimmon-colored lipstick on her generous mouth had been applied with a careless hand. The goo had spread slightly beyond the outline of her lips, yet Anne's self-confidence made this seem irrelevant. She was smoking one of those long Virginia Slims cigarettes, and the bright imprint of her lipstick stood out like a red beacon on the filter end.

Anne actually looked me up and down when I approached her,

weighing me on her elegance scale. She was so disarming that I wanted nothing more than to make a good impression on her.

Moving close to examine the antique cameo earrings I was wearing, her first words to me were, "These are English, nineteenth century or so. Not bad, not bad." I seemed to have passed muster with her, for a moment later I was seated on a stool facing her on a folding chair in the back of the store. Anne took a pencil from behind her ear, and we began to work.

As she talked, I was eyeballing the books on the shelves, getting an idea of which titles I ought to present to her and which to skip. Clearly, the woman was a literary snob. Anne's discerning taste in books made me want to stay focused on everything she had to say. She bought quality fiction from me, and so many books of poetry that I almost wept.

With no customers in the store at one point, we ran next door to a little café, bought cups of coffee and a brownie to share, and then quickly returned.

Anne was so entertaining as we worked that I barely noticed the customer who had come in and was quietly browsing the Classics section. As she was regaling me with stories about her previous jobs in retail bookselling, cackling and dropping cigarette ash on the floor, she suddenly stopped and turned to the customer. He now had a book under his arm that it seemed he was going to purchase.

"Young man," said Anne evenly. "Young man, I'd like a word with you."

The customer, dressed casually in jeans and a sweater, did a double take, thinking Anne might have been speaking to someone else in the store. He finally faced her and waited for her to speak.

"I see you have a copy of *Madame Bovary* under your arm."

"Yes, ma'am, I do. I'm going to purchase it," said the man quizzically.

Anne leapt out of her chair and said, "No, you are *not!*" In a flash, she grabbed the book out from under his arm and held it behind her back. "There's a new translation of this coming out next month, and this one pales in comparison! I won't let you buy it."

The customer stared at Anne, open-mouthed. "Why, *yes,* ma'am," he finally said. "Please order a copy for me."

"I shall, young man, and will send you a postcard when it arrives," Anne spoke to the customer's back as he walked out of the store.

This was the most charmingly outrageous action I'd ever seen taken by a bookstore owner or buyer. It showed the depth of Anne's commitment to her customers and the sanctity of reading itself, and I was in awe. We became friends rather quickly. Once Anne realized that I shared her love of irreverence and deeper love of books, she took me under her wing as a cultural and aesthetic gosling. She also began calling me "Poopsie."

As we were saying our good-byes one day in front of the store, standing in the shadow of the Elks Lodge (moose head nailed to the wall above us), I turned my back on Anne while putting my briefcase in the trunk of my car.

"Maybe it's time for you to start wearing a girdle, Poops," Anne said, assessing the situation before her eyes. "Something with a medium-weight hold to it. You don't need anything tighter than that."

I whirled around to face her. "*Anne!*" I shrieked. "How can you say that?" It was so shocking to me that I froze in place. "I'm too young for a girdle!"

"Poopsie, take it from me. Sometimes age has nothing to do with it."

Walking backward to the door of my car to avoid further scrutiny of my behind, I told Anne I would consider it, but made no promises. After blowing her a kiss, I drove to the 101 freeway entrance and remained deep in derriere thoughts all the way back to Los Angeles.

Anne and I frequently ended up going out for margaritas at the Mexican dive across the street. Anne, with several thousand dollars' worth of jewelry on her neck and perfectly manicured hands, loved nothing more than to sip the tequila concoctions out of plastic cups and munch on greasy homemade tortilla chips and salsa. If we decided to go anywhere further away to imbibe, she liked to drive.

Over the years, I never knew Anne to own anything but the most modest of cars; a midsized Chevy or a Honda Civic, for instance. When she eventually revealed that she was a Quaker, the contradiction between her evident wealth and tightfisted lifestyle made more sense to me. Anne's religious beliefs included both a good measure of thrift and the consciousness of liberal political causes.

She was always challenging me to stretch myself and to think more deeply. The books Anne suggested I read were always valuable additions to my library, including Joyce Carol Oates (*Because It Is Bitter, and Because It Is My Heart*) and Dennis McFarland (*The Music Room*). I also began rereading some of the classics, thanks to her prodding, and was able to find a new depth in the writings of

Thomas Hardy, Mark Twain, and others. When it came to politics, it was Anne who first alerted me to the potential in a young Democratic presidential hopeful I'd never heard of before. His name was Bill Clinton, and I watched the 1992 election returns at a party with Anne while eating Scotch eggs, drinking martinis, and kissing Clinton's face on the TV screen.

Anne Chiquoine Books closed in 1989, but the *grande dame* herself continued on her merry adventurous way. After leaving Ventura to rent a house in Sonoma County, she continued making her annual driving treks to Maine to visit relatives. The postcards she mailed me were full of pride about making these 3,000-mile trips at the age of seventy-five. "Not bad for an old broad!!" she'd pen, or "Writing this from the Holiday Inn in the Ozarks—Russellville, Arkansas!! They *still* haven't raised my rate after seven years!" It goes without saying that Anne was able to talk any Highway Patrol officer out of a speeding ticket when she got pulled over on the highway.

When she was "at home" in Santa Rosa, Anne typed me letters on the reverse sides of stubs from her old business checkbook. I loved seeing the notations on the front, indicating that she'd sent a check to G. P. Putnam's for $30.04, or Doubleday & Company for $42.65. When she deigned to use actual stationery, it would be from a Quality Inn in Salt Lake City, or a Howard Johnson's in Pittsburgh.

It was her volunteer work in Santa Rosa as a summer-school teacher that Anne cared about above all else. Being able to teach young children to read, write, and spell was the most profound way for her to spread her love of books, and she took to it naturally and with great joy. If she saw that the kids were becoming distracted, this pixie of a woman, on the far side of seventy, marched them out to the playground for a game of soccer. Anne formed the team herself and taught the students how to play. "It is here," she wrote me, "that we 'loosen' up and 'kick a beauty' . . . or so they say, upon hearing me yell, 'LET'S GET WITH IT!!' "

The level of education in California frustrated Anne. "No sooner have I received the attention of the wee ones when reading a story and 'guessing at new words' than the headmistress pulls them away for a cooking demonstration. The eager anticipation of the kids is ignored, and the learning process is devoted to boiling eggs??? This education process is appalling!"

It's little wonder that Anne received two marriage proposals from the boys in her class: one was seven years old; the other, nine.

I stayed in touch with Anne for several more years but only saw her one time when we met for lunch during one of her infrequent visits to Ventura. Our letters and cards continued back and forth, no matter where she was. Hers were always filled with encouragement and the hope that I would meet a good man with whom I'd find mutual love, intellectual fire, and, as she described it, "great sex!" She ended almost every message with a request to tell her about the latest changes in the book business; her interest in it never lost its fervor, and she bemoaned the fact that it had become a mutation of its former self. "How it breaks my heart," she told me, "to watch the demise of the book business and all of the corporate takeovers of publishers! And don't even get me started about the crap they call bookstores these days—I refer to the chains, of course."

Anne always shot from the hip. I can only imagine the profanities she would have hurled at the Internet booksellers that hadn't yet left their mark on the industry.

I finally lost track of Anne, hearing only rumors that she'd suffered a stroke and was in a convalescent home in Santa Barbara. After a few years had passed, I began searching for her. What I found filled me with sorrow. Anne had died on December 16, 2002 at the age of eighty-four. Further research on the Internet led me to the Gallaudet University Web site. I knew that Anne's mother had been hearing-impaired all her life, and she and Anne both visited this university for the deaf on many occasions. It came as no surprise to me to read the following announcement on the Gallaudet Web site:

> *Anne Chiquoine, a long time resident of California and a vibrant and inveterate traveler, passed away at the end of 2002. In her will, she bequeathed her $1.4 million estate to Gallaudet University in order to establish the Anne M. Chiquoine and Helen P. Chiquoine Memorial Scholarship Fund.*

Although my friend had died a millionaire, her wealth never stopped her from giving of herself in more ways than anyone could imagine. Anne's indignation about the changing state of the book business has passed itself on to me, a furious belief in doing the right thing for readers and writers alike. Her legacy speaks proudly of respect for the written word, the very thing that sustains me.

BOTH HUNTER'S AND Anne Chiquoine Books are nicely settled in the mental slot where I maintain bookstore obituaries. It makes my skin crawl to realize how extensive this sacred inventory is now. In a notebook that I found a couple of years ago is a list of the book accounts I was calling on in 1985. They're arranged geographically, including all of my territory in Southern California and Arizona, with phone numbers, addresses, and the names of buyers and salesclerks carefully printed in my own hand. I also had notes about the little things that make the difference between a friendly or an adversarial relationship between a book rep and her customers: "Bring extra catalogs for G. to distribute to staff"; "O. likes metaphysical titles—bring applicable galleys"; "Stop at Winchell's for doughnuts—no cream in coffee!"

There was something so charming about this archival "find" that I brought the notebook with me to my armchair and read it from cover to cover. As I savored the memories of twenty years ago, however, the sweet nostalgia gradually turned to despair. Dozens of these bookstores were gone. With dread I counted, turning the pages of my precious history, until the number of closures came to an astonishing eighty-five. This accounted for about two thirds of the bookstores that once prospered and shared their prosperity with me, only to be too fragile in the end to stave off the challenge of the Internet, large book chains, and a changing cultural marketplace.

This is what had caused the gradual but critical drop in my commission earnings during the 1990s. As a single, independent woman, this was a time of terrible anxiety in my life. The fear of not having enough money woke up with me each morning and dragged me to bed at night. Knowing that the closing bookstores weren't going to be replaced with new ones had me dipping into my well of despair.

But in 2002, additional income finally showed up, thanks to my friend Chuck Morrell, a retired Holtzbrink/St. Martin's sales rep in Los Angeles. He called one day to ask if I'd like to partner with him in his author–escort business, and I accepted immediately. The money was good, and I knew the authors would like me. This work wasn't foreign to me. In the past, I'd helped on author tours for various publishers, although I'd never been paid for it before. This would be different. Poverty had made me a professional.

The role of an author escort involves being the driver, mother hen, and, at times, psychotherapist for writers who are sent out on tour by their publishers. We meet their planes and get them safely to interviews, media appearances, and bookstore events. We introduce them to journalists, radio and television hosts, and book buyers. We remind them to eat, to get enough sleep, and to keep in mind that the grueling schedule really will bump up sales of their book. When they're grumpy, we tell them dirty jokes or make them laugh at themselves.

Chuck told me there weren't any jobs lined up at the time, and I'd probably have to wait a few weeks for my first assignment. Patience and hope were all I had going for me. I didn't have to wait long, though, because a few days later I was hired for a last-minute job. Much to my horror, my first assignment was with Jonathan Franzen, the National Book Award-winning author.

It wasn't that I hadn't read his acclaimed novel, *The Corrections*. What made my stomach lurch was the thought that Franzen was a member of the intellectual literati posse, who had wrangled with Oprah Winfrey about going on her show. I'd followed that gossipy story in the press as it unfolded, cringing when he was vilified, because I secretly agreed with his decision to distance himself from the commercial talk-show setting. My preconceived notion of him was that he was a snob with great integrity. It was the snob part that worried me.

As I pulled my old Mercedes—a relic of better days—up to the Argyle Hotel on Sunset, my mind was settling in to the miracle of modern medicine known as Xanax. I'd swallowed one at breakfast, washed down with coffee and rye toast at my dining-room table, and was thus free of panic and prepared to meet the great *auteur* himself at ten that morning.

He was so good-looking that I almost tripped over myself on my way to greet him in the lobby. Franzen—tall, slender, clothes draped perfectly over his body—exuded the confidence of hand-someness in his face, a perfect blend of adolescent charm and grown-up allure. The trademark black-framed glasses highlighted his intense eyes, and his hair fell across his forehead in a whimsi-cal flow of brown locks. The whole package was disarming to me.

We introduced ourselves to one another benignly, cautiously and then drove off to Santa Monica. Franzen was scheduled for an interview on the *Bookworm* radio show with Michael Sil-verblatt, the Oscar Levant of the book business. On the way, I offered him the book-tour munchies I'd selected that morning at my local convenience store. Bottled water, a bag of cashews, a roll of Lifesavers, and a chocolate bar were gathered in a small Saks Fifth Avenue shopping bag that I'd remembered to take with me that morning. Franzen accepted it with the wonder of a child receiving an unexpected gift, taking everything out and examin-ing the different treats with concentration.

We had to wait a while at the radio station, so we sat outside on a wall and swung our feet. I could tell Franzen felt distrustful of me. His reserve and apparently humorless demeanor was what I'd expected, and I quashed the impulse to chatter away nervously. I actually liked the silence between us. If it was arrogance that distanced him from me, so be it.

"Say, those are beautiful shoes," Franzen uttered suddenly, looking down at my feet. "They're sexy!"

I was wearing a pair of red, pointy-toed spike heels that I saved for special occasions. They gave me a certain confidence that helped move me through challenging situations. I knew how attractive they were, but Franzens's compliment gave me an opportunity to knock him off his pedestal.

"Oh, thanks," I said off-handedly. "These are my 'come-fuck-me' shoes."

Franzen put his head to one side and smiled at my cheeky remark. He didn't know what to make of me, which was my point. Maybe I was starting to chip away at his reserve, which I usually end up taking on as a personal challenge. I had ten more hours to go with this guy, and social discomfort and arrogance, no matter how harmless the source, have no place in my life.

The *Bookworm* interview went smoothly, verging on testiness only when Silverblatt began to subtly put words in Franzen's mouth about his writing. There was an edgy moment when the writer became defensive, but the two recovered and continued their discussion unabated. Afterward, they lingered a bit too long, engaged in some lofty chat, and I finally had to take Franzen's arm and tell him it was time to go, lest we be late for our next stop.

Jonathan was expected at Dutton's Bookshop in Brentwood for an informal drop-in. It was past lunchtime, and we were hungry.

Knowing that we didn't have enough time for a meal in a proper restaurant, I timidly asked him if he was opposed to stopping at a fast-food place.

"Oh, I couldn't," Franzen said. "I never eat at those places."

I continued driving down Pico Boulevard in silence.

"Well," Franzen said, "I've eaten fast food, but only on very rare occasions." His stomach began to grumble, so I turned the volume up on the radio. We drove east for a few more blocks.

"*There's a McDonald's!*" Franzen practically yelled, pointing to the yellow arches on the next corner. "Maybe we could stop there."

"Well," I said drolly, "if you insist." I pulled into the parking lot and we got out of the car.

Franzen held the door of the restaurant open for me, and we stepped inside. It smelled horrible and delicious at the same time, as only a McDonald's can when one is desperately hungry.

"I'll get us a place in line," said the gentlemanly Franzen, while I took the opportunity to stop a few yards away simply to stare at him and take in the bizarre moment. After a moment or two, he did a double-take when he caught my eye.

"*What?*" Franzen sputtered, looking serious and intellectual.

"Oh, nothing. I'm just watching the big-shot, National-Book-Award-winning author standing in line to order Quarter-Pounders."

The shift in our behavior with one another was immediate, Franzen cracking up and blushing, me smiling at him warmly for the first time. The remainder of our time together would be relaxed and enjoyable.

When I got back in the car, it occurred to me that I hadn't

taken my receipt from the McDonald's cashier. Franzen's publisher was, of course, reimbursing all my expenses for that day. I told him I'd be right back and was then embarrassed. It was only a few bucks, after all, and I could certainly cover the meal myself.

"Never mind," I said. "It's not important." I drove out of the parking lot.

"But it is! You have to get reimbursed for this!" Franzen emphasized. "I'll write you a receipt."

"Okay. You can use this," I said, amused, handing him the notepad and pencil I always have handy in my car. I watched him studiously writing as we drove to Dutton's Bookshop. When he handed the piece of paper to me, I absentmindedly tossed it into my purse. In the car, all thoughts of nutrition were on hold as we both munched happily away on our McDonald's "food," wiping our greasy fingers on napkins before walking into the store.

After chatting with Doug Dutton, the store's owner, and charming the salesclerks and a few surprised customers, Franzen signed stock and left a little drawing in the "Author Book" that all writers who pass through Dutton's have been doodling in for years. Hands were shaken all around, and we returned to my car for the long drive to Franzen's next stop—the beautiful Central Library in downtown Los Angeles. He was to give a talk in the Taper Auditorium about his new book of essays, *How to Be Alone*, followed by a Q&A session with the audience.

Franzen and I jawed for the next hour like strangers on a train who know they'll probably never see each other again. We talked about our families and childhoods, the complexities of romantic relationships, our personal limitations, and the pride of accomplishment. It was a spontaneous and generous outpouring of whatever came to mind. I took great pleasure in realizing that Franzen was such a good egg, and that we could relate to one another as peers. I felt refreshed.

Franzen's talk and his chat with the audience were delightful, and he received resounding applause at the end. We were then escorted to the Rare Book room upstairs in the library, where a private dinner was given in his honor. The guests included many of the major donors to the library foundation, so Franzen was obliged to table-hop and chat them all up. While he did this, I sat with a couple of his friends who'd shown up. After a few glasses of wine in such rarefied air, we all enjoyed ourselves, and eventually Franzen told me that his friends would drive him back to the hotel and I was free to leave.

"Good-bye, Jonathan!" I said, "I've had such a wonderful time." We hugged affectionately as he thanked me for making his day "so pleasant," and I drove home with the utter satisfaction of time well spent.

Later that night, I found the meal receipt Franzen had written for me. I unfolded the small piece of paper to read the following:

Wendy bought us $7.00 of lunch at MacDonald's on
10/2/2—Franzen

He had misspelled "McDonald's." I laughed out loud.

The relationship between an author and his or her escort is fueled by haste and powerlessness—they have no choice but to be together for a specific amount of time to get a job done, no matter how cranky or tired one may be. Books have to be hawked and promoted, or else they stand little chance of finding their share of readers. Gone are the days when companies could afford to publish books that they loved but had dubious sales potential and no promotion budget to speak of. The financial risks are much higher now, so when authors are paid substantial advances for their books they're expected to hit the road to increase sales. Depending on the author, the experience can be either exhilarating or anguished, or both.

I like to think that I brighten their days when I accompany them around Los Angeles. Unlike me, most author escorts aren't— and never have been—in the book business. Being an old hand at it (and having had a writer for a father), I know how to relate to authors in an empathetic way that makes them know they are understood and appreciated. They are all a part of the crazy, obsessed, and passionate soul I've become in this industry.

Larry Todd and Anne Chiqoine were among the forerunners of hand-selling, the action taken by dedicated booksellers who fall in love with specific books and put them in the hands of their customers. It's a gesture of literary intimacy that worked a half-century ago and continues to make best sellers out of orphaned books that get published without the proper amount of care. The hand-selling that continues in independent bookstores can make them flourish without the budget for an author tour or print advertising; they are the books that bring out the best in all concerned and deserve to be recognized.

As a matter of course, we book reps carry the responsibility of spreading the word for one another about favorite titles. The notion of competition has absolutely no place in the honored context of sharing enthusiasm for writers. Every selling season, I swap my catalogs with those of friends who rep for other publishers. We order review copies for one another and go to bat for the books we find extraordinary.

It's not uncommon for me to be in the middle of a sales call and suddenly remember a novel I've just finished that I'm crazy about. Describing it to the buyer, and suggesting that they order it (or move copies already on hand to a more visible display table in their store), never feels like a betrayal to my own publishers. The book business doesn't exist in a vacuum. It's important to circulate enthusiasm for titles we love, for in doing so we keep the flow of books ongoing and strong. Everyone benefits from this—the bookstore, the publisher, and especially the reader. For me this is the entire point, the true blessing, of being in the business of books.

Eight

TRUE CRIME

> ...A gross and violent injury was inside my head, pushing to get
> out and scream aloud.
> —RUTH RENDELL (WRITING AS BARBARA VINE),
> THE BRIMSTONE WEDDING, 1995

MY PARENTS' CIRCLE of friends included comedians,
writers, magicians, Vegas pit bosses, and various nutcases and
drunks who all contributed to what I came to believe was a normal social milieu. If there was a distortion inherent in this group,
no one ever pointed it out to me. As far as I was concerned, the
people my folks brought home were the sort that all children grew
up knowing. They rotated comfortably in the social wheel of our
lives, and I liked all of them.

Thrown into this mix were three high-ranking sheriff's officers
who were among my father's closest friends. Bill Reed, Jim Warner,
and Dave Bullis were all extremely bright, well-educated men (Bill
held a master's degree from USC in public administration and

made captain in the sheriff's department) who were warm and good-natured as well. They were all about twenty years younger than Dad, and they seemed to take on the surrogate roles of the sons my father never had. The average height and weight of Jim and Bill was six-foot-three, two hundred thirty pounds—they were big lugs who could easily pick me up around the waist with one arm and swing me about until I screamed with laughter. Dave Bullis was another story. At six-foot-seven (or, as he referred to his height, "five-nineteen"), he towered over everyone he met. I never felt safer than when in their loving, protective company.

The constant presence of these cops in my life brought an early awareness of the reality and nature of crime. When they came over for social visits, I waited breathlessly for my first glimpse of a .357 revolver when an open sport coat caught the breeze just so. If I were persistent enough, one of the guys, after carefully removing the bullets from the chamber, would sometimes let me hold the gun. The weight of it in the palm of my hand always startled me, and I learned to hold out both hands before accepting such a weapon in my innocent grasp.

I'm sure my friendship with these three detectives was the inspiration for my love of mysteries. I began reading them when I was a girl, tearing through the Nancy Drew and Hardy Boys series in no time before moving on to the work of Edith Nesbit and Sherlock Holmes. The challenge of solving a puzzle or getting to the bottom of the who, what, where, when, and, most of all, why of a crime—or any perplexing situation, for that matter—made me curl my toes in anxious delight. When I got a little older, I met Miss Marple and Hercule Poirot in Agatha Christie's marvelous books and their bolder, more mature plot lines.

All through my teenage years, I eavesdropped on the late-night conversations my father and his detective friends had when they got off duty and stopped by our house for drinks. I wasn't allowed in the den when they were there, because they discussed their individual cases with Dad, and everything they told him was confidential. Instead, I'd open my bedroom windows, directly above the den, and stick my head out into the night air of Los Angeles to catch parts of sentences that were carried up to me in the breeze.

"so we're trying to get a search warrant for . . . pool of blood, so samples . . . I know this guy did it! . . . footprints on the . . . was still alive, but . . . and the frustrating part is that the knife . . . we're close to finding a . . ."

Some nights, I leaned so far out of the bedroom window that I literally had to catch myself from falling; my curiosity simply couldn't contain itself. I had to take solace in the mystery novels and psychological thrillers that I continued to read, although my tastes became increasingly sophisticated and grim. I began to devour writers such as Raymond Chandler, Edgar Allan Poe, and Wilkie Collins. What I didn't find in my parents' library at home was usually available at the library, so I was never without a choice of mysteries.

The Tate-LaBianca murders occurred in August 1969, each less than three miles from our house on Alta Vista Boulevard. Anyone of a certain age at that time in Los Angeles remembers the sensation of fear and unease as readily as one can conjure the feelings generated on the day JFK was assassinated—vastly different situations, but the mental imprints are equally permanent. The Manson Family murders forever altered my comfort zone. During the three months in which the LAPD was unable to break the case, my sense of personal safety took a beating it had never known before.

My father did his best to ease our minds by staying in phone contact with his cop friends. They had nothing to report, though, except for all the blind alleys the police and sheriff's force had scampered down thus far. We didn't see our detective friends at all during that time. They were consumed with helping to solve the Tate-LaBianca murders.

One day in November, Bill Reed phoned my father while I happened to be in the room. Dad spoke with him for a few minutes, and when he hung up he had a smile on his face.

"Sweetie," he said, "Bill told me that the LAPD is very close to making arrests in the case. They'll be holding a press conference tomorrow or the next day!"

My family was in the bizarre position of having a civilian exclusive on the case, and we were all sworn to secrecy. The very next evening, it was announced that the Manson Family had been rounded up, arrested, and put behind bars. When Vincent Bugliosi's book, *Helter Skelter*, was published five years later, I stayed up all night reading it. To my mind, it surpasses even *In Cold Blood* by Truman Capote, and I consider it the finest true crime book ever written.

WHEN I MOVED into my apartment on Sycamore Avenue in 1976, I never dreamed that my time there would span nearly twenty-five years. As I unpacked my belongings on that hot August afternoon, Jimmy Carter was on the TV in my living room accepting the presidential nomination at the Democratic Convention. When I moved out, Bill Clinton was halfway through his second term. Despite the folly of other presidential leadership in between those years, at least my life in that apartment was framed by two of my heroes.

It was a beautiful space in an even more beautiful building. Constructed in 1928, it was a loving monument to the era of Spanish-style architecture in Los Angeles. My apartment had high, beamed ceilings, French windows, curved archways, and built-in bookcases. The rooms were spacious and welcoming, with, in the living room, a faux fireplace that a gas heater had once occupied. In my foyer was a rounded, half-oval nook in the wall that had probably been designed as a little nest for the household telephone. I painted it various colors over the years, and turned it into an altar that took on different aspects as the people I loved most began to die. My mother, Charlotte, was the first to inspire this when she made her transition in 1978.

The Sycamore apartment became my first sacred home. As time passed, my sense of self—with all its desires, hopes, goodness, fears, and avenues for love—filled every available space within those walls. As my identity grew, so did the unique symbols that represented the span of my curiosity and interests. The framed posters on the walls were gradually replaced by original art. I acquired furniture, rugs, and pretty lamps. My first camera equipment was purchased, the prelude to becoming a professional photographer many years later. I painted the walls a pale melon color in the living room and warm caramel in the bedroom. The kitchenware expanded to accommodate my growing abilities as a cook and entertainer. Because the Sycamore apartment was larger than anywhere else I'd lived, I started having dinner parties on a regular basis.

The only thing I lacked was a spare room for my office. Instead, my rapidly growing book-sales business shared the space in my bedroom that, fortunately, was big enough to vaguely divide into two areas—one for sleeping, the other for working. The queen-sized bed and the dresser and nightstands gave way to a desk, bookcases, file cabinets, and shelving units. Penny Rose, still my devoted best friend, helped me to rearrange that room at least a dozen times while I lived on Sycamore. There was a compulsive drive to create more space. With every UPS shipment of catalogs, supplies, and review copies, new hiding places—under the bed, behind closet doors, even in dresser drawers—concealed the fact that my life was bursting at the seams.

I lived in the front apartment on the ground floor, facing a majestic liquidambar tree across the street. As the years passed, I came to associate the ebb and flow of my interior life with the changing seasons reflected in what I came to call "my" tree. In winter it was barren and took on the color of ash. Spring crept up slowly on it, new leaves barely noticeable until all at once I would see a pale green haze shimmering around it like a halo. A thick, rich growth of deep green leaves adorned the tree through the summer months, as I waited anxiously for the first sign of autumn on its branches.

The depressing symptoms of Seasonal Affective Disorder touched me in an oddly reversed order. Unlike the typical sufferer whose mood lifts when warm weather and long days arrive, in summer I became mired in the oppression of hopelessness instead. But at the first sign of a red or orange leaf on my tree across the street, my spirits would cautiously rise and then, when the colors of autumn consumed the liquidambar, my sense of well-being came to a blessed fruition. In the weeks following Labor Day, when the morning air brought a growing chill and night gradually fell earlier, I spent more time at the living-room windows observing the signs of wonder in my tree.

It was on one such evening in 1981 that a few friends stopped by for drinks. It was the usual raucous group that I was close to in those days, a half-dozen musicians who'd fled their native state of Kansas a few years earlier to pursue fame in Los Angeles. I met them through Dave Srb, my then-boyfriend who had moved in with me for a year before we agreed it would be best to live separately. Dave was the bass player in my friends' band, Snapshots; he wasn't able to join us that night.

We sat around talking, laughing, and drinking vodka on the rocks. At one point, Steve Werner, the singer in the band, walked up the street to his place and returned with an electric laptop keyboard. For the next hour or so, Steve played and sang old R&B songs by the Drifters, the Temptations, Curtis Mayfield—he knew all my favorites and serenaded us that night with his gorgeous voice. When it got close to midnight, I started tidying up before my friends eventually all left. I was so tired. That day, I'd called on a couple of bookstores before playing hostess to my good friends. As I made my way to the bedroom, a freak thunderstorm broke open the skies and let loose with steady showers. At the end of a wonderful evening, I was lulled to sleep by the rain.

There's no polite way to describe a violent crime. Survivors don't have the luxury of euphemisms or the various disguises that language can provide, so for too many of them the event is concealed, even denied. It might go on to exist in a soft-focus realm, too indistinct to ever be examined. The crime becomes a secret that seems to be easily kept, but the place that stores it in one's consciousness eventually festers with guilt, shame, and humiliation. The only way to survive this fate is by squeezing through the crack in the cut-glass window of one's soul.

I woke up from a deep sleep that night when I felt someone in my bed turning me over from my side to my back. There were hands on me, on my thighs, between my legs, on my breasts. My first reaction to this was the groggy thought that Dave must have let himself in to the apartment, that it was my lover's surprise visit in the middle of the night. When I felt the blade of a knife pressing against my neck, though, I realized that I was being raped.

"I'll kill you if you scream!" the man said in a heavy New York accent, quietly, a frantic murmur in the dark.

I was as awake and alert as I had ever been. My consciousness transcended even prayer, and suddenly my survival instincts took over. I did not think; I had no thoughts. Only my body showed any sign of intelligence, and it became a brilliant manifestation of my soul. To survive, it opened itself up to the rapist.

He behaved like the creature that he was, on borrowed time, fearing the knock on the door, the neighbor's pounding on the wall, the helicopter overhead. He told me he was going to fuck me, and he did, and then he repositioned my body and he did it once more, and he aimed himself into the mouth that was my body, holding my face with one hand and the knife with the other as it grazed my neck and my throat.

"You like it, don't you," he said, he didn't ask, he told me that I was liking it and it was an order, a command, and someone inside of me pretended to moan and say yes, I liked it, I loved it, it was the best I'd ever had. I wanted only to live.

And my body focused on his rhythm and stayed with it to please him and to protect my soul, my spirit, and my mind, all of which had left my body and were hovering at some convenient altitude that allowed me to overlook the experience my body was having on my bed on Sycamore Avenue.

And then he was finished, he was finished with me. The bed linens were askew, as a beach is after it takes the fury of a hurricane, blankets, sheets, and pillows tossed about on the floor. Only my body was in perfect alignment, a straight line in the very center of the bed as it froze in place. The rapist got up and began putting on his clothes. It was completely dark in the room, and my glasses were on the nightstand where I'd put them before falling asleep. In the myopic gloom I saw nothing but heard the rustle of clothes and a zipper being pulled up.

"Hey," the rapist murmured, "what's your phone number? Maybe we can see each other again."

The mechanical voice in my body recited my phone number to him, which he then repeated out loud as though memorizing it.

"That's good!" the rapist told me. "I'll give you a call. I want to see you again, okay?"

"Okay!" my voice said. Okay, get out, get out of here, get the hell out of here right now or I'll scream for help, you motherfucker, you. . . . Thought was now returning to me. The man walked out of the room, and I heard him quickly go down the hall and into the kitchen. After that, all I heard was the rain falling outside. I waited to hear the sound of my front door opening and closing, but it never came. My heart throbbed in my chest. I waited and waited some more. For fifteen minutes I lay in the wreckage of my bed listening for the smallest sound, but the aural atmosphere remained the same.

I rose from the bed as quietly as possible, mechanically put my glasses on, slipped on a bathrobe, and tiptoed down the hall to the front of the apartment. In the dim light from the streetlamps, I saw that the living room was empty. In the dining room, the windows were open as I had left them earlier, but one of the screens had been removed and was leaning against the wall. This was how the rapist got in and afterward fled into the night. The terrified minutes I'd spent waiting to hear him leave through the front door were simply a cruel punctuation at the end of the assault. He was long gone.

I stood in the kitchen and began to hyperventilate. Breathing through my mouth at what felt like the speed of light, I manically gasped for air. My breath was loud and rough, as though I'd been running for miles, and my body shook like a drunk going through the D.T.'s. It took me three times to dial my boyfriend's number. I kept dropping the phone, but finally I got through to Dave. Then I began to scream.

Dave got to my apartment in ten minutes and held me while I struggled to tell him I'd been raped. He cried with me and didn't let me go. We realized that my purse was gone, nicked by the rapist when he ran off. I had to call the police. Dave dialed 911 and put the phone in my hand. It was my job to report what happened, and I did. The LAPD showed up in less than five minutes, a female officer and her male partner. They were wonderful—gentle, sensitive, and efficient—and phoned a CSI technician, who arrived to dust for fingerprints and take photographs of both the inside and outside of my dining room. The bed linens were respectfully removed and placed in an evidence bag.

The female officer helped me get dressed, kindly stroking my hair all the while.

She and her partner finally drove me in their squad car to the emergency room at Cedars-Sinai Hospital, while Dave followed behind us. The sun was coming up at the same time the ground was swallowing me.

I went through the motions of the exam by the ER doctor in a state of disassociation: a shot of penicillin, a vaginal swab, ointment for the bruises on my neck. All I remember of the doctor is that he called me "sweetheart" and seemed distraught himself. Before releasing me, he gave me instructions to phone the rape crisis department at the hospital the next day so that I could speak to a counselor. Dave drove me home. He put clean sheets on the bed and we lay there together for a few hours of fitful sleep. Perhaps because Dave was with me, I felt no revulsion toward, or fear of, being in my bedroom again.

The next day I dutifully arranged, and showed up for, my appointment with the rape counselor. She was a volunteer layperson who'd been trained in the most basic of concepts of trauma counseling, and despite my state of confusion I could tell that she was behaving in a routine way, as though every woman who walked through her door fit the same psychological profile. I was a unique individual, though, with unique emotional requirements. The counselor kept insisting that I must be angry, I must be *very angry,* and I had every right to rage on, scream into pillows, hit the wall, and *work it out of my system.*

But I wasn't angry; I was in shock. I had no feelings at all. Feelings are born of thoughts, aren't they, and my mind was at a loss for reason. I could only comprehend what was right in front of me: the walls of an office, a stranger sitting in a chair saying something to me, tissues in a cardboard box on my lap. I didn't belong there. Even as I scheduled another appointment for the following week, I knew I would never return to this office.

The month before, I'd planned a vacation trip to Hawaii to visit a friend. It seemed even more appealing to me after I'd been raped, and I flew to Honolulu a week after the event. The two police officers who helped me that night insisted that it was extremely unlikely that the rapist would return to my apartment. They told me how rarely, if ever, that happened and simply reminded me to lock all my windows before I went to sleep each night. With this in mind, I didn't think twice about arranging for a woman named Robin to house-sit for me while I was gone. She was aware of the attack on me the week before and knew what precautions to take in my apartment.

Hawaii was beautiful, and I collapsed there into the arms of paradise. The warm trade winds settled my mind. It was good to be with my friend Ellen, who nurtured me and made me laugh. We didn't avoid the topic of my rape, but I found that talking about it seemed pointless. It was too soon for analysis of any kind.

We flew to Maui on the third day of my vacation. Ellen had booked us a room at a small hotel right on the beach; and after a full day of sunbathing, cocktails, and dinner, we returned there to watch a bit of television and go to sleep. Eventually I heard Ellen snoring quietly in the bed across from mine, although I wasn't able to sleep. At about three in the morning, I broke out in a rash. I was in agony. In the morning, it was apparent that I had to get myself to a doctor. The rash covered half my body.

We got on the first flight back to Honolulu, picked up the car at the airport, and drove to the emergency room of the nearest hospital. The doctor there gave me a shot of Benedryl and a prescription for an expensive topical cream and sent me packing with the news that I was allergic to the penicillin I'd been given a week earlier after I was raped. It was unbelievable. My body was still being assaulted.

Two days later, the phone rang in Ellen's apartment.

"It's for you," Ellen said, handing me the phone. "It's Robin, your house sitter."

The rapist had come back.

Although Robin was unharmed and safe, she was in a state of panic. That night, she had gone to bed in my apartment at about eleven o'clock. A few hours later, an insistent tapping on the bedroom windows, all of which were locked, awakened her. Robin sat up in bed, fully alert. She saw a shadow moving back and forth outside the curtains.

"It's me!" the man said quietly. "I want to give you back your purse."

Robin ran to the phone on my desk to call 911. "Go away!" she yelled. "I'm not her! I'm calling the police!"

"You have to let me in!" the man cried. "I have your purse. Don't you want it back?"

Robin screamed into the phone to the 911 dispatcher, saying a rapist was outside the window. The police would be there within moments. Hiding behind the bedroom door, she kept screaming at the man outside to go away and finally heard him run toward the alley behind my building. Just then the police pulled up, siren blaring, but they were too late. Once again the rapist escaped into the night. I was three thousand miles away but might as well have been right there in my bedroom. *He came back!* I was the goddamned exception to the rule of statistics, a freak, sweet prey for all of the evil in the world. On the beautiful island, my mind shattered. The vacation was over.

When I got back from Hawaii, the first thing I did was call my sister, Susie, and ask her to loan me the money to have bars put on all the windows in my apartment. Without hesitation, she agreed to this and arranged for the bars to be installed the following day.

Dave and I slept at a friend's house that night, and the next afternoon my apartment was fortified with wrought-iron bars. My relief was instantaneous, and from that point on I began to sleep well again. Yet even after going back to work a few days later (I was a house rep for E. P. Dutton at the time), I knew I was simply going through the motions of exhibiting signs of life. I had acquired the mindset of someone always on the alert for the next bad thing to happen. The very ground beneath me was suspect. My face in the mirror became that of an acquaintance, rather than my former self-image. Thus began a gradual process of shutting down.

Then, a week after returning from Hawaii, the rapist rang me up at three in the morning. I answered the phone in a muddled haze.

"Hi," he said brightly, "it's me!"

"W-w-what? Who is this?" I said sleepily. I was trying to place the voice. Why the hell was this person calling me in the middle of the night?

"*You* know, it's *me*. I've been thinking about you. We had a great time the other night, didn't we?" he said. "I'm playing with myself now. I love hearing your voice!"

I went numb. This wasn't possible—and yet it was; I had given the rapist my phone number, hadn't I? He would have slit my throat if I'd refused. I'd had no choice then, but now I did.

"*Go fuck yourself, you son of a bitch!*" I screamed into the phone and then slammed it down with a psychotic fury. A few moments later I picked the phone up to take it off the hook. The rapist hadn't hung up. I could hear him panting through the indifferent receiver and closed it again with a crash.

Oh my god. Oh my god! I had lost control of my life. I would never escape him. These thoughts roiled through my mind and forced me out of bed; they made me pace around my apartment like a deranged sleepwalker. I wailed, chain-smoked, and shivered so that my teeth were clattering. Finally I knocked myself out with a Tuinal I'd nicked from my father's stash of sleeping pills and fell asleep on the living-room couch.

When I woke up, I acted upon the only option I had left, which was to ask an old family friend for help. When I reached Captain Bill Reed at the Firestone sheriff's station downtown to tell him my story, all I could utter was, "I was raped a few weeks ago, and I'm so scared! I need you!" Then I broke down on the phone. I had never intended to tell Bill about the rape, but at that point it became essential.

"Stay put," Bill said gently. "I'll be at your place in an hour."

When he showed up, he took me in his massive embrace and I hung on to him for dear life. For such a tough cop, Bill exhibited just the kind of tenderness I required in that moment. When he opened his arms to me, I glanced to see if he was wearing the

holster with his gun in it. He was, and I responded whole-
heartedly to the protection of this good man and all that it implied.

Bill was carrying a plastic shopping bag. "What's that?" I asked,
when I'd composed myself.

"I stopped at Home Depot on my way here. Would you mind
if I changed your lock and installed a dead bolt?"

This brought tears to my eyes again. "Are you kidding?" I asked.
"Nothing would make me happier."

Bill went to work on the front door. As I sat on the floor next
to him in the foyer, he slowly laid out his plan for trying to cap-
ture the rapist. "First, I'm going to have one of my detectives contact you. His name is Mike Belger," he said, unscrewing the old
lock on my door.

"He'll phone you later today or first thing in the morning," Bill
continued, bending to stare into the hole where my old lock had
been. "Mike's a great guy—one of the best. I know you'll like him."

I sat looking up at Bill, my hands crossed over bent knees, hanging on his every word like an acolyte. His voice, deep and slow,
had made my heartbeat return to normal.

"Then," Bill said, "we'll put a tap on your phone. That'll take
a few days, but in the meantime Mike will give you a tape recorder
designed to record phone conversations." He examined the new
dead-bolt lock, turning it this way and that, before tentatively
placing it in place in the door. "I know you're not going to like
this, but when the guy calls you again you have to keep him on
the phone for as long as possible. It's the only way to get a trace.
No matter what he says to you, just keep talking."

Bill stopped what he was doing and looked at me earnestly.
"Can you do that, Wendy?"

"Yes," I replied in a tiny voice from the floor.

"Okay—good. Nothing bad is going to happen to you, I promise." He plugged the electric power drill in to a wall socket and began to install the new lock. "I had a few extra keys made for you for this thing," he said, continuing to work. "No one is going to be able to get through this door without a key, believe me."

We sat down at my dining-room table when Bill was finished. "Now, here's what we're going to try and do," he went on. "We'll be tracing the calls, and I want you to set up a meeting with this asshole. Tell him you want your wallet, that he should meet you in a coffee shop to return it."

"I can't do that! How the hell can I do that?" I protested, starting to cry again.

"Please calm down and let me finish," Bill said. He took a deep breath. "Mike Belger and one of my female officers will be sitting at the table next to you, wherever you are. They'll be in plain clothes. At the right moment, they'll cuff the guy and arrest him."

Bill looked at me meaningfully. "Can you do this, Wendy?"

I thought about this setup for a moment. As much as the idea terrified me, the alternative was to continue yielding to the whimsy of the rapist and leave him free to rape other women. This was not an option; I knew that, even in my shattered state of mind.

"Yes, Bill, I can do this," I told him with as much conviction as I could muster. "I trust your judgment on this."

Detective Mike Belger phoned me a few hours later, and I met him for a drink at Port's restaurant on Santa Monica Boulevard. This was my favorite haunt in those days, and the owner, Micaela Livingston, was a good friend of mine. Mike and I were the only people there at five in the afternoon. I ordered a vodka tonic and he a club soda. Within five minutes I knew that Mike was a good soul, and I poured my heart out to him. He was an attractive, smart, sensitive cop in his early forties. Over the next hour, he explained how, with my help, he and his partner would do everything in their power to put this rapist behind bars.

It was a more detailed version of what Bill Reed had already told me, but coming as it was from the man who would actually be participating in this "sting," it made me feel even more assured of the plan. Mike made a point of telling me that during a taped phone conversation, I was to mention the knife the rapist used, and to tell him how frightened I was. Mike had a big binder notebook with him, filled with photos of convicted sex offenders. Although he knew I had never seen the man's face, he had me look through it anyway to see if anyone seemed familiar. It was an exercise in futility. I thought that the rapist was probably white—his hair had felt straight and smooth, and the New York accent seemed a sure giveaway to me. Besides that, though, his face remained a blank in my mind.

After Mike paid the tab, I walked with him to his car and took the tape recorder that was in the trunk. He showed me how to use it on my phone, shook my hand warmly, and said he'd call as soon as the tap was connected to my phone line. When it was, I put the phone next to my bed when I went to sleep each night.

I didn't have to wait long. The first call came in a few nights later, waking me at about four A.M.

Hello?

Yes—I called several times, but you wasn't home. How are you?

Mmmmm . . . how are you?

Oh, pretty good. Hey, I didn't know you had a girlfriend.

Oh. I was in Hawaii, and my friend stayed here. I was just so afraid, because you had that knife—but now I'm back.

You know, I really thought that you really liked me, to tell you the truth.

I feel afraid.

I don't want you to. You know, that's the first time I ever did that.

You never raped anyone before?

No.

Do you have my wallet, and my money?

Yes.

Let's talk again tomorrow when I'm more awake.

Now I'm upset.

You scare me. I didn't understand what was going on, and I still feel afraid.

For what? Why? Nuttin's gonna happen to you!

I want to believe that.

You shouldn't have called the cops, you know.

I didn't know what else to do. I've never woken up with a knife at my throat before.

But tell me something, real honest . . . did you really enjoy being with me?

I really can't tell you for sure. I'm just so confused right now.

I can come over tomorrow if you want me to.

Why don't we talk tomorrow?

I won't come over if you don't want me to.

Why don't we meet somewhere?

Well, I'd really like to see you again like that, you know?

I'm afraid to see you here. If we could meet somewhere. . .

But why are you afraid, doll?

Because I don't know who you are.

No, don't be afraid. It gets me upset. What kind of work do you do?

Uh . . . I'm in sales. What's your name?

Billy. I feel like I want you tonight. I feel . . . I took a shower a couple hours ago and I was sponging myself, playing with myself. It feels like a good thing that we had. I really like you, you're so beautiful. You have a beautiful figure.

Billy, will you call me back when I'm awake? We can talk more about meeting.

What did I do that night that turned you on?

I'm still scared.

What's to be a'scared of? Nuttin's gonna happen. I want to know the real you—how you felt that night, and how you feel now. It'll take your scaredness away if you tell me.

All I feel is fear. Maybe that will change. . . .

You mean you don't want to talk about . . . us?

Not right now. I'll talk to you more when I'm awake. Right now I'm scared. I hope you understand.

It don't feel good when you say that. You know, I'm naked right now.

I'll talk to you tomorrow, Billy.

I got out of bed, went to the bathroom, and threw up. My revulsion toward this man was overwhelming, and having to keep him on the phone for ten minutes was almost more than I could bear. I had forced myself to be pleasant, almost friendly with him during the conversation because I had to keep him on the line. The more garrulous this made him, the more disgusted I felt.

I called Mike Belger the next day and reported the phone call to him. He was already aware of it and told me the phone company had gotten a trace on it. Mike praised me to the heavens and said I was one of the bravest women he'd ever known. "I know this is awful for you, Wendy, but don't give up. If we get two more traces, Pacific Bell will release the phone number to us."

I did the best I could, laying awake at night wondering if and when the phone would ring. A few days later, Billy called again at his usual ghoulish hour before dawn. The first words out of his mouth were "I know you want to see me again." He was a sick fuck. His vulgarity was even worse than the time before, graphic beyond telling, insistent and insane. It took every last bit of my energy and will to allow me to listen without hanging up, respond neutrally to his hideous statements, encourage a meeting between us and drag the conversation out. After ten minutes, I could take no more of it. I hung up on Billy, but the phone company had gotten another trace. I felt a stirring of hope that this ordeal might be over soon.

A few weeks passed without another phone call. My boyfriend, Dave, moved back in, although under different circumstances this wouldn't have happened. In retrospect, I know that our relationship was on the wane then, and could have come to a peaceful, natural ending if not for my rape. Regardless, Dave and I decided to stay together. He was a spiritual man by nature, while in those days I had yet to develop that sort of consciousness. I was analytical, controlling, and emotional. I had worshipped at the temple of psychotherapy, while Dave followed a Presbyterian rhythm.

Bill Reed phoned me one day and said the Sheriff's Department had to remove the tap from my phone. Over a month had passed since the rapist's last phone call, and the department needed to use the tap on another case. It was 1981. Technologically challenged in those days, there wasn't enough equipment to go around for all the criminal cases in Los Angeles. I had no choice but to relinquish my last chance at entrapping "Billy" and resigned myself to this terrible disappointment.

Sometime in the midwinter of the following year, my phone rang in the middle of the night. Dave and I woke up immediately.

"I don't want to talk to him!" I told Dave as the phone trilled repeatedly. "I won't answer it!"

Before I could stop him, Dave picked up the phone. I was stunned and couldn't for the life of me imagine what he had to say to "Billy." As I lay in bed listening to only Dave's side of the conversation, the atmosphere in my bedroom became increasingly surreal.

"No, she won't talk to you," Dave said. A pause followed.

"You know," Dave continued, "I'm not worried any more about whether or not the police find you. You're already in jail. In your heart, I know you're living in a hell that you created because of what you did." The pause was longer.

"Here's what you do, man," said Dave patiently. "I want you to get down on your knees and ask God to forgive you for what you did to her. That's the only way, because she and I can't help you." Another pause.

Suddenly Dave handed me the phone. "Take it," he said quietly. "He wants to apologize to you."

I recoiled from this suggestion as though I'd just been asked to dive into a sewer. My rage blinded me. I took the phone and slammed it down in the receiver. Although years later I fortunately was able to forgive "Billy" and release my entire warehouse of resentment and anger toward him, on this night I'd not yet become that person. All I could feel was hatred.

I never heard from him again. Today I'd like to believe that, if he's still alive, he found the peace of mind that I finally did. Would Dave have been the one responsible for this, or for at least planting the idea of humility in the rapist's mind? I don't know, and I'm not sure if it matters.

My life went on recklessly after that. I lived in a state of denial for the next couple of years, avoiding any kind of therapy or attempt to recover psychologically from the rape. As far as I was concerned, an incident had occurred, had affected me painfully for a period of time, and then had taken its place in the vault of my memory bank. Recovery wasn't an issue for me, because I'd decided to be a victim, rather than a survivor, and lived my life accordingly.

The recreational drugs I experimented with allowed me to avoid having any negative feelings and to create an opaque veneer around my soul. I gathered like-minded people around me who reinforced a meaningless lifestyle and the appearance of frivolity. It was madness. Penny, my dearest friend, distanced herself from me with the realization that any overture of compassion or help was unwanted. Dave was hired for a music gig in Italy that was supposed to last for ten weeks, but he never came back to Los Angeles. Our relationship ended during a transcontinental phone conversation that left me devastated for months, and in that state of mind it never occurred to me that I had become impossible to live with.

For a long time, I maintained the façade that my life was manageable. I went to work every day, selling for my publishers. My father, whose health was failing, took up much of my time as I became his primary caretaker. I behaved like a responsible, devoted daughter, driving him to and from doctor's appointments, making meals for him, and maintaining his household. When I went to New York for sales conferences, I was bright and charming to all I came into contact with. The reality, however, was a much darker truth. Inside, I was dying from the pain of the rape. If depression is a condition of the mind, then despair is a condition of the soul, and mine was engulfed by it.

Things change rapidly. In 1984, a friend casually mentioned how much help she'd been getting from her psychologist, Dr. David Gangsei. In a nanosecond, I realized that I was sick of being in such a numb emotional state. I was ready to make my life better and to begin therapy to work on the terrible effects of the rape. There are no victims in this life—only volunteers. It was time to move on from being a casualty to a survivor.

I met with David Gangsei in his office twice a week for a year. The feelings and memories I thought would take so long to emerge came rushing to the surface right away, and I cried like a baby during those hours. Still, no matter how intense the sorrow, I showed up for every appointment with David. I worked like the dickens with him to heal myself, and it gradually paid off as peace of mind descended upon me.

After the first year, David recommended that I join an eight-week rape survivor's group. Continuing to see him weekly, I also attended group therapy at the Santa Monica Rape Treatment Center on Friday evenings. Four years had already passed since my assault, but to my surprise the other seven women in the group had waited much longer—decades—to seek out help. The shame and guilt attached to their experiences had turned them into long-suffering silent victims. Somehow I'd avoided such a prolonged visit to the purgatory of self-recrimination. For the first time in my life, I began to consider the grace of God, and what it might mean.

Lance Morrow said "All honest thought is a form of prayer." Honesty was the gift that followed years of therapy and the recovery from the rape, and I learned how to be truthful with and about myself. My spiritual life became embedded in this, and as a result everything in my life became richer with meaning, humor, and personal integrity. Drugs became meaningless to me, and I stopped using them. Certain friends fell by the wayside while others gathered closer, and the law of attraction guaranteed the appearance of new people with loving dispositions and generosity of spirit.

After I was raped, my taste in mysteries changed. My curiosity about the cause and motivation of violent behavior grew so that I took to reading books with strong character studies of the psychopathic mind. I'm an Anglophile at heart, so I made a beeline for the Brits—Francis King's *Act of Darkness* to start with, followed by John Harvey's Inspector Resnick mysteries and, surprisingly, certain books by William Trevor. His *Silence in the Garden*, followed many years later by *Felicia's Journey*, showcase his marvelous talent for interpreting the complex reasoning behind acts of crime. P. D. James's two detectives, Cordelia Gray and Adam Dalgliesh, came close to untangling the psychological web of violence but ultimately left me with more questions than answers—which, of course, was not necessarily a bad thing.

It wasn't until I discovered the unmitigated brilliance of Ruth Rendell, though, that the literature of crime and mystery revealed itself to me in all its grandeur. Whether writing as herself or as Barbara Vine, her pseudonym for the darker, more psychological novels that provide a glimpse into Rendell's deeper perception of human nature, she is the incomparable mistress of the genre. It was no coincidence that I became a fan of hers after I was raped. No matter the leaps I made in getting on with my life, I never stopped asking the question "why?" It wasn't a matter of "why *me?*" but a search for answers to why the man who called himself Billy decided, in an uncontrollable state, to attack and rape at all. Rendell's mysteries, more than the others, were the next best thing to an actual confrontation with my nemesis. They had to suffice.

I met Michael Connelly not long after his Edgar-winning first mystery, *The Black Echo*, was published in 1992. It introduced the character of Detective Harry Bosch, a melancholy, complex man who deeply resonated with me. The local rep for Connelly's publisher, Little, Brown, had a dinner party for Mike and his wife, Linda. That night, they were able to meet a few bookstore owners and other reps who had become immediate fans after reading his first book. The Connellys were gracious, unpretentious people whom I liked immensely, and we soon became friends. After *The Black Ice* and *The Last Coyote* were published, Mike's literary star began soaring. I observed with pleasure how fame and fortune did nothing to change the Connellys' natural demeanor of humility and warmth.

My friendship with Mike and Linda included casual dinners both in my home and theirs. One night, they invited a staff writer from the *Los Angeles Times,* Greg Braxton, to join us at their house. I helped Linda prepare the meal and while it was cooking suggested a game of Scrabble to the two writers. Both men pled incompetence at spelling, which shocked the hell out of me and gave me no choice but to taunt them relentlessly until they finally caved in. Never in my life have I played Scrabble with such wimps. If Mike or Greg came up with a word that was more than three letters long, it was a spelling miracle. In the end I creamed them, winning by at least a hundred points, with Greg taking a miserable second. The big loser was my Edgar-winner friend, Mr. Connelly.

Waiting every year for Mike's next crime novel became a ritual that I looked forward to eagerly. I stayed up late into the night reading *The Poet, Trunk Music* (in which Mike gives me a cameo in the character of FBI agent Wendell Werris), *Blood Work,* and so on. Each book hooked me more than the one before, and I soon developed a taste for a different sort of mystery—the police procedural. I'd grown up in the company of cops, after all, which had piqued my curiosity about law-enforcement methodology and investigative work. Mike's books gave me quite an education in these areas.

Several years earlier, I had begun working as a freelance photographer, more for my own creative fulfillment than to supplement my income. When my work achieved a professional quality, Mike hired me to shoot for the photo gallery on his Web site. I was ecstatic. While he always looks after his friends, this really was an exceptional opportunity for me that continues to this day. Because of it, I have the luxury of reading Mike's books in manuscript form months before they're published, being mindful as I do of key scenes (most of which take place in Los Angeles) that are both visually interesting and intimate enough to give his worldwide fan base a sense of Harry Bosch's city.

In the winter of 2005, Mike sent me the manuscript of *The Closers*, his book about an old murder case in Los Angeles that's finally solved by the LAPD's Cold Case unit. As usual, I raced through it with the urgency of a devotee. It tells of a family whose lives are forever altered by the violent death of a loved one, and how such crimes cast a devastating pall on the emotional context of their lives. *The Closers* haunted me in a nearly primal way and lingered in my mind for a long while afterward. There was something about the case it focused on, and the cruel ambiguity of having to wait a lifetime for answers and resolutions, that got under my skin.

A couple of months later, Mike asked if I could take a new portrait of him for the jacket of his next book. Happily accepting the assignment, we then set out to find a date and time that would work for both of us during his upcoming visit from Florida. Mike wasn't available on the first day I suggested, saying he had to "watch a court sentencing on a case involving some of my detective friends."

If I had been a dog, my ears would have perked up when I read that e-mail. A sentencing hearing? Detectives? I was seriously intrigued and asked Mike about it. He quickly sent me a return e-mail.

The case is from the Cold Case squad, which I have been hanging around with for the Harry Bosch stuff.

It was a woman, kidnapped and murdered in the Valley. Many years later the cops found a suspect living in Palm Springs. He still had a knife they thought could have been used to kill the woman. They took it apart and underneath the handle they found blood had seeped into the wood. They got a DNA match to the victim. There was other evidence as well, and in the face of all this the guy pleaded guilty to second-degree murder. The victim left behind a baby who is now a grown woman. She is expected to address the court about the mother she never knew—things like that. I want to be there mostly to congratulate the cops. Both of them, Jackson and Marcia, are characters in *The Closers*.

Putting the pieces together, I realized that this case must have been Mike's inspiration for *The Closers*. My intuition told me that I should be in that courtroom for the hearing—although my motive was an enigma to me. Mike invited me to attend, and we arranged to meet that morning at the San Fernando courthouse.

While driving to the Valley for the hearing, I thought about how interesting it would be to witness it. Surely it wouldn't affect me emotionally, I thought, for I'd never known or even met the woman who was murdered. I would be an objective observer, I imagined.

What happened instead shook me to my core.

After going through security at the front of the building, I entered a small courtroom that held about fifty visitors. Outside in the hall there were news cameras and reporters from various local media, including the *Los Angeles Times*. Mike sat down next to me when he arrived, pointing out the key players in this awful drama as they filed into the room. The two detectives who got the case originally in 1983 were there, as was the pair who finally solved it twenty-two years later—Detectives Rick Jackson and Tim Marcia.

Mike rattled off the names of the Deputy D.A., John Lewin, who plea-bargained to spare the victim's family the agony of a trial, as well as the defense attorney and reporters as they took their seats. A large group of people entered together: the family and friends of the victim. Finally the judge entered the courtroom and took his seat. After calling the court to order and making a few announcements, a deputy brought the murderer, Edmond Marr, into the room.

Marr, a man in his midforties, was wearing an orange jail jumpsuit and had his hands bound in cuffs in front of him. Although his face was devoid of emotion, I took note of a strange handsomeness in it. His bronze skin was of Hispanic descent, with pleasant features on his face and thick, well-cut graying hair. None of this fit into the image of him I'd imagined. I wanted to see a man whose physical nature matched the brutality of the crime he'd committed.

John Lewin walked to the podium and addressed the court, summarizing what had happened to the victim on St. Patrick's Day, 1983. Her name was Elaine Graham, a twenty-nine-year-old wife and mother who by all accounts had been a wonderful woman. She left her home that morning and dropped her two-year-old daughter at a babysitter's before heading on to take a class at Cal State Northridge in the Valley.

Edmond Marr kidnapped Elaine from the parking lot and forced her to drive him in her car to a secluded area of the foothills. There he made her walk up a very steep trail to a spot in the hills that was hidden from view and far from the usual foot-paths taken by hikers. It is assumed that Marr then raped Elaine; it is a fact that he stabbed her to death with a knife. Her body was not found for eight months. For Elaine's loved ones, this was a grievous time of not knowing where she was. By the time her body was recovered, it had skeletized, making it impossible to take samples of any possible evidence. Although her remains were finally buried, the family's anguish never was. It continued taking its toll on them for the next two decades.

When Marr was finally caught, the police found the knife in his home, with Elaine's blood in the wood handle and a DNA matching that of her daughter. Even if he hadn't confessed to the murder, this would have been enough to convict Marr.

The D.A.'s testimony was chilling, setting the perfect tone to introduce the next people called to the podium. Dr. Steven Graham, Elaine's husband, spoke directly to Marr as the defendant kept his head down and stared at the table. Beginning in a calm and steady voice, Graham soon went into a rage toward his wife's murderer. Screaming at Marr about the nightmare he'd put the family through, and referring to him to as a despicable, evil creature, Dr. Graham embodied all the sorrow and pain of the family members sitting in the room. Sobs and low wails were plainly heard, and I began to cry as well.

Elaine's daughter Elise was next called to speak. Now in her midtwenties, she carried herself with the grace and poise of a young woman who had no fear, even while staring at her mother's killer. Like her father, Elise Graham spoke directly to Marr. Unlike her father, she expressed herself in a composed manner that was absolutely chilling.

"People tell me I look just like my mother when she was my age, when you stabbed her to death," she said in a firm voice. "I hear I have her cheekbones. What do you think, Edmond? Do you see her in my face?" she continued, touching her face gently, daring him to look at her. He did not. His head remained lowered. Elise went on to tell him that she had no memory of her mother, and that "you've given me a life sentence of a broken heart."

When she concluded, there wasn't a dry eye in the courtroom. Everyone was crying, including the macho detectives and reputedly impartial journalists. I wept and felt ashamed of myself for the careless thoughts I'd had about this event just hours earlier. This was real life, with real people and gut-level emotions of grief, anger, and loss. I knew that Elaine Graham's loved ones would never be entirely free of their heartbreaking past.

The hearing ended after the judge sentenced Marr, who was then quickly led out of the room. People gathered in the hallway for interviews with the media, and I stood against a wall watching the relief on the faces of the Graham family. I was happy for them. After waiting so many years, they were finally able to confront the man who took from them the most important person in their world. I approached Rick Jackson and Tim Marcia, wanting to thank them for solving the crime and helping the family. They were warm and appreciative, and I explained my connection to Mike Connelly and why I was there for the hearing. As I was leaving, I stopped and turned back to Detective Jackson.

"I'm not sure why I'm asking you this, but—may I have your card?" I said, feeling suddenly unsure of myself.

"Of course!" the detective responded, reaching into his wallet for his LAPD card. "Please call me any time."

My energy was drained beyond all reason, and when I got home I went back to bed. When I woke up two hours later, my first thought was, "*There is evidence from my rape. There is DNA.*"

From the vaginal swab taken in the emergency room, to the semen found on my sheets, evidence would have been tagged and stored in the basement of LAPD headquarters.

I made a cup of coffee, sat in my living room, and considered the mix of emotions I'd felt in the courthouse—a deeply sad empathy with Elise and Dr. Steven Graham, yes, but also a strange envy that gradually crept up on me as I observed their happiness after the hearing. It was the happiness of closure. They'd had their chance to release decades of pain and anger. It was finished for them.

I wanted that closure; yearned for it. Like a slap in the face, it struck me that my rape had affected all of the relationships that had followed in my life. They had all been doomed because my self-confidence had also been raped and plundered. Suddenly I realized that, given the current state of DNA analysis, there was a chance that I could locate "Billy." If he'd been arrested for another crime after he raped me, perhaps the police could help me track him down. My mind raced with the possibilities this offered. I could see this man for the first time, look into his eyes, and tell him how dreadfully his violence had affected my life. I could ask him why he hurt me. I could. . . .

But first I phoned Mike Connelly. He was as drained as I was, needing to talk everything through so we could accumulate some distance from what we had seen and heard that day at the courthouse. This was very helpful to me and brought me back to the present. I had talked about my rape with the Connellys a few years after our friendship had begun, so it felt comfortable to tell Mike about the revelation I'd just had. I talked about it nonstop for five minutes.

"Do you think it would be okay if I phoned Rick Jackson to

ask if he can find the evidence from my case? Do you think he'd mind?" I asked Mike.

He chimed in right away. "It's a great idea, and I hope you do call him. Rick's a great guy, and he'll be happy to help you," Mike offered. "But don't get your hopes up, Wendy. The statute of limitations on your case might have run out already."

It had been nearly twenty-five years since the rape, and this was the last piece of the puzzle for me to solve. No matter the outcome, I owed it to myself to try. That night, I searched through my apartment for the police report that I'd saved since 1981. After two hours, I finally found it.

In the morning I phoned Detective Jackson. Describing my case in detail, and explaining that the sentencing hearing the day before had been the catalyst for my request, I asked if he could determine if the evidence still existed.

"I'll do everything I can to help you, Wendy," Rick told me, "but I have serious doubts about this. The statute of limitations on rape is only six years in California, a crime in itself. But I'll try my best."

I gave him the police report number and Rick promised to get back to me as soon as possible. The pages of the report were yellowed with age, almost brittle in my hands, and as I scanned them there was a sense of disengagement. Who was this Wendy Werris, scribbled about on page after page? I had been thirty years old at the time, unformed, misbegotten, with little if any self-containment. This person came back to me so vaguely that it was hard to realize she ever existed. I had lived many lives since then and hadn't spent much time looking back. The violence of the rape had been absorbed over the years in such a way that I'd been able to transform into a loved and loving woman despite it. The young woman in the police report seemed a stranger.

Rick called me back at the end of the day. The evidence was gone. Nothing tangible remained of my rape. "I'm going to tell you the same thing I told Elise Graham yesterday about losing her mother," Rick said gently. "You'll never completely get over what happened to you, Wendy, but it's time for you to move on. Leave it behind now. I wish you all the best."

I didn't feel disappointed. As I sat there in the sacredness of my home, it occurred to me that I had a good life—a great life, really, and the past no longer held any power over me. Survivors of violent crimes can recover and lead wonderful lives, but although we share the same language as those who've never endured this, we'll always speak it with a quirky, untraceable accent. I've grown very fond of it. That's just the way it goes.

Picking up a box of matches, I walked outside to my patio, stood over the barbeque, and removed the grill. Then, page by page, I burned the police report. The flames flared up and died with each piece of paper, and a great sense of well-being brought a smile to my face. When the last ember died, I uttered aloud, "Good-bye, Billy! Good-bye."

The irony behind all of this does not escape me. My profound sense of closure only came about because I'm in the book business. I happened to read Michael Connelly's first book when it came out in 1992. Each experience after that was connected to the next one in a serendipitous, intentional way that I would not become aware of until the journey came to an end.

We never know what may happen when we pick up a book

to read. The turning of a page might actually change the course of our existence. There is something miraculous about this. Truth strikes at the very heart of books and the readers who turn themselves over with great trust to finding the essence of themselves.

Nine

A REQUIEM; A RENAISSANCE

Depression can be the sand that makes the pearl.

—JONI MITCHELL

MY RAPE HAD been book-ended by the deaths of my parents, Mom in 1978 and Dad in 1987, with a decade in between of both anguish and revelation. My mother died on a full moon in a room at a convalescent hospital that smelled like the end of time. According to the private nurse who was with her, just before the massive stroke that sent Charlotte from this plane to the next, she called out: "*Wendy. Wendy!*"

Those were her last words.

My mother had been sick for years. She suffered from the usual age-related ailments: high blood pressure, a weak heart, too many cigarettes, and a disdain for exercise of any kind that didn't involve shopping. She avoided the doctor like a rebellious child, going a dozen years without a checkup, until one night she went into heart failure and almost died. It was the beginning of her slow decline, which we as a family followed, dumb as oxen, in a state of shock and denial.

My mother was only sixty-three when she died, and the time I still needed to become her friend was erased with her last breath. I'd lost the chance to get to know her in any meaningful way. We'd always had a stormy relationship, perhaps because both of us were the babies in the family, she the youngest of six children, me the youngest of three. Being ranked this way in the architecture of kinship, I became the most stubborn, willful, and devious child in the family. Mom and I tended to share all of these qualities.

In the years leading up to her death, I was so absorbed in my world of drama, recklessness, and boyfriends that I simply took my mother for granted. Her prolonged illness angered and annoyed me. Every episode of heart failure, each visit to the hospital, was experienced by me as an inconvenience to my lifestyle, and I came to resent her. I missed the mark in this relationship over and over again; I overlooked the value of my mother at every turn.

Rather than follow her doctor's orders to ensure a healthier lifestyle, she would pop about twenty milligrams of Valium before leaving the house for a checkup. Naturally, this lowered her typically high blood pressure, the source of all her health issues. She would tell us gleefully that she'd fooled the doctor again, ha ha ha! This charade went on for years, but who did she think she was kidding? Ultimately, she kidded herself to death.

I don't know that my mother got the life she bargained for. Marriage to my father began as a whirligig of mad love, excitement, the allure of show business, and Snag's upward climb to the height of success as a writer. Their honeymoon lasted for six years, until they began having children, and long after that they continued to approach life with a unique verve and sense of fun. My parents had money, confidence, and gratitude enough for my sisters and me to share in spades. Until I became a teenager, our lives were grand.

When my father was offered the job with Jackie Gleason, everything changed. It meant the end of our family unit, because he had to leave Los Angeles to make a living. It was hard on my mother, harder than I could have possibly realized. For eight months out of the year she was alone, managing the household, dealing with her adolescent daughters and all the anguish we ignited, left to fend for herself socially. Mom was angry and depressed for most of the decade that my father shuttled back and forth between L.A. and New York or Miami.

When Gleason wrapped his last season, Dad came home to face long periods of unemployment and dismay at his changing place in show business. Leonard Stern, also one of Gleason's writers and the founder of Price, Stern, Sloan Publishing, explained this phenomenon to me after my father died.

"Picture a film crew sitting in a circle of chairs," he said gently, "with rings of chairs expanding out from the first one. Imagine that the people in each row turn around to face those in the circle behind them.

"The producers are in the first circle. When they turn around, they see the directors. Next, the directors turn to face the actors in the circle behind them. After that, the actors face the writers in the next circle. And when the writers turn around, they look at ... *nothing*. Because they're in the last row, in the position of least importance.

"And this is what happened to Snag, and to more writers from that era than I care to mention," Leonard said.

———∞———

WHEN MY FATHER, Snag Werris, was born, he was handed down a life sentence in show business. A comedy writer by trade, he was raised in the Bronx by my Russian grandparents; he learned how to write jokes while working in vaudeville in the 1930s. At the age of eighteen, he got a summer job at one of the resort hotels in the Catskills, where he was a bellhop by day and an entertainer by night.

The hotel had a big dining hall that doubled as a nightclub in the evenings, and traditional vaudeville shows were staged there six nights a week. These featured singers, dancers, magicians, and comedians, all of whom took this handsome teenager under their wings to teach the tricks of their trades. By the end of his second summer in the Catskills, Snag had learned how to play the piano, harmonize, tap-dance, and perform magic tricks. Still, of all the talents Snag had cultivated, he knew that his greatest gift lay in his writing ability.

This talent, along with an innate sense of humor that belied his dour Russian parents, laid the groundwork for his career. As he traveled through the Borscht Belt in later summers with his mentor, comedian Eddie Davis, to perform as Davis's straight man in his comedy routine, a yellow legal pad and Number One pencils were never far from his reach. Snag scrawled joke after joke, previewing them for Eddie over rye and soda at the close of each day.

Many of the gags were good, but others were awkward and contrived. The merit of each one was based on Eddie's reaction to it. If he laughed out loud, Snag knew the joke was good enough to sell to a comedian in the market for new material (in the 1930s, a writer could get two dollars a joke). If Eddie smiled, the joke would get a rewrite and remain in Snag's bag of tricks. And if Eddie looked right through him, it meant the joke was destined for the nearest trash can. As Snag's mentor, Eddie Davis patiently taught him how to write comedy.

He was also the first person to bring Snag out west to Hollywood, where he got his comedic feet wet while writing for the many burlesque houses there in the 1930s.

Snag met my mother, Charlotte, at the very hotel where he worked in Lakewood, New Jersey. She, along with her large Romanian family, were guests at the resort. By the time Snag carried Charlotte's luggage to the lobby, they had fallen in love. They married at the end of 1938, drove to Hollywood from Brooklyn for their honeymoon, and, when they returned, took a suite of rooms at the Granada Hotel on Ashland Place in Brooklyn. It was their first home as newlyweds.

Snag's career in Manhattan took one giant leap after another. His employers in the 1940s included Frank Sinatra, Jack Benny, and Bing Crosby. They all had their own prime-time radio shows that were recorded in New York and broadcast all over the country to a huge, devoted listening audience. After the evening news, most folks settled in to listen to their favorite stars joke with their celebrity guests, croon a while in the studio with a full orchestra, and perform comedy sketches that Snag wrote.

I imagine the sound of living-room chairs scraping against hardwood floors as they were pulled closer to the radio. Or in the kitchen, where young single women living in walkups in the Village would do their ironing to the rhythm of Hoagy Carmichael, who'd sing a little something between comedy sketches. Better yet, in the bedroom, where husbands would lie on beds in white tank T-shirts while wives, seated in front of vanity mirrors, would remove their makeup with little dabs of Pond's cold cream.

Even though I was yet to be born, I know that some particle of me was there in those rooms listening to the radio and welcoming the energy and vastness of the creative tumult of 1940s New York. I'd like to believe that simply being alive qualifies each of us to align with a singular, homogeneous consciousness. It exists in an orbit where every experience and every mental revolution, every joke and every sob, every calamity and every utterance is processed, stored, and spat out again in the form of our daily expression of life. If this is true, then my father's participation in life is surely a part of who I am.

I was close to Snag in a way my sisters were not. The last to be born after two earlier daughters, my parents were so certain I'd be a boy that they chose the name "William" for me in anticipation of my birth. It's possible that I was aware of this in the womb, because I turned myself around in there in the breech position. I wasn't going to budge. Because of this, my mother had to have a Caesarean delivery. From the start, I was the willful, determined, and reckless child, while my sisters followed a safer, more traditional path.

When I was about five years old, Snag and I began a Friday night ritual that didn't include anyone else in the family: we watched the fights on TV. At 6:45, I'd hear Snag calling to me from the living room: "Honey, the boxing starts in a few minutes!"

I'd stop whatever I was doing and run down the hall in my socks so that I could slide on the hardwood floor, jump over the two steps that led into our sunken living room, and make a racket when I landed. *Thump*. Inevitably, Snag would flinch when I entered the room with such graceless panache, but he was always happy to see me.

We sat together in his leather armchair in front of the small RCA black-and-white set, me half-on and half-off his lap. My feet would kick the front of the chair in my excitement as we waited for the fights to begin. Snag would have his glass of vodka on the rocks on the end table and smoke an endless stream of Kent cigarettes. My mother would often bring a bowl of popcorn in for us, which I kept on my lap and shared with my dad.

When the show finally began, we whistled along to the Gillette jingle. It was almost unbearably happy for me, this entitlement of private time that bonded me to my dad. The fights were broadcast live from the Olympic Stadium in downtown Los Angeles in stunning black and white. I loved seeing the boxers—loved their swings, lunges, tippy-toed dances back and forth across the ring. I loved the sound of gloves meeting muscle or cartilage or slick cheekbones. The yelling and booing of the crowd was music to my little ears. Best of all, though, were the knockouts. As soon as the boxer hit the floor, Snag and I began our chant:

"*Thousand and one! thousand and two! thousand and three!*" and so on, until either the bell rang to call the fight, or the boxer wobbled up off the mat before the ten seconds were up. Occasionally my mother would walk into the room because Snag and I were making so much damn noise. His behavior was as silly as mine, and our laughter and enthusiastic outbursts were right on par with one another.

"Will you keep it *down*, for God's sake? I'm trying to have a phone conversation!" my mother would yell before turning on her heel and stomping out of the room. Naturally, this triggered more fits of hysteria from us.

Out of emotional necessity, I've pitched many childhood memories into the black hole of detachment. My recollections of those Friday nights with my father, however, have only become more beloved to me with the passage of time. They remain as testament to having once been loved with the depth of a bottomless well.

I suppose I was the next best thing to a son for Snag; certainly I was always aware that there was a sense of failure associated with my birth as a girl. When the doctor went to the waiting room after my delivery and announced to Snag, "*Mazel tov!* You have another girl!" my father was as shocked as my mother. I grew up hearing this story. Snag always got a lot of laughs at the punch line, when he explained how embarrassed he and my mother had been when they had to call their families and tell them I was a *girl*. A girl! What the hell went wrong? Ha, ha, ha! The ersatz son!

I waited until after my mother died, in 1978, to finally question Snag about this.

"Were you disappointed when I was born, Dad?" I asked, while having dinner with him one night. We were at Musso and Frank's Grill in Hollywood, which Snag had been patronizing since 1938. "I mean, were you sorry that I turned out to be a girl?"

"*Yes!*" he said, without hesitation, and I felt my face grow red as a beet, tears threatening to spill and my mind painfully stilled. I sat there with my mouth open, stunned by this revelation. "We just assumed you'd be a boy, honey," he continued. "But after the initial disappointment, I came to accept it." With that he shrugged and returned to his dinner, as though this was meaningless banter that required no further discussion. Snag had ignored the social nicety that suggests that if you can't be kind, at least be vague. In fact, he had just initiated the existential burlesque that framed our relationship for the next nine years.

Snag's words that night hit me hard, slamming into my romantic relationships, most of which were with men who worked in some artistic field. Their lifestyles were similar to my father's: unpredictable and dramatic. I tried to replenish my empty heart with any version of love that crossed my path, the result of a false belief that I wasn't really wanted in this world. Until I later came to believe otherwise, I mostly chose lovers based on their willingness to leave.

The decline of Dad's career in the 1970s was difficult for my mother, who also had to adjust to his increasing dependence on alcohol and sleeping pills. In his unfailing efforts to write another script on spec, or create a game show or a list of gags for Johnny Carson to use, my father drank vodka into the wee hours of the morning while my mother fell asleep without him night after night. Because he had to take a handful of sleeping pills to get to sleep, it was almost impossible for Mom to wake him before one in the afternoon. Although I know my father, a hapless alcoholic, didn't intend to hurt her, this behavior drove Charlotte further and further into herself.

By 1978, Mom was in a convalescent hospital. Her initial stroke had left her unable to walk or speak clearly. Dad and my sisters remained optimistic that she'd be coming home as soon as she was "well." I felt alone in understanding that my mother didn't have much longer to live.

On one of my last visits to her in the hospital, she was extremely agitated. "I want to die!" she told me. "I want to die and be with God!"

I didn't argue with her, or give her a lecture on maintaining a survivor's attitude. Something in me knew to simply remain silent and look upon her with a gentle acceptance. A powerful message passed between us. Charlotte didn't want to live a compromised life, and I accepted her decision.

When I got the call from the hospital at four in the morning to tell me that my mother had passed, I phoned Penny. She picked me up and drove to the grim facility on Fairfax Avenue. While we waited for the mortuary van to come and collect the body, Penny sat with me in Mom's room. Viewing the face of my dead mother, the first corpse I'd ever seen, it struck me that she had become young again. Every line in her face, and the grimace of pain and stress I'd gotten used to seeing in her after the stroke, had disappeared. It was my mother, and yet it was not. It was her body, but she had clearly abandoned it. She was becoming an apparition. I wept freely.

It was up to me to deliver this news to my father. My sisters lived far away, and we agreed that he must be told in person. Alone with him in his apartment, I quietly said, "Mom died. She died a few hours ago, Dad."

From his forehead down, my father began to crumble. It was

a concise and perfectly timed collapse of all his limbs and mus-cles, and in the moment it took to grab him some detached part of my mind watched with awe at the sight of this. I'd read accounts of this in nineteenth-century novels—"*At the sight of him, she crum-bled. . . . He began to crumble while reading the letter. . . .*"—but I'd never actually witnessed it. That the person before me was my father made it all the more surreal.

"My heart is breaking," Dad cried. "*It's breaking!*" He stood there on the very precipice of his heart. Watching him fall apart, I understood for the first time that the deepest love we can embody also carries with it the capacity for our most profound sorrow.

Dad outlived my mother by nine lonely years.

For me, the decade between my parents' deaths was a yin-yang rendering of life. As I was recovering from one loss, I was prepar-ing for another: the death of my father. Mom's illness lasted through most of my twenties. Dad began his decline when I turned thirty, and my life revolved around his diminishing existence for the next seven years.

During a time when others my age were thinking about mar-riage and starting a family, I was bidding adieu to the idea of both. I chose to spend those years examining death rather than life, or the idea that death is an essential *part* of life. Understanding the nature of my mortality, while grasping the concept of having an eternal mind, took precedence over living a traditional life. Each of us embraces happiness in a unique way. I found mine through self-examination. The poet-songwriter Greg Brown suggests: "What is real but compassion, as we move from birth to death?" Through the most difficult years of my life, this idea made it pos-sible to still accept my share of grace.

During that time, the book business continued to support me, acting as an especially loyal ally while I walked through the valley of Madame Death. When I felt stripped of any identity, save that of a potential suicide, UPS would deliver cartons of new catalogs from my publishers, or my phone would ring and I'd hear the voice of a friendly bookseller asking for help with a special order. As depressed as I was, I could still rise to any occasion where books were concerned. They were the most obliging part of my life, and some of my favorites from that era remain: *Sophie's Choice* (William Styron), *Good As Gold* (Joseph Heller), *August* (Judith Rossner), and *The Prince of Tides* (Pat Conroy).

Repping continued to be my greatest stimulant, and as the decade of the 1980s continued—and with it the growth of my business—I found myself in the enviable position of being in demand. When publishers wanted to take on reps, or replace their current ones, invariably they contacted my commission group to see if we might be interested in their lines. It was a deeply gratifying time in my career, and I was making more money than I could keep track of. I spent it shamelessly, on myself and on others.

My work schedule revolved around my father. A few years after my mother died, he was mugged in the alley behind his apartment while taking out the trash. One of the attackers struck Dad in the eye, detaching a cornea. The unthinkable happened, and my father began to go blind. For a man so passionate about words, reading, and writing, it was the cruelest outcome.

Driving him became my second job. We went to doctors' appointments all over Los Angeles, supermarkets for shopping, the dry cleaners, the bank. I will not say I always did this willingly. My father's demands were massively difficult for me. One night, while having drinks in my home with a first date, Dad called in a panic. He was having an episode of heart failure, and I heard him gasping for air on the phone. Grabbing my purse and a jacket, I told my date I had to leave.

"Where are you going?" he asked.

"I have to take my father to the hospital—*right now!*"

My date insisted on coming with me. We got Dad in the car, and I drove down the streets at sixty miles an hour, stopping at red lights only long enough to see if there were cars coming before burning rubber through the intersections. My father's lungs were filling with fluid, and the sound was terrifying. What he used to do for my mother, I was now doing for him. We reached the hospital in time, and Dad was admitted and released after a few days, his health relatively stable.

This was not an isolated incident, only one of many. Once he called me while I was in the midst of having a dinner party, and I had to leave my guests sitting around the dining table to fend for themselves. I no longer remember how many times I made that Indy 500 drive to the emergency room, but I can tell you that, as a rep, at least there were always books in the trunk of my car to read in the waiting room.

Dad's greatest joy after my mother died was a home-cooked meal. He came to my place on Sycamore for dinner every week. We always followed the same routine: I'd drive the four blocks to his place to pick him up, gently get him into the car, and then help him up the few steps to my apartment when we arrived. Settled in the living room with the news on the TV, I'd bring him a double scotch on the rocks. "Not too much!" he'd always tell me, but I knew that if I didn't pour enough he'd complain.

I always made comfort food for him—dishes like meatloaf, roast chicken, or broiled salmon. These were his favorite things, the things my mother used to make for him. Mashed potatoes and fresh vegetables would complete the entrée. We always ended with coffee and cake.

Dad was a slow eater, and it used to drive me mad when I finished my meal half an hour before him. Oblivious to this, he would talk as slowly as he ate, usually at the same time. A conversation, then, would go something like this:

"Honey," he'd begin, "did I ever tell you . . . about the time . . . that Sinatra and me (chew, chew, swallow, sip drink, pause) were in the club car . . . on the train (hiccup, chewchewchew, breathe, swallow, sip drink, stare into space) together at two in the morning?"

I'd heard this story a thousand times, but still I said, "No, Dad. You and Frank Sinatra? Please tell me!"

"Well," he continued, "it just so happened (chew, pick teeth, chew chew, swallow, swirl ice in glass now devoid of Scotch) we were on the road . . . in Sinatra's private train (smack lips, pause, inhale, chew chew, wipe mouth with napkin) . . . and one night . . . I couldn't sleep . . . so I joined . . . honey, can I have another drink? (fork to lips, chew, swallow, lose train of thought). . . ."

"Dad!! You're on the train with Sinatra, you can't sleep, and for God's sake *WHAT HAPPENED NEXT*?" I'd say, now at the end of my rope.

"Oh!" he exclaimed. "Let's see . . . so I'm in one corner of the club car . . . in my pajamas and bathrobe . . . and there's Frank (move piece of chicken with sourdough roll, sigh loudly, hiccup, sip scotch) . . . at the other end of the car, he's in his bathrobe, too, and we acknowledge one another . . . and sit in silence . . . Oh, am

I full! That was delicious! . . . and watch the full moon outside the windows. . . ."

At this point I would thrust myself out of my chair and start washing the dishes, while Dad trailed off into his own little world. He spent too much time alone, not being the kind of man who would start dating after the death of my mother. If my sisters and I asked him about this, he would say: "She was the love of my life—the only one. How could I ever get married again?" We let him be. None of us could begin to fathom the depth of his grief.

Dad passed the time with a group of young comedy writers who'd become his protégés. They visited him in his apartment with their material to read aloud and be critiqued by the man they referred to as "Maestro." Occasionally he flew to New York to visit his sister, my Aunt Shirley. At home he'd watch Johnny Carson every night, and when he began to go blind he'd pull the armchair up to about two feet from the TV screen. And, until the bitter end, he kept writing jokes, for Bob Hope, for Carson, for Milton Berle. He still wrote them on yellow legal pads, his handwriting ever larger with the dimming of his sight.

My father's life ended badly, without grace or ease. His heart was so weak that he had circulation problems throughout his body. A month before the end, his left leg was amputated below the knee. That night, after the surgery, I went to his hospital room. Standing in the doorway, I watched him sleeping. I saw the shadow falling on the space where his leg used to be. As I stumbled to the chair, I began to faint, and a nurse, entering the room behind me, grabbed me before I fell. Once I was in the chair, she had me put my head between my knees and then brought a glass of orange juice for me to drink. In reality, it was her kindness that revived me.

As with my mother, I knew Dad wouldn't make it out of the hideous quagmire of his illness. I began waiting for him to die. There was a constant ache in my throat from the effort, day after day, of swallowing my tears. His last days were pitiful. I wanted to die with him.

On the last day of his life, I went to see him at the hospital. He was in a coma, breathing erratically and with great effort. With each exhalation, the length of time before he took another breath lengthened. I began to count the seconds. Five. Seven. Eight. It was frightening to watch this end-of-life procession of heartbeats, and I knew I wasn't strong enough to endure the image of Dad's last breath.

I took his hand in mine and said, "I love you, Dad. Thank you for everything you gave to me, and for your love. I'll always be proud to be your daughter." I leaned down and kissed his cheek. "Go with God, Dad," I whispered and walked out of the room. I drove right back home, and the phone was ringing as I walked inside. When I answered, a nurse at the hospital told me that Dad had died a few minutes after I left. It was February 27, 1987.

My father's funeral service began with the playing of Frank Sinatra's album *Come Fly With Me*. The funeral director thought it odd—inappropriate, even—but my sisters and I insisted, and we got our way. We also had the mortuary place Dad's tap shoes on top of his casket, later to be buried with him. Our friend Kevin Hartigan, one of Dad's young protégés, gave the eulogy, a funny and loving tribute to the man who was always there to help his friends with a gag, or to get through a personal problem.

Kevin read a letter to the mourners that Dad had received from George Seaton, the man who had both written and directed the beloved film *Miracle on 34th Street*. My father's other passion in life was the magical arts, and Seaton's letter was written shortly after Dad had been elected president of the Society of American Magicians.

> *As I've always said publicly, I think you're without a doubt an outstanding illusionist. I remember years ago one of your first tricks was creating the illusion of a writer at work. You did this magnificently and convincingly. Most men who attempt this sort of thing do it in private. I have known many who seek the solitude of a den or a study, and then return to the studio the next day and give the illusion of having worked. You, however, performed the feat on an open set, in front of hundreds of witnesses. Before their very eyes, with merely a pencil and paper or a typewriter, you convincingly gave the impression of a writer creating.*
>
> *Congratulations,*
> *George*

People howled with laughter; people broke down and cried.

There was one gesture the day of the funeral that most strikingly reminded me of how much Dad had been loved. Jackie Gleason, whose own poor health made it impossible for him to travel from Florida for the funeral, sent, in his absence, a bouquet of carnations. Jackie had famously always worn one as a boutonnière when he was on stage. The carnations, in memory of my father, were all red, save for one pure white bloom in the center of the arrangement. That's the light of Dad's soul, I thought, holding the flowers up to my face to inhale their sharp, sweet fragrance.

There was a card that arrived with this display. It read:

> *Show business has lost a great friend.*
> —JACKIE GLEASON

It had, indeed, and my heart would not be able to find any way out of its sorrow for many months.

Kinescopes of Jackie's television shows, from *Cavalcade of Stars* to the *Jackie Gleason Show*, were still under wraps in Dad's apartment. The Museum of Television and Radio had, for years, been trying to persuade my father to donate them to its collection. This footage hadn't been seen since the shows first aired, decades earlier, and Dad possessed the only known copies. Every Friday night after the taping of *Cavalcade of Stars* in New York, my father would give two bottles of Four Roses scotch to the young man who ran the film library at the studio. In return, Dad got a kinescope of that week's show. His stubbornness was a huge inconvenience for the museum. Dad stood firm in his belief that the museum should reward him greatly for the kinescopes, despite having paid practically nothing for them himself. However, that wasn't how it worked.

Now everything belonged to us, his daughters, and we agreed that Dad's life's work belonged in a public venue. It would give millions of fans the chance to view these remarkable shows that primarily featured Jackie, but several other comedians and performers as well.

Less than a week after the funeral, Bob Batcha, then the president of the museum, and Ron Simon, its curator, flew to Los Angeles to box up almost a hundred cans of film reels and ship them back to New York. In return, they promised to transfer all of the footage to video and make three extra sets for my sisters and me. Among the collection were the very first *Honeymooners* sketches as they appeared on *Cavalcade of Stars*, featuring a very young Art Carney with Gleason. The Snag Werris Collection was the largest donation of its kind ever made to the museum, a legacy from my father that I'm achingly proud of.

My sisters and I embarked on the month-long task of clearing out Dad's apartment. In life, his eccentricities were apparent to us; in death, we found out just how wacky he had been. We found cases of wine corks (no wine; just the corks), nails, and rubber bands. One box was filled with salt and pepper shakers he'd nicked from restaurants; another with little packets of Sweet'n Low and sugar with a similar provenance. There was cash hidden in odd places. We found it in the napkin holder on his dining table, stuffed behind dividers in filing cabinets, and in the far back corner of a kitchen cupboard.

Stashed behind bookcases, at the bottom of a laundry basket, and in the top drawer of his ungainly metal joke file were unopened half-gallons of Plain Wrap vodka with their familiar and embarrassing blue and white stripes.

Then there were the office supplies: two boxes of carbon paper, a case of Atlas Stationers No. 1 pencils (the dark, soft kind that aren't made any more), six reams of onionskin paper so old that it fell apart when I touched it, and rolls of postage stamps from the Eisenhower presidency. We also found blank yellow legal pads piled as high as my shoulders.

I returned to work and went about sleepwalking through the days. Like the weeks and months following my rape, life seemed to have no boundaries. My perceptions were one-dimensional and flat in a way that frightened me. In orphanhood, I had become a stranger to myself.

By night I paced through my apartment weeping, gasping, choking on grief. I missed my Da! I wanted my Pop! It slowly dawned on me that he had been the defining presence in my life, the one who forced me to look inward because so much of his character had manifested in my own. Without realizing it, my father had given me the gift of knowing myself. Where I had once envied my sisters for getting married, I was suddenly proud of being the only one of us to still bear the Werris name, my badge of honor and redemption. Strangely enough, in this way I had become a facsimile of the son Dad always wanted.

My parents are buried together at a cemetery that, ironically, faces the Warner Brothers studio lot where Dad once worked. I seldom visit their graves any more, believing as I now do that they—and all of my loved ones who've made their transition to the next experience—go with me wherever I am. That's my kind of truth. That's love.

I WENT THROUGH a kind of resurrection after my father died. All through his protracted illness, he had been the only purpose in my life. After almost ten years of emergencies and medical drama, my default state of mind was *always on alert*. Gradually, it occurred to me that I was now allowed to relax. Relief settled over my entire life like a blanket of fine cashmere. My father was free, and I was free. I was happy for both of us. There was no guilt attached to this. It was a wonderful passage in my life that I relished.

Shortly after Dad's death in 1987, I received a call from my friend Ione Graves. She had been the house rep for Oxford University Press in L.A. for many years and, as I mentioned earlier, took selling trips with me through the Southwest. We had cavorted our way through Arizona and New Mexico with great panache. I was surprised to hear that she was moving to Philadelphia and changing careers.

"Oxford's going to replace me with a commission rep, Wendy," Ione said, "and I want to recommend you to the sales manager. What do you think?"

My first thought was that I'd be very unhappy when Ione, one of my closest friends, left Los Angeles. The entire book community here was fond of her, and Ione's departure would be a big loss for everyone. On the other hand, the opportunity to add Oxford University Press to my stable of I-5 Associates lines was wildly attractive to me. Being the oldest and most venerable publisher in the world, it wasn't something I could afford to pass up. I told Ione I was interested and left the rest up to her.

At the same time my, father's modest estate was finally settled and I received my portion. It gave me the chance to experience my childhood dream of staying at the Plaza Hotel in New York, where I'd be headed in a few weeks for my usual round of May sales conferences. I booked a room there, a little sheepishly because I normally stayed at an affordable, midrange hotel. Like all the other commission reps who had to pay their own expenses during these biannual trips, I always hustled to find the best deal possible.

Jonathan Weiss was the sales director at Oxford at the time. He phoned me one morning shortly before I was to leave for New

York and asked if we could set up an interview for Ione's job while I was there. Delighted by this, I assured him that I'd be available to meet with him.

"You could come to the office if you'd like," Jonathan said. "Where are you staying in New York?"

"Oh," I sniffed, "I'll be at the Plaza."

Jonathan paused before responding. "*What?* You're kidding me. Would it be all right to have the interview there? We could meet in the Oak Room downstairs."

Preening my feathers, I agreed to this. "Just call me from a house phone when you get there."

Walking into my room at the Plaza a week later, I stopped in the doorway and gasped, hand over heart. It was exquisite. Burgundy satin drapes hung from valences on the tall windows, which overlooked Central Park. The carpeting, which covered a room nearly as big as my entire apartment on Sycamore Avenue, was deeply plush and patterned in a lovely fleur-de-lis design in gold, blue, and red. I took my shoes off so my feet could sink into its grandeur and wandered about the room. The king-sized bed, covered with an embroidered silk spread and matching pillow shams, gently took my weight as I fell onto it. In the corner was a sitting area that featured a beautiful antique desk, with armchairs covered in pale yellow silk on either side of it.

I did what any mature thirty-six-year-old woman would: I jumped up and down on the bed. Then I picked up the phone and, as Eloise might have done when her nanny was out of hearing range, ordered a banana split with extra hot-fudge sauce from room service. When I hung up, I said, "*Thanks, Pop,*" out loud to the empty room, and then burst into tears. "*Thanks. . . .*"

Well, to hell with the Oak Room. When Jonathan Weiss called from downstairs to say that he was in the lobby, I brashly insisted that we have the interview in my room. "You've gotta see this place! It's big enough for the whole Oxford staff!"

We shook hands warmly at the door, and I took in Jonathan's open and pleasant face, pressed khakis, and blue checked shirt. He, however, was too busy gawking at the room to really look my way. "My god!" he yelped. "Did you get a good rate?" I fell out laughing. Little did I know that this was a typical Weiss entrance into a room, or that his management style embodied a naturally occurring cost-consciousness that was almost maniacal.

We sat in the comfortable armchairs and enjoyed the coffee that room service delivered. Our interview was wonderful. Jonathan seemed impressed with my long summary of all the publishers I'd repped for, the large western territory I was familiar with, and the comfortable and respectful relationships I had with booksellers. In turn, he described the nature of Oxford's publishing program, their sales expectations for my territory, and the profound importance of their backlist titles. I picked his brains about the differences between general trade books—the only kind I'd sold—and university press publishing, with its emphasis on scholarly books in the sciences and humanities.

Two hours later, Jonathan hired me. "I haven't interviewed anyone else," he said frankly. "But I like you. Your résumé is great, and you're one of the few people I know who started in the business the same time as me, and has held their own.

"Besides," he continued, "anyone with the balls to stay at the Plaza during sales conference has to be a great sales rep."

That was almost twenty years ago, and Jonathan remained my

boss at Oxford for the first half of my tenure with the company. Publishing began to change drastically in the nineties. Nearly all of the wonderful old trade houses were gradually sold off to corporate mega-powers, and the face of publishing was tweaked into a permanently bewildered expression. The only part of the industry that seemed resistant to this worrisome, bottom-line mentality was the university press sector, and it soon became apparent to me that being part of it would offer the most secure environment I could find.

Oxford was the beginning of my career shift as I slowly began to acquire more university presses to rep. George Carroll, ever my mad accomplice in the book business, had taken on Oxford on a commission basis a year or so before I did. Between him and Jonathan Weiss, I had a crash course in the qualities unique to university press publishing.

Unlike the model of commercial houses that concentrates on established, popular markets, Oxford—like all other university presses—aims to advance knowledge in ways that are meaningful to a more serious, specialized market. The print runs are smaller; the publicity efforts result in more of a regional, rather than national, public awareness. For the most part, the authors aren't household names, but their prestigious credentials and award-winning books continue to sell in backlist far longer than most titles that reach the best-seller lists and are soon forgotten.

For a girl like me, so accustomed to selling popular fiction, how-to guides, mystery novels, and self-help titles in every arena, Oxford presented an intimidating challenge. I was up for it, however, and found the books exceptional in every sense. Truthfully, I'm not much of a nonfiction reader, save for the life stories and memoirs of people who interest me (Harry Crosby, Diane Arbus, Geoffrey Wolfe, and Maxwell Perkins, to name a few), but Oxford's extensive list of books on history, science, physics, and politics made me want to learn more about all these subjects. I'd long been using their dictionaries and other reference books and already knew they were the best on the market.

I adapted well to Oxford, and from my first sales conference the sensational people I met there made me feel that I belonged. They brought an elegance to my perception of books, and perhaps I gave them a feisty, irreverent sense of the business from my point of view. At any rate, it worked for all concerned.

Considering what was happening to the book industry I knew and loved, it became clear that to move away from trade publishing would be wise as an independent rep. I found in the university presses a relative freedom from the corporate hand. In the past, there were instances where I lost lines because they were either sold to, or suddenly distributed by, large publishers. While nothing is guaranteed, the chance of a university press, with its nonprofit status, falling victim to a takeover by an outside company is slim beyond measure.

It's also true that I came to prefer the publishing atmosphere of academic presses. There's a reverence about their books that I feel secure with. In some ways, they run a backward ship, with discount schedules and order minimums that can't always compete with commercial houses. Still, these staid practices remind me in part of the time when I was a very young woman learning about the dignified book business that used to be. In fact, today I rep for university presses exclusively, having found a new niche for myself in an ever-evolving career that is still rich in the element of surprise.

Ten

PICKWICK BOOKSHOP REDUX

The only success worth one's powder was success in the line of one's idiosyncrasy—what was talent, but the art of being completely whatever one happened to be?

—HENRY JAMES

I'M SEATED IN the purple armchair in my living room, staring into the lens of a video camera. The expression on my face is slightly mental.

"It's five o'clock on April 17, 2004," I say to the glass eye. "This is the day of our Pickwick Bookshop reunion, and I'm nervous.

"So I'm chain-smoking [here I pause to light a cigarette] and drinking [I take a sip of the Pinot Grigio that I favor], waiting for the first people to arrive." As I begin to rise from the chair to turn the camera off, I say: "I'll continue this later."

I have no idea what later will look like, for it's been thirty-three years since I've seen most of my Pickwick comrades, looked them in the face, affectionately touched them on the arm to make a point or make them laugh. Six months earlier, when I had the idea for this reunion, the challenge seemed monumental and insane. How would I find these people? How many could I track down? Who was alive; who had passed on? How would they respond to me? What was I setting myself up for?

Like the penguins on their annual, predestined trek across the tundra, once I'd made my decision, I had no choice but to continue on the slippery march to find my onetime mates.

Penny Rose was still, after more than three decades, my best and dearest friend, true sister, and literary tormentor. In contrast to my own writing technique, she had the discipline of a Gnostic monk, and her short stories and essays were being published in literary journals all over the country. I, on the other hand, had swapped writing for photography many years earlier, a move that might have been hurried by writer's block, but which allowed a hidden talent to emerge that led to my images being widely printed, first in the prestigious *American Photo* magazine.

I didn't write a word for a dozen years and then had the idea for the book you're reading, which scared the crap out of me. Without Penny's psychological battering, I would never have started it, let alone finished. "You're a writer, you fucking moron!" she'd repeat loudly and often. "Now, get off your ass and *write!*"

Penny and I had always adored Mr. Latting. He was our favorite floor manager at Pickwick, dressed every day in natty tweeds and bow ties or ascots at his neck. His bushy brows often revealed more in one subtle movement than the eyes themselves.

We had taken him out to lunch some years back, and he and I had never stopped exchanging Christmas cards, so I knew that he must be alive and well (if elderly). When I called the only number

I had for him, I was delighted to hear him say "Good afternoon!" Mr. Latting sounded as archly aristocratic as he used to at
Pickwick, his voice fey and astringent. Here was a man who
enjoyed being himself more than anyone else I'd ever known.

"Oh, Ben!" I said, having long ago dropped the formal saluta-
tion; "It's *Miss Werris!* It's Wendy."

"*Hwell* (for this is how he pronounced it), as I live and breathe!
How are *thee*?" Ben said.

"Doing very *hwell*, Ben," I told him, and we proceeded to catch
up and compare notes on the previous several years. He was still
living in a tiny two-story duplex near downtown L.A., his health
was good, and, at eighty-four, he was able to get himself to the
Music Center several times a year for his beloved operas.

I got to the point. "I want to have a Pickwick Bookshop
reunion, Ben. Will you help me organize it?"

"Oh, my! My, my, *my*!" he replied. "Perhaps we should check
our *hory-scopes* before we begin?"

Mr. Latting was in.

For the next three months, with Ben's assistance, I hunted
hither and yon for my former mad, eccentric colleagues from the
bookstore. Each time I hit the jackpot, a rousing orchestral finish
boomed in my head! It was nothing short of thrilling to recon-
nect with the people who had never been far from my consciousness despite all the years apart, and the feeling was entirely
mutual.

In a matter of seconds, each phone conversation would resonate
with instant recall of memories and the uniquely powerful sensation that had defined my years at Pickwick Bookshop. No other
life experience could touch it. Perhaps if we'd all survived a plane

crash together, or an earthquake, sharing a profound, singular moment in time, the resonance would be similar.

I found Bob Glasscock, the astrologer who had introduced me to Linda Goodman and told my fortune with the turn of a crystal. He'd returned to his hometown of Little Rock and was writing screenplays. Joni Miller, the backlist buyer I worked for, whose anxiety attacks I thwarted with Cadbury chocolate bars, lived in a fourth-floor walkup in the East Village, working freelance for Workman Publishing as the editor of their annual *Collectible Teapot & Tea Calendar*. She'd also been a board member of the James Beard Foundation in New York for many years and had amassed one of the largest collections of vintage cookbooks in the world.

When I found Shirley Arnold in San Diego, it took ten minutes to refresh her memory before she could place me, but I took no offense. I was overwhelmed simply to have found her and still imagined her with the same long red fingernails, dressed in a tight, sexy skirt and spike heels as on the day she hired me to work at Pickwick in 1970.

The real mystery, though, lay in what might have happened to Hugh Callens. He was the dear, alcoholic hillbilly who ran the metaphysical section at the store, taught me how to drink mai tais, and was always laughing out of the side of his handlebar moustache. I was fairly certain he was dead, either by his own hand or cirrhosis of the liver. It was inconceivable that he'd survived all those years of self-abuse that I imagined would have continued long after I left Pickwick.

Like a little kid at a Passover *seder*, I hunted for Hugh as though he was the *affikomen matzoh*, hidden under a sofa or up high in the kitchen cupboard.

If I could only remember what state he was from! Somewhere in the south, I knew, although—if he was alive—he could be living anywhere. There were no listings for him in California, so I devoted an entire cocktail hour to a white pages Web site and methodically ran his name through every state in alphabetical order. By the time I scrolled through South Dakota, it seemed a hopeless effort.

But when I got to Tennessee, there he was. I screamed.

When I called the number listed, an elderly man with a southern twang answered the phone.

"Yes, hello, sir," I said politely. "I'm looking for Hugh Callens. I'm an old friend of his from the Pickwick Bookshop days." Waiting for his response, I held my breath, anxious about Hugh's fate.

"This is his father," the man said. "Ah'm Hugh senior. He don't live with his mother and me; he has his own place in Nashville. Nah, who'dja say you were again?"

So relieved I could have burst, I patiently explained the nature of my call, and that I was putting together a reunion for the old gang. "Please tell me how Hugh is! I haven't spoken to him in over thirty years."

Mr. Callens explained that Hugh had moved back to Tennessee in the early 1980s, that he'd gone back to college and received first his bachelor's degree and then a master's in clinical social work. Hugh had been working for the state as a psychiatric social worker for several years, all of his clients being "mentally ill."

What? Thirty years ago, Hugh had fit into the same classification as the people he now mentored. It was almost impossible not to burst out laughing, so bizarre and unexpected was this news. After his father told me he couldn't give out Hugh's home telephone number, I begged him to give his son my message. After repeating my number aloud as he wrote it down, Mr. Callens was compelled to ask me a question.

"Young lady," he began ominously, "are you a Christian?"

All at once I remembered that Hugh's father was a Southern Baptist minister. Should I lie, or tell this man the truth? I was desperate to speak to Hugh and didn't want to jeopardize my chances. Honesty is a blessing and a curse; bullshit only works about half the time. I decided on a combination of the two.

"No, sir, I'm not a Christian, but I'm sure I love God as much as you do. Actually, I'm a Jew," I said with confidence. It was doubtful that Mr. Callens had ever spoken to a Jew in his life.

He paused just long enough for me to know I'd shocked him. "Well," he said, "that's fine. *That's just fine*! After all, aren't the Jews supposed to be the chosen people?"

Wouldn't you know it—a goddamned trick question. My mind spun. "Well, Mr. Callens," I finally spouted, "everything's debatable, *isn't it?*"

Without giving him a chance to respond, I quickly reminded him again to give Hugh my message and ended the call by saying, "Thank you, sir—and God bless you!"

Ten minutes later, my phone rang. It was Hugh. I could barely catch my breath when I heard his voice; but when I did, we chattered away like a couple of fruitcakes, jumping back and forth in time and juggling topics as quickly as we could think of them. Hugh had been sober for about twenty years. He had hit bottom one night when, drunk, he passed out on Hollywood Boulevard while waiting for a bus, falling into the street. When his bus came along, the driver had to slam on the brakes to avoid hitting

Hugh, who lay there in a stupor. He'd just used up his last life as an alcoholic. The bus driver was a kindly man who roused Hugh, got him on the bus, and drove him home safely. Hugh never had another drink.

The reunion gathered steam. I called Musso and Frank's Grill—still in business in Los Angeles—to make a reservation for twenty-five people. It was the most appropriate gathering place for us because of its location—two blocks from where the bookstore used to be, an ultimate nostalgia factor. Penny and I used to treat ourselves to lunch at Musso's about once a month, always on a payday, and each order the cheapest thing on the menu (unless Louis Epstein, our old boss, was buying). In those days, Penny and I especially liked the "Appetizer Frank." The entire thing consisted of a half head of romaine lettuce, the round side up, smothered in Thousand Island dressing. Thirty-five years ago it had cost three dollars, the equivalent of over ten bucks today.

After finding most of the Pickwick comrades I'd been looking for, and designing and mailing the invitations, there was a period in which I waited in a still, strange calm. I had reopened the past in a way that, for years, had been contrary to how I approached my life. I was grateful for all that had gone before and had integrated all of it into my rich consciousness, but I no longer referred to my past as a point of reference. Everything I required, it seemed, was now right in front of me; the present moment held all the answers and knowledge to make my life move along purposefully.

The Pickwick reunion, however, had me moving aside the inner veils that clouded who I had been before. I found myself examining the events in my life that led to such profound changes in the woman who my old friends and colleagues probably remembered as she was in her twenties. I had arrived at an entirely different state of being since they last saw me. Without any sense of conceit or vanity, I was in awe of the person I'd become.

I transformed into an adult while I worked at Pickwick Bookshop, coaxed along by my unique co-workers. These people, and the effect they had on my evolution, never strayed far from my mind. How could I possibly forget Joni Miller, the woman responsible for creating the first Women's Studies and Black History sections in a bookstore? Or Daniel Dorse, who teased Ray Bradbury every time the great writer was in the store by calling him "Mr. [Isaac] Asimov" or "Mr. [Frank] Herbert"? What about Steve Clark, who ran the art book section at Pickwick? One day Jack Palance came into the store, approached Steve, and growled: "Where are the art books?" Steve immediately asked in return, "*Where would you like them?*" The actor was struck dumb by this reply.

"It was the Emerald City of bookstores and now it's gone," wrote Sam Frank in the *Los Angeles Times* on July 9, 1995. "B. Dalton Hollywood, formerly known as Pickwick Bookshop, closed on May 20. I was walking along the squalid section of Hollywood Boulevard east of Highland on May 26 when I was shocked to see a sign in the front window saying, 'going out of business.' "

Although I was aware that the store had closed, seeing this piece in the Book Review that Sunday made the hair on my arms stand up. I rarely visited Pickwick after B. Dalton took over when I left in 1972, but the store remained in the back of my mind as a permanent icon for my entrance into the book business. Like my parents before they passed, I thought the store would always be there.

Sam Frank went on to say, "The official reason B. Dalton Hollywood closed, according to Dalton publicist Ann Rucker, is that 'over the last four years, there haven't been enough people . . . shopping in the area to enable us to keep the store open any longer.' " My heart broke into pieces as I read this.

In conclusion, Frank wrote, "Whatever the new business is that replaces B. Dalton (Pickwick) Hollywood, and whatever they will be selling, the demise of a great bookstore speaks dark volumes . . . and now there is just a wistful memory of a treasure island of books." In fact, the business that operated there for many years afterward was a cheap Hollywood souvenir shop that carried the tackiest collection of "keepsake" items imaginable. Following that, the Erotic Museum took residence within the hallowed walls of the former Pickwick Bookshop. It remains there today as the tenant, which strikes me as an almost appropriate homage to the store's ghostly Dickens/Bukowski collaboration.

As I waited for the Pickwickians to arrive at my front door, memories had begun to set my entire body to tingling. One by one they appeared: Daniel Dorse, Hugh Callens, Ben Latting, David Pabian, and John Effinger. George Carroll came straight from the airport, having flown in from Seattle for the fete. Ben held court as we all gathered around the elder statesman of Pickwick, who wore the gold pendant bestowed on him the night of Mr. E's retirement dinner in 1973.

While everyone carried on conversations at fever pitch, I walked the room with the video camera, capturing outrageous bytes of emotional greetings and hysterical laughter. Someone took over when I wanted to make a statement on-camera. Sitting on my couch with George, I explained that Pickwick was the genesis for my two closest friendships today, with Penny Rose *and* the big lug sitting next to me. "They've both been in my life since 1970," I declare proudly, nearly spilling my second glass of wine on George's trousers. Our business partnership reached its natural end in 1998, which likely contributed to the even closer friendship we have today.

We met the rest of the group at Musso and Frank's, looking virtually the same as it always had—red leather banquettes and fading murals on the walls. There was a twenty-foot table set for us near the bar, and it required three cantankerous waiters to tend it. They all remembered Pickwick when it was just down the street from the restaurant.

I ordered one of the vodka martinis Musso's is famous for, and suddenly Shirley Arnold walked into the room. "Oh, my God!" I yelled, in a pitch that others might have used to scream "*fire!*" in a restaurant. Everyone turned to watch me embrace Shirley in a bear hug. She looked almost exactly like the gorgeous vamp of thirty-five years before. Jeff Rogart, a former floor manager at the store and still in the book business, now at HarperCollins, flew in from his home in Connecticut for the reunion. Nick Clemente, who had been Pickwick's advertising director, still looked like a larger-than-life Teddy Bear. He arrived with his wife Jeanine, who had been his assistant at the store. They were followed by a few more late stragglers.

Hugh Callens regaled us with stories of his drunken cons at Pickwick, including his clandestine version of "customer service" during the Christmas shopping rush. In a voice close to a whisper, Hugh would ask people toward the end of the lines if they were making a cash purchase. When someone said "yes," he'd pull them out of line, eyeball the books they were holding and decide on a *fair price*.

"Tell you what," Hugh would say to the customer, "I'll take fifteen dollars for your books *and* gift-wrap them myself in the back. You won't have to stand in this damn line. Save yourself some money, too."

Unbelievably, he got away with this every time, pocketing the cash and returning the gift-wrapped books in a Pickwick bag to the grateful customer in no time at all. When Hugh finished telling this story, we practically gave him a standing ovation at Musso and Frank's. What gall! Only he could have pulled this off.

We drove the waiters crazy, of course, none of us sitting in our chairs for more than a few moments at a time. The din of laughter and conversation was almost deafening, interrupted from time to time by little shrieks of recognition and shock. There were no speeches or pontifications. The energy among us was too wild, uncontrolled, and disorganized for any formalities. We simply ran with the joy that grabbed us that night.

There were people missing among us, though. Poor Joni had been hit by a taxi a few months earlier in New York and wasn't allowed to fly. Alan Kahn, with whom I never lost touch and who remains a close friend and mentor, was out of the country on business and couldn't join us either. He'd become the most successful of all of us, having worked his way up from being the book buyer for the Pickwick chain to a prominent executive position with Barnes & Noble.

Lloyd Harkema, the sycophantic floor manager who used to grovel at the feet of an embarrassed Alfred Hitchcock when he was shopping at Pickwick, had been murdered during a robbery in his home in the 1980s. Learning of this was an enormous shock to all of us.

Louis Epstein—the beloved Mr. "E"—was eighty-nine when he died in 1991. His obituary in the *L.A. Times* read, in part: "'If a customer comes into Pickwick and asks for a book I don't have,' Epstein once said, 'I'm ashamed.'" Mr. E's lifelong reverence for books had drawn everyone around the table at Musso's into the business in the first place. It was the greatest honor to work for him and to have known him. Each of us seated there had carried this reverential tradition deeply into our own lives. I think of him often, and with great love.

By the end of the evening, we all agreed that in the gospel of Pickwick Bookshop, none of us of had actually ever left the store—and Pickwick, blessedly, has never left us.

Life has revealed itself in a language known only to me, and comprised of my own private alphabet. You, too, have such a language. The discovery of it is found in the sum total of every experience we've known—all the loves, losses, agonizing pain, and ecstatic joys. You will find in this book a unique translation of a life well lived, because of the generosity of books, because of the grand life tour they have given me. The business will never again be what it once was. It's not possible to find the cultivated sensibility of the past in most publishers and bookstores today, because economic realities no longer allow for it. Of course, to implicate books for the failures of the industry is absurd. Their value remains unchanged and sanctified. Books were the mold from which my life was formed and, ultimately, made whole. For all of this, I am grateful.

EPILOGUE

> Life has no other discipline to impose, if we would but realize it, than to accept life unquestioningly. Everything we shut our eyes to, everything we run away from, everything we deny, denigrate or despise, serves to defeat us in the end. What seems nasty, painful, evil, can become a source of beauty, joy and strength, if faced with an open mind. Every moment is a golden one for him who has the vision to recognize it as such.
>
> —HENRY MILLER

MY CONVENTIONAL WISDOM has taught me that if you do anything long enough, it's likely that you'll find yourself at a fork in the freeway of your life. The first time this happened to me was in 1970, when I had to choose between Pickwick Bookshop and a university education. It next happened after I'd been in the book business for fifteen years, ten of those as a publishers' rep, and the mental activities in my head sounded like tambourines playing to the beat of a career change.

I was always an advocate of psychotherapy, having started that process when I was nineteen and continuing well into my thirties—right around the time I thought I'd had enough of the book business, bless its good soul. Since I'd never finished college, it seemed the perfect time for me to go back to school, get my degree, and work toward the only other thing I was inclined to do: become a psychologist. I enrolled at Antioch University and spent the next eighteen months absorbed in psychology classes that by their very nature brought me to an intense period of introspection. The books I was assigned to read, by psychology masters including Carl Rogers, B. F. Skinner, Rollo May, and Carl Jung, all engaged me in ideas about my psychological roots and the purposes of my own discontent.

When I graduated from Antioch with a Bachelor of Arts in psychology, I realized that not only was I skeptical of my ability to be a good therapist, but my life in the book business was not yet finished. With a new vision of myself, the strong suits and those that still required some mending, I stayed on the only career path I'd ever known.

This worked for many years. With a sense of optimism and renewed faith in the book business, I managed to survive the breakup of my business partnership, the loss of lines and income, and the pathos of corporate takeovers in the publishing industry. My hope sustained itself even in light of another round of bookstores in my territory going out of business. I kept nursing the idea that things would get better, the industry would turn itself around, and my remaining accounts would thrive and grow their businesses. Even though I was no longer in a commission group, the better to attract new publishers, I even believed I'd acquire more lines to sell.

For me, hope needs the fuel of possibility to burn brightly, and at some vague point I began to turn my back on it. Most of my sales calls would begin with a litany of woe and disappointment from the buyer or owner of the store. The tragedy of 9/11 marked a turning point for retail book sales all over the country. The anxiety that hung over the book industry was like a toxic cloud, with all concerned affected by it. Many people were being laid off, and among my own publishers a series of upheavals and personnel shifts had left me pondering just who it was I worked for, and why. The book business was beginning to lose its grip on me.

In 2000, a change in ownership forced me to move out of the apartment on Sycamore that had been my home for twenty-four years. What began as a traumatic experience turned into a great, transforming gift. My new home, which seemed to find me, provides a space twice as big as, and a thousand times more gratifying than, my former space. Best of all, I have a large private patio that allows for a beautiful urban garden and a sacred space for my musings and contemplations. It's on the ground floor and faces the street. From one day to the next, I never know who I'll see strolling by.

I was sitting on the patio one day while in the throes of conflicting thoughts about my role in the book business. With my face turned to the warm sun and my feet up on a chair, I suddenly felt a presence at the wrought-iron gate. I opened my eyes. A Buddhist monk dressed in flowing saffron robes was standing there quietly, smiling at me. Remaining motionless, I returned his smile.

"I am looking for Wendy Werris," the young man said in a halting Asian accent.

"That would be me," I said, rising from my chair. I walked over to the gate, opened it, and faced the monk. He seemed as calm as a hydrangea bloom rooted in paradise.

"I would like to buy a book from you," he said, handing me a sheet of paper. It was an e-mail he'd printed out, written entirely in a foreign script save for my name, my address, and the title of a book on Buddhism published by a press I represent. This scenario startled me. While I'd received many calls on my home telephone from individuals wanting to place orders with me rather than through the proper bookstore channels, this was the first time that someone—a Buddhist monk with a shaved head, no less— had ever come right to my home to buy a book.

"Oh, I'm so sorry. I don't keep books in my house," I said gently. "You have to go to a bookstore for this."

The monk looked at me with great purpose in his eyes. "I must have this book. My master in Thailand . . . it is his request."

It's rare to meet someone so focused on his intention, but it was there in this man, and it was rather disarming. Everything in his being seemed centered and definite. He knew who and what he was, and his awareness was the result of his relationship with his master. I saw something of myself in him, a knowingness that had come and gone in the course of my career: the book business had once been my master, but now I doubted the truth in that. The presence of the monk made me realize this, and I knew he was the creation of my subconscious mind.

I went inside and wrote down the name and address of a local bookstore on a piece of paper; it specializes in titles on Eastern religion and philosophy. "This is where you should go for the book," I told the monk back on my patio. He took the paper and slipped it inside his bright orange robes.

"What if they do not have it? What will I then do for my master?"

I smiled at him. "If that's the case, they'll order the book for you. You'll have it in a few weeks, and your master will be pleased."

"Thank you," the monk said. "Thank you very much." Before he turned to leave, we bowed to one another. *Peace, brother*, I said silently.

After being a book rep for so many years, I've learned a little bit about a lot of things. It comes from having to know enough about the books I'm selling to condense the information down into a sentence or two; a selling point, if you will. My mind is filled with tidbits of information about how Hanae Mori, the Japanese fashion designer, made the costumes for Nureyev when he performed in the classic *Cinderella* ballet, or that the poet Conrad Aiken was the first person to bring the work of Emily Dickinson to popular attention. If it ever came up in conversation at a dinner party, I could also probably chime in on particle physics or something that happened when the Freedom Riders were changing the face of civil rights in 1961. Stuff like that. Little bits about sports records, or how to use a thesaurus.

What I care about most today, though, is learning a lot about one thing: how to live a happy life. Like the monk in saffron robes, my desire is to know my good intentions, bring them to fruition, and express as much love and gratitude as possible. When I decide to leave the book business, one thing is certain: the book business will never leave me.

And so it is.

ACKNOWLEDGMENTS

LOVING THANKS . . .

to my sisters, Susan Grey and Laurie Marcus, for their support during the writing of this book, and for allowing me to unlock their memories of our family.

to my beloved Pickwick crew for their generosity of spirit and spot-on recollections, especially Shirley Arnold, Hugh Callens, Daniel Dorse, Alan Kahn, Ben Latting, Joni Miller, and David Pabian.

to Detective Rick Jackson, Los Angeles Police Department, Cold Case Homicide Unit, and Captain (Ret.) William F. Reed, County of Los Angeles Sheriff's Department, for their tender care. You're my heroes.

to Peter Ginna for the gracious gift of his literary expertise.

to George Carroll for his enduring friendship.

to those who've left this plane for the next: Barry Cowsill, the beautiful free spirit who succumbed to Hurricane Katrina; Betty Shapian, who broke the mold for all book publicists that followed; Steve Roven, M.D., righteous soul and eternal brother; and Wendy Wasserstein, with whom I spent a lifetime in three glorious days, for telling me to finish this book.

to the circle of friends who cajoled, cradled, and comforted me through the rough bits while I was writing: Nick Adams, Alicia Contreras, Sophie Herxheimer, Rikki Klieman, Gladys Monaster, Nancy Oliver, Tony Parsons, Hela Roven, Dr. David Walker, and Tom Willshire.

to Charlie Winton, for welcoming me into the fold in 1983 and believing in me ever since.

to Linda and Maggie Bass, for keeping Micky alive with me.

to John Smart for so consciously being my friend, and for making me laugh harder than anyone else.

to Adelaide Docx, for mapping the geography of this book.

to Philip Turner, my sensational editor, for showing me the way.

Finally, to the Goddess of all literary agents, B. J. Robbins. This wouldn't have happened without you, and my love and gratitude are beyond measure.

AN ALPHABETICAL LIFE

LIST OF PUBLISHERS repped by WW, 1976–2006

Arbor House

Bellerophon

Bob Adams

Bobbs-Merrill

Bradbury

Carcanet

Carroll & Graf

Cherry Lane Music

Chilton

Chronicle

Cobb Group

Cornell University Press

Council Oak

Creative Homeowner Press

Dartnell

Daydream

E. P. Dutton

M. Evans

Georgi

Getty Trust

Golden Turtle

Graphic Arts

Grove Press

Green Tiger

Gulf

Human Kinetics

IDG

International Polygonics

Irwin

Jewish Lights

Kensington

Kodansha

Laughing Elephant

Lawrence Hill

Leisure Press

LPC Distributors

Microcosm

Microsoft Press

Millbrook

Nolo

Ohio State University Press

Orbis

Oxford University Press

Phaidon

Peter Pauper

PME

Probus

Publishers Group West

Redjacket

Roaring Brook

Samuel French

Sasquatch

Seven Locks

State University of New York Press

Sterling

Talman

Tokyo Pop

Two Continents

University of Georgia Press

University of Hawaii Press

University of Idaho Press

University of Minnesota Press

University of Nevada Press

University of Toronto Press

University of Utah Press

Walker

Warner Juvenile Books

Wordware

Zephyr

▌ INDEX

Index

Index

Index